Annual Editions:
Technologies, Social Media, and Society, 22/e
Liz Friedman and Daniel Mittleman

http://create.mheducation.com

This McGraw-Hill Create text may include materials submitted to
McGraw-Hill for publication by the instructor of this course.
The instructor is solely responsible for the editorial content of such
materials. Instructors retain copyright of these additional materials.

ISBN-10: 1259873439   ISBN-13: 9781259873430

Contents

Detailed Table of Contents

entrepreneurs won't catch on if those devices can't connect to each other automatically, lack intuitive programmability, or aren't appealing designed."

The Murky Ethics of Driverless Cars, Tom Jacobs, *Pacific Standard*, 2016
"A new study explores a moral dilemma facing the creators of self-driving vehicles: In an accident, whose lives should they prioritize?"

Preface

A NOTE TO THE READER

In vetting articles for *Technologies, Social Media, and Society* from the sea of contenders, we have tried to continue in the tradition of the previous editors. The writers are journalists, computer scientists, lawyers, economists, policy analysts, and academics, the kinds of professions you would expect to find represented in a collection on the social implications of computing. They write for newspapers, business and general circulation magazines, academic journals, professional publications and, more and more, for websites. Their writing is mostly free from both the unintelligible jargon and the breathless enthusiasm that prevents people from forming clear ideas about computing and social media policy. This is by design, of course, and we hope that after reading the selections you agree. *Annual Editions: Technologies, Social Media, and Society* is organized around important dimensions of society rather than of computing. This book's major themes are the economy, community, politics considered broadly, and the balance of the risk and reward of new technology.

The units are organized to lead us through several of the critical issues of our day. You may notice that many of these issues (nature of community and friendships, causes of unemployment, intellectual property, freedom of speech, as examples) only tangentially seem to be technology or social media issues. This, too, is by design and serves as evidence for how intertwined technology policy has become with other social and economic policy decisions in the world today.

We are living during a very exciting time, comparable to the 25 or so years that followed the invention of Gutenberg's printing press. The principal modes for communication and collaboration in our society are changing faster than we know how to make public policy or evolve culture to deal with them. As such, business models, property rules, international treaty rules, and a myriad of other economic and social norms are experiencing both evolution and revolution, often with unanticipated or controversial outcomes. At the same time, these technological advances are empowering masses of people around the world who just a generation ago had little or no access to real opportunity. And technological advances are making available incredible new gains in medicine and productivity.

A word of caution. Each article has been selected because it is topical, interesting, and (insofar as the form permits) nicely written. To say that an article is interesting or well-written, however, does not mean that it is right. This is as true of both the facts presented in each article and the point of view of the author. We hope you will approach these articles as you might a good discussion among friends. You may not agree with all opinions, but you will come away nudged in one direction or another by reasoned arguments, holding a richer, more informed view of important issues.

This book includes several features we hope will be helpful to students and professionals. Included with each article are Learning Outcomes, Critical Thinking study/discussion questions, and Internet References. The Internet References include links to articles and videos that guide a deeper dive into the topic at hand. The use of videos further supports multiple learning styles among the students using this reader.

Though some of the critical thinking questions can be answered from within the article, many more invite further investigation, in essence, allowing each reader to construct their own understanding of the article topic. We hope the articles we gathered for this volume, along with the materials provided with them, initiate further discussion and further interest in these controversial issues of our day. They are intended to get the discussion flowing, not to provide definitive answers.

We want *Annual Editions: Technologies, Social Media, and Society* to spark your interest for exploring some of the most important discussions of the time: those about the promises and risks engendered by new developments in information technology and social media.

We invite college course instructors to join us at http://mittlemanfriedman.org.

Editors

Liz Friedman is the Assistant Dean of Student Services in the College of Computing and Digital Media at DePaul University. In addition to her primary work as a college administrator, Dr. Friedman teaches coursework examining the impact of computing technology on our lives and careers. She earned her PhD in Higher, Adult, and Lifelong Education from Michigan State University in 2004.

Danny Mittleman is an Associate Professor in the College of Computing and Digital Media at DePaul University. He teaches coursework in Virtual Collaboration, Social Media, and Social Impact of Technology. Dr. Mittleman is the author of over 55 academic publications, and several dozen more conference and invited presentations. His research focuses on the design of virtual and physical spaces for work collaboration, as well as the design of collaborative work process. He has spoken on these topics at NASA, The World Bank, the Federal Reserve, NCSA, the Department of Defense, and multiple Fortune 500 corporations. Today all of his free time—and then some—are devoted toward raising his triplet sons.

Academic Advisory Board

Members of the Academic Advisory Board are instrumental in the final selection of articles for each edition of ANNUAL EDITIONS. Their review of articles for content, level, and appropriateness provides critical direction to the editors and staff. We think that you will find their careful consideration well reflected in this volume.

Ghassan Alkadi
Southeastern Louisiana University

David Allen
Temple University

Peggy Batchelor
Furman University

Beverly Bohn
Park University

Maria I. Bryant
College of Southern Maryland

Cliff Cockerham
Whites Creek High School

Arthur I. Cyr
Carthage College

Peter A. Danielson
University of British Columbia

Michael J. Day
Northern Illinois University

Therese DonGiovanni O'Neil
Indiana University of Pennsylvania

Kenneth Fidel
DePaul University

Norman Garrett
Eastern Illinois University

David C. Gibbs
University of Wisconsin—Stevens Point

Keith Harman
Oklahoma Baptist University

Marc D. Hiller
University of New Hampshire

Malynnda A. Johnson
Carroll University

Patricia A. Joseph
Slippery Rock University

John Karayan
Woodbury University

Donna Kastner
California State University—Fullerton

Edward Kisailus
Canisius College

Eugene J. Kozminski
Aquinas College

Christine Kukla
North Central College

Rick Lejk
University of North Carolina—Charlotte

Xiangdong Li
New York City College of Technology

David Little
High Point University

Michael Martel
Ohio University

Ottis L. Murray
University of North Carolina—Pembroke

Morris Pondfield
Towson University

Scott Rader
University of St. Thomas

Ramona R. Santa Maria
Buffalo State College, SUNY

Thomas Schunk
SUNY Orange County Community College

Keith Stearns
University of Wisconsin—Eau Claire

Edwin Tjoe
St. John's University

Lawrence E. Turner
Southwestern Adventist University

Lih-Ching Chen Wang
Cleveland State University

Fred Westfall
Troy University

Rene Weston-Eborn
Weber State College

Nathan White
McKendree University

Unit 1

UNIT

Prepared by: Liz Friedman, *DePaul University* and
Daniel Mittleman, *DePaul University*

Introduction

No technological change is all good or all bad. Most every change has both positive and negative consequences. Consider the case of a major technology shift from a century ago—the invention and mass adoption of the automobile.

The automobile permitted us to travel faster and farther than previously possible by horse. And because of that, the automobile meant the end of horse-drawn carriages. That trade off, for many, was positive; it certainly changed man's relationship to the horse. The automobile created or advanced whole new fields of work from highway construction to petroleum engineering. It created jobs for gas station attendants, parking valets, mechanics, and car salesmen. It also eliminated many jobs for blacksmiths, stable boys, and street sweeps.

More than that, however, the automobile opened up the practicality of suburban living, shopping malls, and super highways. It enabled much of what we now think of as Americana such as carpooling, road trips, and drive-through restaurants. But it also fed America's need for oil, which has contributed to hostilities in the Middle East, oil spills in Alaska and the Gulf of Mexico, controversy around overland oil pipelines, and climate change.

What follows this opening essay is a book of readings: a collection of recent newspaper, magazine, and journal articles as well as extended blog posts from notable authors. It is possible to step through the collected articles reading each as a disconnected essay, much as you might read a typical monthly magazine with only a loose theme, if any at all, connecting the articles.

You might decide you like some of the articles: they amuse you, they stimulate you to think, or they contain information you can put to practical use. And you might decide you dislike other articles that bore you, or don't seem at all relevant to your life interests, or both. In truth, you could read the articles in this book in just that fashion. But to do so would miss the point of the whole exercise of the course you are currently taking.

What this book—and presumably your course—is about is the evaluation of recent technological advances on our economics, our politics, our culture, and on us. These readings address a myriad of intertwining issues about social media, privacy, security, and business. Getting one's head around the ideas from these articles—and the implications that stem from the ideas—is not a simple matter.

What differentiates this book—this reader—from a magazine, and what differentiates you reading this material inside a course rather than on your own, is the use of a framework or model to help make sense of the complexities.

Neil Postman, an education theorist and writer, presented a useful framework for addressing these issues in a 1988 speech. In short, Postman presented five ideas:

1. All technological change is a trade-off. That is, every new technology introduces advantages and disadvantages.
2. Advantages and disadvantages of new technologies are never distributed evenly among the world's populace. Every technological change creates winners and losers.
3. Embedded within each new technology is one—maybe more—underlying new idea. Often this idea is not immediately apparent; sometimes it is fairly abstract. But the idea will be there and its impact may turn out to dwarf the technology itself.
4. Technological change is not additive, it is ecological. That is, a new technology cannot simply be added to our world; its adoption changes our world.
5. Adopted technologies become mythic. The existence of new technologies, once they diffuse to regular use, are taken for granted as though they have always been there and they cannot possibly be removed.

These ideas can be applied as a framework to evaluate almost every technology topic in this reader. As you read each article consider the following questions:

- What are the advantages and disadvantages this new technology presents?
- Who are the winners and losers as this technology diffuses into regular use?
- What grand idea(s) underlies this new technology and how does this idea impact our economic, social, cultural, or political institutions?
- How is diffusion of this technology changing structures, patterns, or norms in our world?

Perhaps some articles do not focus on the technology itself, but on the ideas, patterns, or outcomes already occurring. Even so, applying Postman's framework is an excellent approach to making sense of the reading.

In the case of the automobile, Postman's ideas provide a strong structure for analysis. The automobile clearly had its advantages: faster travel led to more mobility and greater opportunity for many. On the other hand, it has contributed to air pollution and a breakdown of urban neighborhoods. Postman suggests that embedded in every new technology is one or more powerful abstract ideas. Early automobile pioneers might have imagined American suburbia, but they could not foresee it as it has evolved. Nor could they have predicted the global political ramifications that the demand for a consistent, low-priced oil and gas supply would portend. Clearly the automobile changed our world. But it did so not by adding a new tool to it, rather by enabling enormous shifts in societal structures.

Some questions to consider in this unit:

- How is technological change influenced by economics?
- How do technology advancements combat and contribute to social inequality?

Article

Prepared by: Liz Friedman, *DePaul University* and
Daniel Mittleman, *DePaul University*

What World Are We Building

Danah Boyd

Learning Outcomes

After reading this article, you will be able to:

- Identify biases in search engine results.
- Evaluate the role cultural prejudices play in big data and how that influences prediction.
- Distinguish between intentional and unintentional discrimination in machine learning.

1. Internet

I grew up in small town Pennsylvania, where I struggled to fit in. As a geeky queer kid, I rebelled against hypocritical dynamics in my community. When I first got access to the Internet, before the World Wide Web existed, I was like a kid in a candy store. Through early online communities, I met people who opened my eyes to social issues and helped me appreciate things that I didn't even understand. Looking back, I think of the Internet as my saving grace because the people that I met—the *strangers* that I met—helped me take the path that I'm on today. I fell in love with the Internet as a portal to the complex, interconnected society that we live in.

I studied computer science, wanting to build systems that connected people and broke down societal barriers. As my world got bigger, though, I quickly realized that the Internet was a platform and that what people did with that platform ran the full spectrum. I watched activists leverage technology to connect people in unprecedented ways while marketers used those same tools to manipulate people for capitalist gain. I stopped believing that technology alone could produce enlightenment.

In the late 90s, the hype around the Internet became bubbalicious, and it started to be painfully clear to me that economic agendas could shape technology in powerful ways. After the dot-com bubble burst in 2000, I was part of a network of people

determined to build systems that would enable people to connect, share, and communicate. By then I was also a researcher trained by anthropologists, curious to know what people would do with this new set of tools called social media.

In the early days of social network sites, it was exhilarating watching people grasp that they were part of a large global network. Many of my utopian-minded friends started dreaming again of how this structure could be used to break down social and cultural barriers. Yet, as these tools became more popular and widespread, what unfolded was not a realization of the idyllic desires of many early developers, but a complexity of practices that resembled the mess of everyday life.

2. Inequity All Over Again

While social media was being embraced, I was doing research, driving around the country talking with teenagers about how they understood technology in light of everything else taking place in their lives. I watched teens struggle to make sense of everyday life and their place in it. And I watched as privileged parents projected their anxieties onto the tools that were making visible the lives of less privileged youth.

As social media exploded, our country's struggle with class and race got entwined with technology. I will never forget sitting in small town Massachusetts in 2007 with a 14-year-old white girl I call Kat. Kat was talking about her life when she made a passing reference to why her friends had all quickly abandoned MySpace and moved to Facebook: because it was safer, and MySpace was boring. Whatever look I gave her at that moment made her squirm. She looked down and said,

I'm not really into racism, but I think that MySpace now is more like ghetto or whatever, and . . . the people that have Facebook are more mature . . . The people who use MySpace—again, not in a racist way—but are usually more like [the] ghetto and hip-hop/rap lovers group.

As we continued talking, Kat became more blunt and told me that black people use MySpace and white people use Facebook.

Fascinated by Kat's explanation and discomfort, I went back to my field notes. Sure enough, numerous teens had made remarks that, with Kat's story in mind, made it very clear that a social division had unfolded between teens using MySpace and Facebook during the 2006–2007 school year. I started asking teens about these issues and heard many more accounts of how race affected engagement. After I posted an analysis online, I got a response from a privileged white boy named Craig:

> *The higher castes of high school moved to Facebook. It was more cultured, and less cheesy. The lower class usually were content to stick to MySpace. Any high school student who has a Facebook will tell you that MySpace users are more likely to be barely educated and obnoxious. Like Peet's is more cultured than Starbucks, and Jazz is more cultured than bubblegum pop, and like Macs are more cultured than PC's, Facebook is of a cooler caliber than MySpace.*

This was not the first time that racial divisions became visible in my research. I had mapped networks of teens using MySpace from single schools only to find that, in supposedly "integrated" schools, friendship patterns were divided by race. And I'd witnessed and heard countless examples of the ways in which race configured everyday social dynamics which bubbled up through social media. In our supposedly post-racial society, social relations and dynamics were still configured by race.

In 2006–2007, I watched a historic practice reproduce itself online. I watched a digital white flight. Like U.S. cities in the 1970s, MySpace got painted as a dangerous place filled with unsavory characters, while Facebook was portrayed as clean and respectable. With money, media, and privileged users behind it, Facebook became the dominant player that attracted everyone. And among youth, racial divisions reproduced themselves again, shifting, for example, to Instagram (orderly, safe) and Vine (chaotic, dangerous).

Teenagers weren't creating the racialized dynamics of social media. They were reproducing what they saw everywhere else and projecting onto their tools. And they weren't alone. Journalists, parents, politicians, and pundits gave them the racist language they reiterated.

And today's technology is valued—culturally and financially—based on how much it's used by the most privileged members of our society.

3. Statistical Prejudice

Thirteen years ago I was sitting around a table with a group imagining how to build tools that would support rich social dynamics. None of us, I think, imagined being where we are now. Sure, there were those who wanted to be rich and famous, but no one thought that a social network site would be used by over a billion people and valued in the hundreds of billions of dollars. No one thought that every major company would have a "social media strategy" within a few years. No one saw that the technologies we were architecting would reconfigure the political and cultural landscape. None of us were focused on what we now call "big data."

"Big data" is amorphous and fuzzy, referencing, first, a set of technologies and practices for analyzing large amounts of data. But, these days, it's primarily a certain *phenomenon* that promises that if we just had more data, we could solve all of the world's problems. The problem with "big data" isn't whether or not we have data, but whether or not we have the ability to make meaning from and produce valuable insights with it. This is trickier than one might imagine.

One of the perennial problems with the statistical and machine learning techniques that underpin "big data" analytics is that they rely on data entered as input. When the data you input is biased, what you get out is just as biased. These systems learn the biases in our society, and they spit them back out at us.

Consider the work done by computer scientist Latanya Sweeney. One day she was searching for herself on Google when she noticed that the ads displayed were for companies offering criminal record background checks with titles like "Latanya Sweeney, Arrested?" which implied that she might have a criminal record. Suspicious, she started searching for other, more white-sounding names, only to find that the advertisements offered in association with those names were quite different. She set about to test the system more formally and found that, indeed, searching for black names was much more likely to produce ads for criminal justice-related products and services.

The story attracted a lot of media attention. But what the public failed to understand was that Google wasn't intentionally discriminating or selling ads based on race. Google was indifferent to the content of the specific ad that showed up with a name search. All it knew is that people clicked on those ads for some searches but not others, and so it was better to serve them up when the search queries had a statistical property similar to queries where a click happens. In other words, because racist viewers were more likely to click on these ads when searching for black names, Google's algorithm quickly learned to serve up these ads for names that are understood as black. Google was trained to be "racist" by its racist users.

Our cultural prejudices are deeply embedded in countless datasets, the very datasets that our systems are trained to learn on. Students of color are much more likely to have disciplinary school records than white students. Black men are far more likely to be stopped and frisked by police, arrested for drug possession or charged with felonies, even as their white counterparts engage in the same behaviors. Poor people are far more likely to have health problems, live further away from work, and struggle to make rent. Yet all of these data are used to fuel personalized learning algorithms, to inform risk-assessment tools for judicial decision-making, and to generate credit and insurance scores. And so the system "predicts" that people who are already marginalized are higher risks, thereby constraining their options and making sure they are, indeed, higher risks.

This was not what my peers set out to create when we imagined building tools that allowed you to map who you knew or enabled you to display interests and tastes.

Lest you think that I fear "big data," let me take a moment to highlight the potential. I'm on the board of Crisis Text Line, a phenomenal service that allows youth in crisis to communicate with counselors via text message. We've handled millions of conversations with youth who are struggling with depression, disordered eating, suicidal ideation, and sexuality confusion. The practice of counseling is not new, but the potential shifts dramatically when you have millions of messages about crises that can help train a system designed to help people. Because of the analytics that we do, counselors are encouraged to take specific paths to suss out how they can best help the texter. Natural language processing allows us to automatically bring up resources that might help a counselor or encourage them to pass the conversation to a different counselor who may be better suited to help a particular texter. In other words, we're using data to empower counselors to better help youth who desperately need our help. And we've done more active rescues during suicide attempts than I like to count (*so many* youth lack access to basic mental health services).

The techniques we use at Crisis Text Line are the exact same techniques that are used in marketing. Or personalized learning. Or predictive policing. Predictive policing, for example, involves taking prior information about police encounters and using that to make a statistical assessment about the likelihood of crime happening in a particular place or involving a particular person. In a very controversial move, Chicago has used such analytics to make a list of people most likely to be a victim of violence. In an effort to prevent crime, police officers approached those individuals and used this information in an effort to scare them to stay out of trouble. But surveillance by powerful actors doesn't build trust; it erodes it. Imagine that same information being given to a social worker. Even better, to a community liaison. Sometimes, it's not the data that's disturbing, but how it's used and by whom.

4. The World We're Creating

Knowing how to use data isn't easy. One of my colleagues at Microsoft Research—Eric Horvitz—can predict with startling accuracy whether someone will be hospitalized based on what they search for. What should he do with that information? Reach out to people? That's pretty creepy. Do nothing? Is that ethical? No matter how good our predictions are, figuring out how to use them is a complex social and cultural issue that technology doesn't solve for us. In fact, as it stands, technology is just making it harder for us to have a reasonable conversation about agency and dignity, responsibility, and ethics.

Data is power. Increasingly we're seeing data being used to assert power over people. It doesn't have to be this way, but one of the things that I've learned is that, unchecked, new tools are almost always empowering to the privileged at the expense of those who are not.

For most media activists, unfettered Internet access is at the center of the conversation, and that is critically important. Today we're standing on a new precipice, and we need to think a few steps ahead of the current fight.

We are moving into a world of prediction. A world where more people are going to be able to make judgments about others based on data. Data analysis that can mark the value of people as worthy workers, parents, borrowers, learners, and citizens. Data analysis that has been underway for decades but is increasingly salient in decision-making across numerous sectors. Data analysis that most people don't understand.

Many activists will be looking to fight the ecosystem of prediction—and to regulate when and where prediction can be used. This is all fine and well when we're talking about how these technologies are designed to do harm. But more often than not, *these tools will be designed to be helpful,* to increase efficiency, to identify people who need help. Their positive uses will exist alongside uses that are terrifying. What do we do?

One of the most obvious issues is the limited diversity of people who are building and using these tools to imagine our future. Statistical and technical literacy isn't even part of the curriculum in most American schools. In our society where technology jobs are highpaying and technical literacy is needed for citizenry, less than 5% of high schools offer AP computer science courses. Needless to say, black and brown youth are much less likely to have access, let alone opportunities. If people don't understand what these systems are doing, how do we expect people to challenge them?

We must learn how to ask hard questions of technology and of those making decisions based data-driven tech. And opening the black box isn't enough. Transparency of data, algorithms, and technology isn't enough. We need to *build assessment into* any system that we roll-out. You can't just put millions of dollars of surveillance equipment into the hands of the police in the hope of creating police accountability, yet, with police body-worn cameras, that's exactly what we're doing. And we're not even trying to assess the implications. This is probably the fastest roll-out of a technology *out of hope,* and it won't be the last. How do we get people to look beyond their hopes and fears and actively interrogate the trade-offs?

Technology plays a central role—more and more—in every sector, every community, every interaction. It's easy to screech in fear or dream of a world in which every problem magically gets solved. To make the world a better place, we need to start paying attention to the different tools that are emerging and learn to frame hard questions about how they should be put to use to improve the lives of everyday people.

We need those who are thinking about social justice to understand technology and those who understand technology to commit to social justice.

Critical Thinking

1. How have social class and race become entwined with technology?

2. What are the ethical concerns with data as power?

3. How do we tackle the limited diversity of the people who build the tools for our future?

Internet References

Facebook's Bias Is Built-In, and Bears Watching
https://goo.gl/KfcYEv

It's Not Just Facebook. Tech Companies Need to Open Up about Their Biases.
https://goo.gl/5LA1iU

When Big Data Becomes Bad Data
https://goo.gl/Os653I

Danah Boyd is the founder and president of Data & Society, a Principal Researcher at Microsoft, and a Visiting Professor at New York University. Her research is focused on making certain that society has a nuanced understanding of the relationship between technology and society, especially as issues of inequity and bias emerge.

Prepared by: Liz Friedman, *DePaul University* and
Daniel Mittleman, *DePaul University*

Article

The Fourth Industrial Revolution

What It Means and How to Respond

KLAUS SCHWAB

Learning Outcomes

After reading this article, you will be able to:

- Identify the four main effects that the Fourth Industrial Revolution will have on business.

- Differentiate between long-term gains of technological innovation and potential inequality, particularly in the labor market.

- Analyze the impact of new technologies and platforms on citizens ability to engage with government.

We stand on the brink of a technological revolution that will fundamentally alter the way we live, work, and relate to one another. In its scale, scope, and complexity, the transformation will be unlike anything humankind has experienced before. We do not yet know just how it will unfold, but one thing is clear: the response to it must be integrated and comprehensive, involving all stakeholders of the global polity, from the public and private sectors to academia and civil society.

The First Industrial Revolution used water and steam power to mechanize production. The Second used electric power to create mass production. The Third used electronics and information technology to automate production. Now a Fourth Industrial Revolution is building on the Third, the digital revolution that has been occurring since the middle of the last century. It is characterized by a fusion of technologies that is blurring the lines between the physical, digital, and biological spheres.

There are three reasons why today's transformations represent not merely a prolongation of the Third Industrial Revolution but rather the arrival of a Fourth and distinct one: velocity, scope, and systems impact. The speed of current breakthroughs has no historical precedent. When compared with previous industrial revolutions, the Fourth is evolving at an exponential rather than a linear pace. Moreover, it is disrupting almost every industry in every country. And the breadth and depth of these changes herald the transformation of entire systems of production, management, and governance.

The possibilities of billions of people connected by mobile devices, with unprecedented processing power, storage capacity, and access to knowledge, are unlimited. And these possibilities will be multiplied by emerging technology breakthroughs in fields such as artificial intelligence, robotics, the Internet of Things, autonomous vehicles, 3-D printing, nanotechnology, biotechnology, materials science, energy storage, and quantum computing.

Already, artificial intelligence is all around us, from self-driving cars and drones to virtual assistants and software that translate or invest. Impressive progress has been made in AI in recent years, driven by exponential increases in computing power and by the availability of vast amounts of data, from software used to discover new drugs to algorithms used to predict our cultural interests. Digital fabrication technologies, meanwhile, are interacting with the biological world on a daily basis. Engineers, designers, and architects are combining computational design, additive manufacturing, materials engineering, and synthetic biology to pioneer a symbiosis between microorganisms, our bodies, the products we consume, and even the buildings we inhabit.

Challenges and Opportunities

Like the revolutions that preceded it, the Fourth Industrial Revolution has the potential to raise global income levels and improve the quality of life for populations around the world. To date, those who have gained the most from it have been consumers able to afford and access the digital world; technology has made possible new products and services that increase the efficiency and pleasure of our personal lives. Ordering a cab, booking a flight, buying a product, making a payment, listening to music, watching a film, or playing a game—any of these can now be done remotely.

In the future, technological innovation will also lead to a supply-side miracle, with long-term gains in efficiency and productivity. Transportation and communication costs will drop, logistics and global supply chains will become more effective, and the cost of trade will diminish, all of which will open new markets and drive economic growth.

At the same time, as the economists Erik Brynjolfsson and Andrew McAfee have pointed out, the revolution could yield greater inequality, particularly in its potential to disrupt labor markets. As automation substitutes for labor across the entire economy, the net displacement of workers by machines might exacerbate the gap between returns to capital and returns to labor. On the other hand, it is also possible that the displacement of workers by technology will, in aggregate, result in a net increase in safe and rewarding jobs.

We cannot foresee at this point which scenario is likely to emerge, and history suggests that the outcome is likely to be some combination of the two. However, I am convinced of one thing—that in the future, talent, more than capital, will represent the critical factor of production. This will give rise to a job market increasingly segregated into "low-skill/low-pay" and "high-skill/high-pay" segments, which in turn will lead to an increase in social tensions.

In addition to being a key economic concern, inequality represents the greatest societal concern associated with the Fourth Industrial Revolution. The largest beneficiaries of innovation tend to be the providers of intellectual and physical capital—the innovators, shareholders, and investors—which explains the rising gap in wealth between those dependent on capital versus labor. Technology is therefore one of the main reasons why incomes have stagnated, or even decreased, for a majority of the population in high-income countries: the demand for highly skilled workers has increased while the demand for workers with less education and lower skills has decreased. The result is a job market with a strong demand at the high and low ends but a hollowing out of the middle.

This helps explain why so many workers are disillusioned and fearful that their own real incomes and those of their children will continue to stagnate. It also helps explain why middle classes around the world are increasingly experiencing a pervasive sense of dissatisfaction and unfairness. A winner-takes-all economy that offers only limited access to the middle class is a recipe for democratic malaise and dereliction.

Discontent can also be fueled by the pervasiveness of digital technologies and the dynamics of information sharing typified by social media. More than 30 percent of the global population now uses social media platforms to connect, learn, and share information. In an ideal world, these interactions would provide an opportunity for cross-cultural understanding and cohesion. However, they can also create and propagate unrealistic expectations as to what constitutes success for an individual or a group, as well as offer opportunities for extreme ideas and ideologies to spread.

The Impact on Business

An underlying theme in my conversations with global CEOs and senior business executives is that the acceleration of innovation and the velocity of disruption are hard to comprehend or anticipate and that these drivers constitute a source of constant surprise, even for the best connected and most well informed. Indeed, across all industries, there is clear evidence that the technologies that underpin the Fourth Industrial Revolution are having a major impact on businesses.

On the supply side, many industries are seeing the introduction of new technologies that create entirely new ways of serving existing needs and significantly disrupt existing industry value chains. Disruption is also flowing from agile, innovative competitors who, thanks to access to global digital platforms for research, development, marketing, sales, and distribution, can oust well-established incumbents faster than ever by improving the quality, speed, or price at which value is delivered.

Major shifts on the demand side are also occurring, as growing transparency, consumer engagement, and new patterns of consumer behavior (increasingly built upon access to mobile networks and data) force companies to adapt the way they design, market, and deliver products and services.

A key trend is the development of technology-enabled platforms that combine both demand and supply to disrupt existing industry structures, such as those we see within the "sharing" or "on demand" economy. These technology platforms, rendered easy to use by the smartphone, convene people, assets, and data—thus creating entirely new ways of consuming goods and services in the process. In addition, they lower the barriers for businesses and individuals to create wealth, altering the personal and professional environments of workers. These new platform businesses are rapidly multiplying into many new services, ranging from laundry to shopping, from chores to parking, from massages to travel.

On the whole, there are four main effects that the Fourth Industrial Revolution has on business—on customer expectations, on product enhancement, on collaborative innovation, and on organizational forms. Whether consumers or businesses, customers are increasingly at the epicenter of the economy, which is all about improving how customers are served. Physical products and services, moreover, can now be enhanced with digital capabilities that increase their value. New technologies make assets more durable and resilient, while data and analytics are transforming how they are maintained. A world of customer experiences, data-based services, and asset performance through analytics, meanwhile, requires new forms of collaboration, particularly given the speed at which innovation and disruption are taking place. And the emergence of global platforms and other new business models, finally, means that talent, culture, and organizational forms will have to be rethought.

Overall, the inexorable shift from simple digitization (the Third Industrial Revolution) to innovation based on combinations of technologies (the Fourth Industrial Revolution) is forcing companies to reexamine the way they do business. The bottom line, however, is the same: business leaders and senior executives need to understand their changing environment, challenge the assumptions of their operating teams, and relentlessly and continuously innovate.

The Impact on Government

As the physical, digital, and biological worlds continue to converge, new technologies and platforms will increasingly enable citizens to engage with governments, voice their opinions, coordinate their efforts, and even circumvent the supervision of public authorities. Simultaneously, governments will gain new technological powers to increase their control over populations, based on pervasive surveillance systems and the ability to control digital infrastructure. On the whole, however, governments will increasingly face pressure to change their current approach to public engagement and policymaking, as their central role of conducting policy diminishes owing to new sources of competition and the redistribution and decentralization of power that new technologies make possible.

Ultimately, the ability of government systems and public authorities to adapt will determine their survival. If they prove capable of embracing a world of disruptive change, subjecting their structures to the levels of transparency and efficiency that will enable them to maintain their competitive edge, they will endure. If they cannot evolve, they will face increasing trouble.

This will be particularly true in the realm of regulation. Current systems of public policy and decision-making evolved alongside the Second Industrial Revolution, when decision-makers had time to study a specific issue and develop the

necessary response or appropriate regulatory framework. The whole process was designed to be linear and mechanistic, following a strict "top down" approach.

But such an approach is no longer feasible. Given the Fourth Industrial Revolution's rapid pace of change and broad impacts, legislators and regulators are being challenged to an unprecedented degree and for the most part are proving unable to cope.

How, then, can they preserve the interest of the consumers and the public at large while continuing to support innovation and technological development? By embracing "agile" governance, just as the private sector has increasingly adopted agile responses to software development and business operations more generally. This means regulators must continuously adapt to a new, fast-changing environment, reinventing themselves so they can truly understand what it is they are regulating. To do so, governments and regulatory agencies will need to collaborate closely with business and civil society.

The Fourth Industrial Revolution will also profoundly impact the nature of national and international security, affecting both the probability and the nature of conflict. The history of warfare and international security is the history of technological innovation, and today is no exception. Modern conflicts involving states are increasingly "hybrid" in nature, combining traditional battlefield techniques with elements previously associated with nonstate actors. The distinction between war and peace, combatant and noncombatant, and even violence and nonviolence (think cyberwarfare) is becoming uncomfortably blurry.

As this process takes place and new technologies such as autonomous or biological weapons become easier to use, individuals and small groups will increasingly join states in being capable of causing mass harm. This new vulnerability will lead to new fears. But at the same time, advances in technology will create the potential to reduce the scale or impact of violence, through the development of new modes of protection, for example, or greater precision in targeting.

The Impact on People

The Fourth Industrial Revolution, finally, will change not only what we do but also who we are. It will affect our identity and all the issues associated with it: our sense of privacy, our notions of ownership, our consumption patterns, the time we devote to work and leisure, and how we develop our careers, cultivate our skills, meet people, and nurture relationships. It is already changing our health and leading to a "quantified" self, and sooner than we think it may lead to human augmentation. The list is endless because it is bound only by our imagination.

I am a great enthusiast and early adopter of technology, but sometimes I wonder whether the inexorable integration of technology in our lives could diminish some of our quintessential human capacities, such as compassion and cooperation. Our relationship with our smartphones is a case in point. Constant connection may deprive us of one of life's most important assets: the time to pause, reflect, and engage in meaningful conversation.

One of the greatest individual challenges posed by new information technologies is privacy. We instinctively understand why it is so essential, yet the tracking and sharing of information about us is a crucial part of the new connectivity. Debates about fundamental issues such as the impact on our inner lives of the loss of control over our data will only intensify in the years ahead. Similarly, the revolutions occurring in biotechnology and AI, which are redefining what it means to be human by pushing back the current thresholds of life span, health, cognition, and capabilities, will compel us to redefine our moral and ethical boundaries.

Shaping the Future

Neither technology nor the disruption that comes with it is an exogenous force over which humans have no control. All of us are responsible for guiding its evolution, in the decisions we make on a daily basis as citizens, consumers, and investors. We should thus grasp the opportunity and power we have to shape the Fourth Industrial Revolution and direct it toward a future that reflects our common objectives and values.

To do this, however, we must develop a comprehensive and globally shared view of how technology is affecting our lives and reshaping our economic, social, cultural, and human environments. There has never been a time of greater promise or one of greater potential peril. Today's decision-makers, however, are too often trapped in traditional, linear thinking, or too absorbed by the multiple crises demanding their attention, to think strategically about the forces of disruption and innovation shaping our future.

In the end, it all comes down to people and values. We need to shape a future that works for all of us by putting people first and empowering them. In its most pessimistic, dehumanized form, the Fourth Industrial Revolution may indeed have the potential to "robotize" humanity and thus to deprive us of our heart and soul. But as a complement to the best parts of human nature—creativity, empathy, stewardship—it can also lift humanity into a new collective and moral consciousness based on a shared sense of destiny. It is incumbent on us all to make sure the latter prevails.

Critical Thinking

1. How does the Fourth Industrial Revolution influence a segregated marketplace?
2. What are ways that the introduction of new technologies disrupts business?
3. How will advances in biotechnology and AI redefine what it means to be human?

Internet References

Change Is the Only Thing That's Constant: Digital Disruption Demands Adaptability
   https://goo.gl/ekYCp9

The Fourth Industrial Revolution Redefines the Relationship between Business and Tech
   http://www.information-age.com/technology/applications-and-development/123461886/fourth-industrial-revolution-redefines-relationship-between-business-and-tech

Why Perceived Inequality Leads People to Resist Innovation
   https://goo.gl/OZPBgl

KLAUS SCHWAB is Founder and Executive Chairman of the World Economic Forum.

Article

Prepared by: Liz Friedman, *DePaul University* and
Daniel Mittleman, *DePaul University*

A World without Work

For centuries, experts have predicted that machines would make workers obsolete. That moment may finally be arriving. Could that be a good thing?

DEREK THOMPSON

Learning Outcomes

After reading this article, you will be able to:

- Explain how technology might put pressure on the value and availability of work.

- Distinguish between futures of consumption, communal creativity, and contingency.

- Identify ways in which a world without work would make politics more contentious.

1. Youngstown, U.S.A.

The end of work is still just a futuristic concept for most of the United States, but it is something like a moment in history for Youngstown, Ohio, one its residents can cite with precision: September 19, 1977.

For much of the 20th century, Youngstown's steel mills delivered such great prosperity that the city was a model of the American dream, boasting a median income and a home-ownership rate that were among the nation's highest. But as manufacturing shifted abroad after World War II, Youngstown steel suffered, and on that gray September afternoon in 1977, Youngstown Sheet and Tube announced the shuttering of its Campbell Works mill. Within 5 years, the city lost 50,000 jobs and $1.3 billion in manufacturing wages. The effect was so severe that a term was coined to describe the fallout: *regional depression.*

Youngstown was transformed not only by an economic disruption but also by a psychological and cultural break-down. Depression, spousal abuse, and suicide all became much more prevalent; the caseload of the area's mental-health

center tripled within a decade. The city built four prisons in the mid-1990s—a rare growth industry. One of the few downtown construction projects of that period was a museum dedicated to the defunct steel industry.

This winter, I traveled to Ohio to consider what would happen if technology permanently replaced a great deal of human work. I wasn't seeking a tour of our automated future. I went because Youngstown has become a national metaphor for the decline of labor, a place where the middle class of the 20th century has become a museum exhibit.

"Youngstown's story is America's story, because it shows that when jobs go away, the cultural cohesion of a place is destroyed," says John Russo, a professor of labor studies at Youngstown State University. "The cultural breakdown matters even more than the economic breakdown."

In the past few years, even as the United States has pulled itself partway out of the jobs hole created by the Great Recession, some economists and technologists have warned that the economy is near a tipping point. When they peer deeply into labor-market data, they see troubling signs, masked for now by a cyclical recovery. And when they look up from their spreadsheets, they see automation high and low—robots in the operating room and behind the fast-food counter. They imagine self-driving cars snaking through the streets and Amazon drones dotting the sky, replacing millions of drivers, warehouse stockers, and retail workers. They observe that the capabilities of machines—already formidable—continue to expand exponentially, while our own remain the same. And they wonder: *Is any job truly safe?*

Futurists and science-fiction writers have at times looked forward to machines' workplace takeover with a kind of giddy excitement, imagining the banishment of drudgery and its replacement by expansive leisure and almost limitless personal freedom. And make no mistake: if the capabilities of computers continue to multiply while the price of computing continues to decline, that will mean a great many of life's necessities and luxuries will become ever cheaper, and it will mean great wealth—at least when aggregated up to the level of the national economy.

But even leaving aside questions of how to distribute that wealth, the widespread disappearance of work would usher in a social transformation unlike any we've seen. If John Russo is right, then saving work is more important than saving any particular job. Industriousness has served as America's unofficial religion since its founding. The sanctity and preeminence of work lie at the heart of the country's politics, economics, and social interactions. What might happen if work goes away?

T HE U.S. LABOR FORCE has been shaped by millennia of technological progress. Agricultural technology birthed the farming industry, the industrial revolution moved people into factories, and then globalization and automation moved them back out, giving rise to a nation of services. But throughout these reshufflings, the total number of jobs has always increased. What may be looming is something different: an era of technological unemployment, in which computer scientists and software engineers essentially invent us out of work, and the total number of jobs declines steadily and permanently.

This fear is not new. The hope that machines might free us from toil has always been intertwined with the fear that they will rob us of our agency. In the midst of the Great Depression, the economist John Maynard Keynes forecast that technological progress might allow a 15-hour workweek, and abundant leisure, by 2030. But around the same time, President Herbert Hoover received a letter warning that industrial technology was a "Frankenstein monster" that threatened to upend manufacturing, "devouring our civilization." (The letter came from the mayor of Palo Alto, of all places.) In 1962, President John F. Kennedy said, "If men have the talent to invent new machines that put men out of work, they have the talent to put those men back to work." But 2 years later, a committee of scientists and social activists sent an open letter to President Lyndon B. Johnson arguing that "the cybernation revolution" would create "a separate nation of the poor, the unskilled, the jobless," who would be unable either to find work or to afford life's necessities.

The job market defied doomsayers in those earlier times, and according to the most frequently reported jobs numbers, it has so far done the same in our own time. Unemployment is currently just over 5 percent, and 2014 was this century's best year for job growth. One could be forgiven for saying that recent predictions about technological job displacement are merely forming the latest chapter in a long story called *The Boys Who Cried Robot*—one in which the robot, unlike the wolf, never arrives in the end.

The end-of-work argument has often been dismissed as the "Luddite fallacy," an allusion to the 19th-century British brutes who smashed textile-making machines at the dawn of the industrial revolution, fearing the machines would put hand-weavers out of work. But some of the most sober economists are beginning to worry that the Luddites weren't wrong, just premature. When former Treasury Secretary Lawrence Summers was an MIT undergraduate in the early 1970s, many economists disdained "the stupid people [who] thought that automation was going to make all the jobs go away," he said at the National Bureau of Economic Research Summer Institute in July 2013. "Until a few years ago, I didn't think this was a very complicated subject: the Luddites were wrong, and the believers in technology and technological progress were right. I'm not so completely certain now."

2. Reasons to Cry Robot

What does the "end of work" mean, exactly? It does not mean the imminence of total unemployment, nor is the United States remotely likely to face, say, 30 or 50 percent unemployment within the next decade. Rather, technology could exert a slow but continual downward pressure on the value and availability of work—that is, on wages and on the share of prime-age workers with full-time jobs. Eventually, by degrees, that could create a new normal, where the expectation that work will be a central feature of adult life dissipates for a significant portion of society.

After 300 years of people crying wolf, there are now three broad reasons to take seriously the argument that the beast is at the door: the ongoing triumph of capital over labor, the quiet demise of the working man, and the impressive dexterity of information technology.

- *Labor's losses.* One of the first things we might expect to see in a period of technological displacement is the diminishment of human labor as a driver of economic growth. In fact, signs that this is happening have been present for quite some time. The share of U.S. economic output that's paid out in wages fell steadily in the 1980s, reversed some of its losses in the 1990s, and then continued falling after 2000, accelerating during the Great Recession. It now stands at its lowest level since the government started keeping track in the mid-20th century.

A number of theories have been advanced to explain this phenomenon, including globalization and its accompanying loss of bargaining power for some workers. But Loukas Karabarbounis and Brent Neiman, economists at the University of Chicago, have estimated that almost half of the decline is the result of businesses' replacing workers with computers and software. In 1964, the nation's most valuable company, AT&T, was worth $267 billion in today's dollars and employed 758,611 people. Today's telecommunications giant, Google, is worth $370 billion but has only about 55,000 employees—less than a tenth the size of AT&T's workforce in its heyday.

- *The spread of nonworking men and underemployed youth.* The share of prime-age Americans (25 to 54 years old) who are working has been trending down since 2000. Among men, the decline began even earlier: the share of prime-age men who are neither working nor looking for work has doubled since the late 1970s, and has increased as much throughout the recovery as it did during the Great Recession itself. All in all, about one in six prime-age men today are either unemployed or out of the workforce altogether. This is what the economist Tyler Cowen calls "the key statistic" for understanding the spreading rot in the American workforce. Conventional wisdom has long held that under normal economic conditions, men in this age group—at the peak of their abilities and less likely than women to be primary caregivers for children—should almost all be working. Yet fewer and fewer are.

Economists cannot say for certain why men are turning away from work, but one explanation is that technological change has helped eliminate the jobs for which many are best suited. Since 2000, the number of manufacturing jobs has fallen by almost 5 million, or about 30 percent.

Young people just coming onto the job market are also struggling—and by many measures have been for years. Six years into the recovery, the share of recent college grads who are "underemployed" (in jobs that historically haven't required a degree) is still higher than it was in 2007—or, for that matter, 2000. And the supply of these "non-college jobs" is shifting away from high-paying occupations, such as electrician, toward low-wage service jobs, such as waiter. More people are pursuing higher education, but the real wages of recent college graduates have fallen by 7.7 percent since 2000. In the biggest picture, the job market appears to be requiring more and more preparation for a lower and lower starting wage. The distorting effect of the Great Recession should make us cautious about overinterpreting these trends, but most began before the recession, and they do not seem to speak encouragingly about the future of work.

- *The shrewdness of software.* One common objection to the idea that technology will permanently displace huge numbers of workers is that new gadgets, like self-checkout kiosks at drugstores, have failed to fully displace their human counterparts, like cashiers. But employers typically take years to embrace new machines at the expense of workers. The robotics revolution began in factories in the 1960s and '70s, but manufacturing employment kept rising until 1980, and then collapsed during the subsequent recessions. Likewise, "the personal computer existed in the '80s," says Henry Siu, an economist at the University of British Columbia, "but you don't see any effect on office and administrative-support jobs until the 1990s, and then suddenly, in the last recession, it's huge. So today you've got checkout screens and the promise of driverless cars, flying drones, and little warehouse robots. We know that these tasks can be done by machines rather than people. But we may not see the effect until the next recession, or the recession after that."

Some observers say our humanity is a moat that machines cannot cross. They believe people's capacity for compassion, deep understanding, and creativity are inimitable. But as Erik Brynjolfsson and Andrew McAfee have argued in their book *The Second Machine Age,* computers are so dexterous that predicting their application 10 years from now is almost impossible. Who could have guessed in 2005, 2 years before the iPhone was released, that smartphones would threaten hotel jobs within the decade, by helping homeowners rent out their apartments and houses to strangers on Airbnb? Or that the company behind the most popular search engine would design a self-driving car that could soon threaten driving, the most common job occupation among American men?

In 2013, Oxford University researchers forecast that machines might be able to perform half of all U.S. jobs in the next two decades. The projection was audacious, but in at least a few cases, it probably didn't go far enough. For example, the authors named psychologist as one of the occupations least likely to be "computerisable." But some research suggests that people are more honest in therapy sessions when they believe that they are confessing their troubles to a computer, because a machine can't pass moral judgment. Google and WebMD already may be answering questions once reserved for one's therapist. This doesn't prove that psychologists are going the way of the textile worker. Rather, it shows how easily computers can encroach on areas previously considered "for humans only."

AFTER 300 YEARS of breathtaking innovation, people aren't massively unemployed or indentured by machines. But to suggest how this could change, some economists have pointed to the defunct career of the second-most-important species in U.S. economic history: the horse.

For many centuries, people created technologies that made the horse more productive and more valuable—like plows for agriculture and swords for battle. One might have assumed that the continuing advance of complementary technologies would make the animal ever more essential to farming and fighting, historically perhaps the two most consequential human activities. Instead came inventions that made the horse obsolete—the tractor, the car, and the tank. After tractors rolled onto American farms in the early 20th century, the population of horses and mules began to decline steeply, falling nearly 50 percent by the 1930s and 90 percent by the 1950s.

Humans can do much more than trot, carry, and pull. But the skills required in most offices hardly elicit our full range of intelligence. Most jobs are still boring, repetitive, and easily learned. The most-common occupations in the United States are retail salesperson, cashier, food and beverage server, and office clerk. Together, these four jobs employ 15.4 million people—nearly 10 percent of the labor force, or more workers than there are in Texas and Massachusetts combined. Each is highly susceptible to automation, according to the Oxford study.

Technology creates some jobs too, but the creative half of creative destruction is easily overstated. Nine out of 10 workers today are in occupations that existed 100 years ago, and just 5 percent of the jobs generated between 1993 and 2013 came from "high tech" sectors like computing, software, and telecommunications. Our newest industries tend to be the most labor-efficient: they just don't require many people. It is for precisely this reason that the economic historian Robert Skidelsky, comparing the exponential growth in computing power with the less-than-exponential growth in job complexity, has said, "Sooner or later, we will run out of jobs."

Is that certain—or certainly imminent? No. The signs so far are murky and suggestive. The most fundamental and wrenching job restructurings and contractions tend to happen during recessions: we'll know more after the next couple of downturns. But the possibility seems significant enough—and the consequences disruptive enough—that we owe it to ourselves to start thinking about what society could look like without universal work, in an effort to begin nudging it toward the better outcomes and away from the worse ones.

To paraphrase the science-fiction novelist William Gibson, there are, perhaps, fragments of the post-work future distributed throughout the present. I see three overlapping possibilities as formal employment opportunities decline. Some people displaced from the formal workforce will devote their freedom to simple leisure; some will seek to build productive communities outside the workplace; and others will fight, passionately and in many cases fruitlessly, to reclaim their productivity by piecing together jobs in an informal economy. These are futures of *consumption, communal creativity,* and *contingency.* In any

combination, it is almost certain that the country would have to embrace a radical new role for government.

3. Consumption: The Paradox of Leisure

Work is really three things, says Peter Frase, the author of *Four Futures,* a forthcoming book about how automation will change America: the means by which the economy produces goods, the means by which people earn income, and an activity that lends meaning or purpose to many people's lives. "We tend to conflate these things," he told me, "because today we need to pay people to keep the lights on, so to speak. But in a future of abundance, you wouldn't, and we ought to think about ways to make it easier and better to not be employed."

Frase belongs to a small group of writers, academics, and economists—they have been called "post-workists"—who welcome, even root for, the end of labor. American society has "an irrational belief in work for work's sake," says Benjamin Hunnicutt, another post-workist and a historian at the University of Iowa, even though most jobs aren't so uplifting. A 2014 Gallup report of worker satisfaction found that as many as 70 percent of Americans don't feel engaged by their current job. Hunnicutt told me that if a cashier's work were a video game—grab an item, find the bar code, scan it, slide the item onward, and repeat—critics of video games might call it mindless. But when it's a job, politicians praise its intrinsic dignity. "Purpose, meaning, identity, fulfillment, creativity, autonomy—all these things that positive psychology has shown us to be necessary for well-being are absent in the average job," he said.

The post-workists are certainly right about some important things. Paid labor does not always map to social good. Raising children and caring for the sick is essential work, and these jobs are compensated poorly or not at all. In a post-work society, Hunnicutt said, people might spend more time caring for their families and neighbors; pride could come from our relationships rather than from our careers.

The post-work proponents acknowledge that, even in the best post-work scenarios, pride and jealousy will persevere, because reputation will always be scarce, even in an economy of abundance. But with the right government provisions, they believe, the end of wage labor will allow for a golden age of well-being. Hunnicutt said he thinks colleges could reemerge as cultural centers rather than job-prep institutions. The word *school,* he pointed out, comes from *skholē,* the Greek word for "leisure." "We used to teach people to be free," he said. "Now we teach them to work."

Hunnicutt's vision rests on certain assumptions about taxation and redistribution that might not be congenial to many Americans today. But even leaving that aside for the moment, this vision is problematic: it doesn't resemble the world as it is currently experienced by most jobless people. By and large, the jobless don't spend their downtime socializing with friends or taking up new hobbies. Instead, they watch TV or sleep. Time-use surveys show that jobless prime-age people dedicate some of the time once spent working to cleaning and childcare. But men in particular devote most of their free time to leisure, the lion's share of which is spent watching television, browsing the Internet, and sleeping. Retired seniors watch about 50 hours of television a week, according to Nielsen. That means they spend a majority of their lives either sleeping or sitting on the sofa looking at a flatscreen. The unemployed theoretically have the most time to socialize, and yet studies have shown that they feel the most social isolation; it is surprisingly hard to replace the camaraderie of the water cooler.

Most people want to work and are miserable when they cannot. The ills of unemployment go well beyond the loss of income; people who lose their job are more likely to suffer from mental and physical ailments. "There is a loss of status, a general malaise and demoralization, which appears somatically or psychologically or both," says Ralph Catalano, a public-health professor at UC Berkeley. Research has shown that it is harder to recover from a long bout of joblessness than from losing a loved one or suffering a life-altering injury. The very things that help many people recover from other emotional traumas—a routine, an absorbing distraction, and a daily purpose—are not readily available to the unemployed.

The transition from labor force to leisure force would likely be particularly hard on Americans, the worker bees of the rich world: Between 1950 and 2012, annual hours worked per worker fell significantly throughout Europe—by about 40 percent in Germany and the Netherlands—but by only 10 percent in the United States. Richer, college-educated Americans are working *more* than they did 30 years ago, particularly when you count time working and answering e-mail at home.

In 1989, the psychologists Mihaly Csikszentmihalyi and Judith LeFevre conducted a famous study of Chicago workers that found people at work often wished they were somewhere else. But in questionnaires, these same workers reported feeling better and less anxious in the office or at the plant than they did elsewhere. The two psychologists called this "the paradox of work": many people are happier complaining about jobs than they are luxuriating in too much leisure. Other researchers have used the term *guilty couch potato* to describe people who use media to relax but often feel worthless when they reflect on their unproductive downtime. Contentment speaks in the present tense, but something more—pride—comes only in reflection on past accomplishments.

The post-workists argue that Americans work so hard because their culture has conditioned them to feel guilty when they are not being productive, and that this guilt will fade as work ceases to be the norm. This might prove true, but it's an untestable hypothesis. When I asked Hunnicutt what sort of modern community most resembles his ideal of a post-work society, he admitted, "I'm not sure that such a place exists."

Less passive and more nourishing forms of mass leisure could develop. Arguably, they already are developing. The Internet, social media, and gaming offer entertainments that are as easy to slip into as is watching TV, but all are more purposeful and often less isolating. Video games, despite the derision aimed at them, are vehicles for achievement of a sort. Jeremy Bailenson, a communications professor at Stanford, says that as virtual reality technology improves, people's "cyber-existence" will become as rich and social as their "real" life. Games in which users climb "into another person's skin to embody his or her experiences firsthand" don't just let people live out vicarious fantasies, he has argued, but also "help you live as somebody else to teach you empathy and pro-social skills."

But it's hard to imagine that leisure could ever entirely fill the vacuum of accomplishment left by the demise of labor. Most people do need to achieve things through, yes, *work* to feel a lasting sense of purpose. To envision a future that offers more than minute-to-minute satisfaction, we have to imagine how millions of people might find meaningful work without formal wages. So, inspired by the predictions of one of America's most famous labor economists, I took a detour on my way to Youngstown and stopped in Columbus, Ohio.

4. Communal Creativity: The Artisans' Revenge

Artisans made up the original American middle class. Before industrialization swept through the U.S. economy, many people who didn't work on farms were silversmiths, blacksmiths, or woodworkers. These artisans were ground up by the machinery of mass production in the 20th century. But Lawrence Katz, a labor economist at Harvard, sees the next wave of automation returning us to an age of craftsmanship and artistry. In particular, he looks forward to the ramifications of 3-D printing, whereby machines construct complex objects from digital designs.

The factories that arose more than a century ago "could make Model Ts and forks and knives and mugs and glasses in a standardized, cheap way, and that drove the artisans out of business," Katz told me. "But what if the new tech, like 3-D-printing machines, can do customized things that are almost as cheap? It's possible that information technology and robots eliminate traditional jobs and make possible a new artisanal economy . . . an economy geared around self-expression, where people would do artistic things with their time."

In other words, it would be a future not of consumption but of creativity, as technology returns the tools of the assembly line to individuals, democratizing the means of mass production.

Something like this future is already present in the small but growing number of industrial shops called "makerspaces" that have popped up in the United States and around the world. The Columbus Idea Foundry is the country's largest such space, a cavernous converted shoe factory stocked with industrial-age machinery. Several hundred members pay a monthly fee to use its arsenal of machines to make gifts and jewelry; weld, finish, and paint; play with plasma cutters and work an angle grinder; or operate a lathe with a machinist.

When I arrived there on a bitterly cold afternoon in February, a chalkboard standing on an easel by the door displayed three arrows, pointing toward BATHROOMS, PEWTER CASTING, and ZOMBIES. Near the entrance, three men with black fingertips and grease-stained shirts took turns fixing a 60-year-old metal-turning lathe. Behind them, a resident artist was tutoring an older woman on how to transfer her photographs onto a large canvas, while a couple of guys fed pizza pies into a propane-fired stone oven. Elsewhere, men in protective goggles welded a sign for a local chicken restaurant, while others punched codes into a computer-controlled laser-cutting machine. Beneath the din of drilling and wood-cutting, a Pandora rock station hummed tinnily from a Wi-Fi-connected Edison phonograph horn. The foundry is not just a gymnasium of tools. It is a social center.

Alex Bandar, who started the foundry after receiving a doctorate in materials science and engineering, has a theory about the rhythms of invention in American history. Over the past century, he told me, the economy has moved from hardware to software, from atoms to bits, and people have spent more time at work in front of screens. But as computers take over more tasks previously considered the province of humans, the pendulum will swing back from bits to atoms, at least when it comes to how people spend their days. Bandar thinks that a digitally preoccupied society will come to appreciate the pure and distinct pleasure of making things you can touch. "I've always wanted to usher in a new era of technology where robots do our bidding," Bandar said. "If you have better batteries, better robotics, more dexterous manipulation, then it's not a far stretch to say robots do most of the work. So what do we do? Play? Draw? Actually talk to each other again?"

You don't need any particular fondness for plasma cutters to see the beauty of an economy where tens of millions of people make things they enjoy making—whether physical or digital, in buildings or in online communities—and receive feedback and appreciation for their work. The Internet and the cheap availability of artistic tools have already empowered millions of people to produce culture from their living rooms. People upload more than 400,000 hours of YouTube videos and 350 million new Facebook photos every day. The demise of the formal economy could free many would-be artists, writers, and craftspeople to dedicate their time to creative interests—to live as cultural producers. Such activities offer virtues that many organizational psychologists consider central to satisfaction at work: independence, the chance to develop mastery, and a sense of purpose.

After touring the foundry, I sat at a long table with several members, sharing the pizza that had come out of the communal oven. I asked them what they thought of their organization as a model for a future where automation reached further into the formal economy. A mixed-media artist named Kate Morgan said that most people she knew at the foundry would quit their jobs and use the foundry to start their own business if they could. Others spoke about the fundamental need to witness the outcome of one's work, which was satisfied more deeply by craftsmanship than by other jobs they'd held.

Late in the conversation, we were joined by Terry Griner, an engineer who had built miniature steam engines in his garage before Bandar invited him to join the foundry. His fingers were covered in soot, and he told me about the pride he had in his ability to fix things. "I've been working since I was 16. I've done food service, restaurant work, hospital work, and computer programming. I've done a lot of different jobs," said Griner, who is now a divorced father. "But if we had a society that said, 'We'll cover your essentials, you can work in the shop,' I think that would be utopia. That, to me, would be the best of all possible worlds."

5. Contingency: "You're on Your Own"

One mile to the east of downtown Youngstown, in a brick building surrounded by several empty lots, is Royal Oaks, an iconic blue-collar dive. At about 5:30 p.m. on a Wednesday, the place was nearly full. The bar glowed yellow and green from the lights mounted along a wall. Old beer signs, trophies, masks, and mannequins cluttered the back corner of the main room, like party leftovers stuffed in an attic. The scene was mostly middle-aged men, some in groups, talking loudly about baseball and smelling vaguely of pot; some drank alone at the bar, sitting quietly or listening to music on headphones. I spoke with several patrons there who work as musicians, artists, or handymen; many did not hold a steady job.

"It is the end of a particular kind of wage work," said Hannah Woodroofe, a bartender there who, it turns out, is also a graduate student at the University of Chicago. (She's writing a dissertation on Youngstown as a harbinger of the future of work.) A lot of people in the city make ends meet via "post-wage arrangements," she said, working for tenancy or under the table, or trading services. Places like Royal Oaks are the new union halls: People go there not only to relax but also to find tradespeople for particular jobs, like auto repair. Others go to exchange fresh vegetables, grown in urban gardens they've created amid Youngstown's vacant lots.

When an entire area, like Youngstown, suffers from high and prolonged unemployment, problems caused by unemployment move beyond the personal sphere; widespread joblessness shatters neighborhoods and leaches away their civic spirit. John Russo, the Youngstown State professor, who is a co-author of a history of the city, *Steeltown* USA, says the local identity took a savage blow when residents lost the ability to find reliable employment. "I can't stress this enough: this isn't just about economics; it's psychological," he told me.

Russo sees Youngstown as the leading edge of a larger trend toward the development of what he calls the "precariat"—a working class that swings from task to task in order to make ends meet and suffers a loss of labor rights, bargaining rights, and job security. In Youngstown, many of these workers have by now made their peace with insecurity and poverty by building an identity, and some measure of pride, around contingency. The faith they lost in institutions—the corporations that have abandoned the city, the police who have failed to keep them safe—has not returned. But Russo and Woodroofe both told me they put stock in their own independence. And so a place that once defined itself single-mindedly by the steel its residents made has gradually learned to embrace the valorization of well-rounded resourcefulness.

Karen Schubert, a 54-year-old writer with two master's degrees, accepted a part-time job as a hostess at a café in Youngstown early this year, after spending months searching for full-time work. Schubert, who has two grown children and an infant grandson, said she'd loved teaching writing and literature at the local university. But many colleges have replaced full-time professors with part-time adjuncts in order to control costs, and she'd found that with the hours she could get, adjunct teaching didn't pay a living wage, so she'd stopped. "I think I would feel like a personal failure if I didn't know that so many Americans have their leg caught in the same trap," she said.

Among Youngstown's precariat, one can see a third possible future, where millions of people struggle for years to build a sense of purpose in the absence of formal jobs, and where entrepreneurship emerges out of necessity. But while it lacks the comforts of the consumption economy or the cultural richness of Lawrence Katz's artisanal future, it is more complex than an outright dystopia. "There are young people working part-time in the new economy who feel independent, whose work and personal relationships are contingent, and say they like it like this—to have short hours so they have time to focus on their passions," Russo said.

Schubert's wages at the café are not enough to live on, and in her spare time, she sells books of her poetry at readings and organizes gatherings of the literary-arts community in Youngstown, where other writers (many of them also underemployed) share their prose. The evaporation of work has deepened the local arts and music scene, several residents told me, because people who are inclined toward the arts have so much time to spend with one another. "We're a devastatingly poor and hemorrhaging population, but the people who live here are fearless and creative and phenomenal," Schubert said.

Whether or not one has artistic ambitions as Schubert does, it is arguably growing easier to find short-term gigs or spot employment. Paradoxically, technology is the reason. A constellation of Internet-enabled companies matches available workers with quick jobs, most prominently including Uber (for drivers), Seamless (for meal deliverers), Homejoy (for house cleaners), and TaskRabbit (for just about anyone else). And online markets like Craigslist and eBay have likewise made it easier for people to take on small independent projects, such as furniture refurbishing. Although the on-demand economy is not yet a major part of the employment picture, the number of "temporary-help services" workers has grown by 50 percent since 2010, according to the Bureau of Labor Statistics.

Some of these services, too, could be usurped, eventually, by machines. But on-demand apps also spread the work around by carving up jobs, like driving a taxi, into hundreds of little tasks, like a single drive, which allows more people to compete for smaller pieces of work. These new arrangements are already challenging the legal definitions of *employer* and *employee,* and there are many reasons to be ambivalent about them. But if the future involves a declining number of full-time jobs, as in Youngstown, then splitting some of the remaining work up among many part-time workers, instead of a few full-timers, wouldn't necessarily be a bad development. We shouldn't be too quick to excoriate companies that let people combine their work, art, and leisure in whatever ways they choose.

Today the norm is to think about employment and unemployment as a black-and-white binary, rather than two points at opposite ends of a wide spectrum of working arrangements. As late as the mid-19th century, though, the modern concept of "unemployment" didn't exist in the United States. Most people lived on farms, and while paid work came and went, home industry—canning, sewing, carpentry—was a constant. Even in the worst economic panics, people typically found productive things to do. The despondency and helplessness of unemployment were discovered, to the bafflement and dismay of cultural critics, only after factory work became dominant and cities swelled.

The 21st century, if it presents fewer full-time jobs in the sectors that can be automated, could in this respect come to resemble the mid-19th century: an economy marked by episodic work across a range of activities, the loss of any one of which would not make somebody suddenly idle. Many bristle that contingent gigs offer a devil's bargain—a bit of additional autonomy in exchange for a larger loss of security. But some might thrive in a market where versatility and hustle are rewarded—where there are, as in Youngstown, few jobs to have, yet many things to do.

6. Government: The Visible Hand

In the 1950s, Henry Ford II, the CEO of Ford, and Walter Reuther, the head of the United Auto Workers union, were touring a new engine plant in Cleveland. Ford gestured to a fleet of machines and said, "Walter, how are you going to get these robots to pay union dues?" The union boss famously replied: "Henry, how are you going to get them to buy your cars?"

As Martin Ford (no relation) writes in his new book, *The Rise of the Robots,* this story might be apocryphal, but its message is instructive. We're pretty good at noticing the immediate effects of technology's substituting for workers, such as fewer people on the factory floor. What's harder is anticipating the second-order effects of this transformation, such as what happens to the consumer economy when you take away the consumers.

Technological progress on the scale we're imagining would usher in social and cultural changes that are almost impossible to fully envision. Consider just how fundamentally work has shaped America's geography. Today's coastal cities are a jumble of office buildings and residential space. Both are expensive and tightly constrained. But the decline of work would make many office buildings unnecessary. What might that mean for the vibrancy of urban areas? Would office space yield seamlessly to apartments, allowing more people to live more affordably in city centers and leaving the cities themselves just as lively? Or would we see vacant shells and spreading blight? Would big cities make sense at all if their role as highly sophisticated labor ecosystems were diminished? As the 40-hour workweek faded, the idea of a lengthy twice-daily commute would almost certainly strike future generations as an antiquated and baffling waste of time. But would those generations prefer to live on streets full of high-rises, or in smaller towns?

Today, many working parents worry that they spend too many hours at the office. As full-time work declined, rearing children could become less overwhelming. And because job opportunities historically have spurred migration in the United States, we might see less of it; the diaspora of extended families could give way to more closely knitted clans. But if men and women lost their purpose and dignity as work went away, those families would nonetheless be troubled.

The decline of the labor force would make our politics more contentious. Deciding how to tax profits and distribute income could become the most significant economic-policy debate in

American history. In *The Wealth of Nations*, Adam Smith used the term *invisible hand* to refer to the order and social benefits that arise, surprisingly, from individuals' selfish actions. But to preserve the consumer economy and the social fabric, governments might have to embrace what Haruhiko Kuroda, the governor of the Bank of Japan, has called the visible hand of economic intervention. What follows is an early sketch of how it all might work.

In the near term, local governments might do well to create more and more-ambitious community centers or other public spaces where residents can meet, learn skills, bond around sports or crafts, and socialize. Two of the most common side effects of unemployment are loneliness, on the individual level, and the hollowing-out of community pride. A national policy that directed money toward centers in distressed areas might remedy the maladies of idleness and form the beginnings of a long-term experiment on how to reengage people in their neighborhoods in the absence of full employment.

We could also make it easier for people to start their own, small-scale (and even part-time) businesses. New-business formation has declined in the past few decades in all 50 states. One way to nurture fledgling ideas would be to build out a network of business incubators. Here Youngstown offers an unexpected model: its business incubator has been recognized internationally, and its success has brought new hope to West Federal Street, the city's main drag.

Near the beginning of any broad decline in job availability, the United States might take a lesson from Germany on job-sharing. The German government gives firms incentives to cut all their workers' hours rather than lay off some of them during hard times. So a company with 50 workers that might otherwise lay off 10 people instead reduces everyone's hours by 20 percent. Such a policy would help workers at established firms keep their attachment to the labor force despite the declining amount of overall labor.

Spreading work in this way has its limits. Some jobs can't be easily shared, and in any case, sharing jobs wouldn't stop labor's pie from shrinking: it would only apportion the slices differently. Eventually, Washington would have to somehow spread wealth, too.

One way of doing that would be to more heavily tax the growing share of income going to the owners of capital and use the money to cut checks to all adults. This idea—called a "universal basic income"—has received bipartisan support in the past. Many liberals currently support it, and in the 1960s, Richard Nixon and the conservative economist Milton Friedman each proposed a version of the idea. That history notwithstanding, the politics of universal income in a world without universal work would be daunting. The rich could say, with some accuracy, that their hard work was subsidizing the idleness of millions of "takers." What's more, although a universal income might replace lost wages, it would do little to preserve the social benefits of work.

The most direct solution to the latter problem would be for the government to pay people to do something, rather than nothing. Although this smacks of old European socialism, or Depression-era "makework," it might do the most to preserve virtues such as responsibility, agency, and industriousness. In the 1930s, the Works Progress Administration did more than rebuild the nation's infrastructure. It hired 40,000 artists and other cultural workers to produce music and theater, murals and paintings, state and regional travel guides, and surveys of state records. It's not impossible to imagine something like the WPA—or an effort even more capacious—for a post-work future.

What might that look like? Several national projects might justify direct hiring, such as caring for a rising population of elderly people. But if the balance of work continues to shift toward the small-bore and episodic, the simplest way to help everybody stay busy might be government sponsorship of a national online marketplace of work (or, alternatively, a series of local ones, sponsored by local governments). Individuals could browse for large long-term projects, like cleaning up after a natural disaster, or small short-term ones: an hour of tutoring, an evening of entertainment, an art commission. The requests could come from local governments or community associations or nonprofit groups; from rich families seeking nannies or tutors; or from other individuals given some number of credits to "spend" on the site each year. To ensure a baseline level of attachment to the workforce, the government could pay adults a flat rate in return for some minimum level of activity on the site, but people could always earn more by taking on more gigs.

Although a digital WPA might strike some people as a strange anachronism, it would be similar to a federalized version of Mechanical Turk, the popular Amazon sister site where individuals and companies post projects of varying complexity, while so-called Turks on the other end browse tasks and collect money for the ones they complete. Mechanical Turk was designed to list tasks that cannot be performed by a computer. (The name is an allusion to an 18th-century Austrian hoax, in which a famous automaton that seemed to play masterful chess concealed a human player who chose the moves and moved the pieces.)

A government marketplace might likewise specialize in those tasks that required empathy, humanity, or a personal touch. By connecting millions of people in one central hub, it might even inspire what the technology writer Robin Sloan has called "a Cambrian explosion of mega-scale creative and intellectual pursuits, a generation of Wikipedia-scale projects that can ask their users for even deeper commitments."

THERE'S A CASE to be made for using the tools of government to provide other incentives as well, to help people avoid the typical traps of joblessness and build rich lives and vibrant communities. After all, the members of the Columbus Idea Foundry probably weren't born with an innate love of lathe operation or laser-cutting. Mastering these skills requires discipline; discipline requires an education; and an education, for many people, involves the expectation that hours of often frustrating practice will eventually prove rewarding. In a post-work society, the financial rewards of education and training won't be as obvious. This is a singular challenge of imagining a flourishing post-work society: How will people discover their talents, or the rewards that come from expertise, if they don't see much incentive to develop either?

Modest payments to young people for attending and completing college, skills-training programs, or community-center workshops might eventually be worth considering. This seems radical, but the aim would be conservative—to preserve the status quo of an educated and engaged society. Whatever their career opportunities, young people will still grow up to be citizens, neighbors, and even, episodically, workers. Nudges toward education and training might be particularly beneficial to men, who are more likely to withdraw into their living rooms when they become unemployed.

7. Jobs and Callings

Decades from now, perhaps the 20th century will strike future historians as an aberration, with its religious devotion to overwork in a time of prosperity, its attenuations of family in service to job opportunity, its conflation of income with self-worth. The post-work society I've described holds a warped mirror up to today's economy, but in many ways it reflects the forgotten norms of the mid-19th century—the artisan middle class, the primacy of local communities, and the unfamiliarity with widespread joblessness.

The three potential futures of consumption, communal creativity, and contingency are not separate paths branching out from the present. They're likely to intertwine and even influence one another. Entertainment will surely become more immersive and exert a gravitational pull on people without much to do. But if that's all that happens, society will have failed. The foundry in Columbus shows how the "third places" in people's lives (communities separate from their homes and offices) could become central to growing up, learning new skills, and discovering passions. And with or without such places, many people will need to embrace the resourcefulness learned over time by cities like Youngstown, which, even if they seem like museum exhibits of an old economy, might foretell the future for many more cities in the next 25 years.

On my last day in Youngstown, I met with Howard Jesko, a 60-year-old Youngstown State graduate student, at a burger joint along the main street. A few months after Black Friday in 1977, as a senior at Ohio State University, Jesko received a phone call from his father, a specialty-hose manufacturer near Youngstown. "Don't bother coming back here for a job," his dad said. "There aren't going to be any left." Years later, Jesko returned to Youngstown to work, but he recently quit his job selling products like waterproofing systems to construction companies; his customers had been devastated by the Great Recession and weren't buying much anymore. Around the same time, a left-knee replacement due to degenerative arthritis resulted in a 10-day hospital stay, which gave him time to think about the future. Jesko decided to go back to school to become a professor. "My true calling," he told me, "has always been to teach."

One theory of work holds that people tend to see themselves in jobs, careers, or callings. Individuals who say their work is "just a job" emphasize that they are working for money rather than aligning themselves with any higher purpose. Those with pure careerist ambitions are focused not only on income but also on the status that comes with promotions and the growing renown of their peers. But one pursues a calling not only for pay or status, but also for the intrinsic fulfillment of the work itself.

When I think about the role that work plays in people's self-esteem—particularly in America—the prospect of a *no-work* future seems hopeless. There is no universal basic income that can prevent the civic ruin of a country built on a handful of workers permanently subsidizing the idleness of tens of millions of people. But a future of *less work* still holds a glint of hope, because the necessity of salaried jobs now prevents so many from seeking immersive activities that they enjoy.

After my conversation with Jesko, I walked back to my car to drive out of Youngstown. I thought about Jesko's life as it might have been had Youngstown's steel mills never given way to a steel museum—had the city continued to provide stable, predictable careers to its residents. If Jesko had taken a job in the steel industry, he might be preparing for retirement today. Instead, that industry collapsed and then, years later, another recession struck. The outcome of this cumulative grief is that Howard Jesko is not retiring at 60. He's getting his master's degree to become a teacher. It took the loss of so many jobs to force him to pursue the work he always wanted to do.

Critical Thinking

1. What would a transition from labor force to leisure force look like?

2. What is the impact of on-demand apps like uber on the workplace?

3. What social and cultural changes might be brought to bear if technological progress eliminates work as we know it?

Internet References

A World Without Work? If Work Is Service, the Opportunities to Work Are Infinite
 https://goo.gl/6ZnP4Q

The Jobs We'll Lose to Machines—and the Ones We Won't (TED Talk)
 https://goo.gl/Y1H2aD

The Political Economy of a World Without Work
 https://goo.gl/z7wJ8k

Would a Work-Free World Be So Bad?
 https://goo.gl/skb0st

DEREK THOMPSON is a senior editor at *The Atlantic*, where he writes about economics, labor markets, and the entertainment business.

Article

Prepared by: Liz Friedman, *DePaul University* and
Daniel Mittleman, *DePaul University*

As Data Overflows Online, Researchers Grapple with Ethics

Vindu Goel

Learning Outcomes

After reading this article, you will be able to:

- Assess the controversial research known as the "Facebook emotion experiment."
- Discuss the role of ethics in the manipulation of personal data on the Internet.
- Acknowledge the absence of adequate federal guidance for large-scale research on Internet users.

Scholars are exhilarated by the prospect of tapping into the vast troves of personal data collected by Facebook, Google, Amazon and a host of start-ups, which they say could transform social science research.

Once forced to conduct painstaking personal interviews with subjects, scientists can now sit at a screen and instantly play with the digital experiences of millions of Internet users. It's the frontier of social science—experiments on people who may never even know they are subjects of study, let alone explicitly consent.

"This is a new era," said Jeffrey T. Hancock, a Cornell University professor of communication and information science. "I liken it a little bit to when chemistry got the microscope."

User Experiments JULY 28

But the new era has brought some controversy with it. Professor Hancock was a co-author of the Facebook study in which the social network quietly manipulated the news feeds of nearly 700,000 people to learn how the changes affected their emotions. When the research was published in June, the outrage was immediate.

Now Professor Hancock and other university and corporate researchers are grappling with how to create ethical guidelines for this kind of research. In his first interview since the Facebook study was made public, Professor Hancock said he would help develop such guidelines by leading a series of discussions among academics, corporate researchers, and government agencies like the National Science Foundation.

"As part of moving forward on this, we've got to engage," he said. "This is a giant societal conversation that needs to take place."

Scholars from M.I.T. and Stanford University are planning panels and conferences on the topic, and several academic journals are working on special issues devoted to ethics.

Microsoft Research, a quasi-independent arm of the software company, is a prominent voice in the conversation. It hosted a panel last month on the Facebook research with Professor Hancock and is offering a software tool to scholars to help them quickly survey consumers about the ethics of a project in its early stages.

The Federal Trade Commission, which regulates companies on issues like privacy and fair treatment of Internet users, is also planning to get involved. Although the agency declined to comment specifically on the Facebook study, the broader issues touch on principles important to the agency's chairwoman, Edith Ramirez.

"Consumers should be in the driver's seat when it comes to their data," Ms. Ramirez said in an interview. "They don't want to be left in the dark and they don't want to be surprised at how it's used."

Facebook, which has apologized for its experiment, declined further comment, except to say, "We're talking with academics and industry about how to improve our research process."

Much of the research done by the Internet companies is in-house and aimed at product adjustments, like whether people prefer news articles or cat videos in their Facebook feeds or how to make Google's search results more accurate.

But bigger social questions are studied as well, often in partnership with academic institutions, and scientists are eager to conduct even more ambitious research.

The Facebook emotion experiment was in that vein. The brainchild of a company data scientist, Adam D. I. Kramer, but designed and analyzed with help from Professor Hancock and another academic researcher, Jamie E. Guillory, it was intended to shed light on how emotions spread through large populations. Facebook deliberately changed the number of positive and negative posts in the subjects' news feeds over a week in January 2012, then looked at how the changes affected the emotional tone of the users' subsequent Facebook posts.

In another well-known experiment, Facebook sent voting reminders to 61 million American users on Election Day in 2010. Some users also saw a list of their friends who said they had already voted, and the researchers found that the specific social nudge prompted more of those people to go to the polls. The study prompted some to suggest that Facebook had the power to sway election results.

Social scientists presented a message like this one to more than 60 million Facebook users during the 2010 Congressional elections.

Such testing raises fundamental questions. What types of experiments are so intrusive that they need prior consent or prompt disclosure after the fact? How do companies make sure that customers have a clear understanding of how their personal information might be used? Who even decides what the rules should be?

Existing federal rules governing research on human subjects, intended for medical research, generally require consent from those studied unless the potential for harm is minimal. But many social science scholars say the federal rules never contemplated large-scale research on Internet users and provide inadequate guidance for it.

For Internet projects conducted by university researchers, institutional review boards can be helpful in vetting projects. However, corporate researchers like those at Facebook don't face such formal reviews.

Sinan Aral, a professor at the Massachusetts Institute of Technology's Sloan School of Management who has conducted large-scale social experiments with several tech companies, said any new rules must be carefully formulated.

"We need to understand how to think about these rules without chilling the research that has the promise of moving us miles and miles ahead of where we are today in understanding human poplulations," he said. Professor Aral is planning a panel discussion on ethics at an M.I.T. conference on digital experimentation in October. (The professor also does some data analysis for The New York Times Company.)

Some scientists had been thinking about these issues for several years, but the discussions have boiled over since the Facebook experiment.

"It's the case study we're all talking about," said Lucy Bernholz, a visiting scholar at Stanford's Center on Philanthropy and Civil Society, who is organizing a conference in September on the ethics of digital data, including what limits should be placed on its use.

Mary L. Gray, a senior researcher at Microsoft Research and associate professor at Indiana University's Media School, who has worked extensively on ethics in social science, said that too often, researchers conducting digital experiments work in isolation with little outside guidance.

She and others at Microsoft Research spent the last two years setting up an ethics advisory committee and training program to provide guidance to researchers in the company's labs who are working with human subjects. She is now working with Professor Hancock to bring such thinking to the broader research world.

"If everyone knew the right thing to do, we would never have anyone hurt," she said. "We really don't have a place where we can have these conversations."

Dr. Gray advocates a simple litmus test for researchers: If you're afraid to ask your subjects for their permission to conduct the research, there's probably a deeper ethical issue that must be considered.

For Professor Hancock, solutions could include an opt-in process for projects that involve big changes in an Internet user's experience, and a debriefing system to inform users about smaller tests after the fact.

Companies won't willingly participate in anything that limits their ability to innovate quickly, he said, so any process has to be "effective, lightweight, quick, and accountable."

While some would say the risks of the Facebook study were obvious, Professor Hancock said the researchers didn't realize that manipulating the news feed, even modestly, would make some people feel violated.

He learned otherwise from hundreds of anguished and angry e-mails he received after the work was published. "They said, 'You can't mess with my emotions. It's like messing with me. It's mind control.'"

Critical Thinking

1. Is Professor Jeffrey T. Hancock's likening of this "new era" to "when chemistry got the microscope" a valid metaphor? Why or why not?
2. How much of a concern should it be that Facebook may have the power to sway election results?
3. Does Professor Hancock's contention that the researchers did not realize that manipulating the news feed would make people feel violated help to remove at least some of the researchers' culpability? Explain.

Internet References

New York Times: "Facebook Tinkers With Users' Emotions in News Feed Experiment, Stirring Outcry"
   www.nytimes.com/2014/06/30/technology/facebook-tinkers-with-users-emotions-in-news-feed-experiment-stirring-outcry.html?_r=0

Washington Post: "Was the Facebook emotion experiment unethical?"
   www.washingtonpost.com/blogs/monkey-cage/wp/2014/07/01/was-the-facebook-emotion-experiment-unethical

WIRED: "Everything You Need to Know About Facebook's Controversial Emotion Experiment"
   www.wired.com/2014/06/everything-you-need-to-know-about-facebooks-manipulative-experiment

Unit 2

UNIT

Prepared by: Liz Friedman, *DePaul University* and
Daniel Mittleman, *DePaul University*

Social Media and Community

Almost every American college student knows that the First Amendment to the Constitution guarantees the right to practice any religion and to exercise free speech. What many may not know are the other rights specified by the First Amendment: the right to peaceably assemble and the right to petition the government. The founders of the American government recognized that to establish and maintain a free and open society, not only must the ability to speak be protected but the ability to gather in groups, form associations, and network must also be protected. Without these latter protections, citizens would not be able to form the critical mass necessary to feel safe standing up and petitioning the government.

A French social observer, Emile Durkheim (1858–1917), argued that a vital society must have members who feel a sense of community. Community is easily evident in pre-industrial societies where kinship ties, shared religious beliefs, and customs reinforce group identity and shared values. Not so today in the United States, where a mobile population commutes long distances and retreats each evening to the sanctity and seclusion of individualized homes. Contemporary visitors to the United States are struck by the cornucopia of cultural options available to Americans. They find a dizzying array of religions, beliefs, philosophical and political perspectives, models of social interaction, entertainment, and now, digital gadgets. Today, we have the technical means to communicate almost instantly and effortlessly across great distances. And with that, the bounds of traditional association are being abandoned and replaced by online interactions on Facebook, Tumblr, LinkedIn, and other social media.

On the positive side, social media is a vehicle for people to express their views, connect with others, and learn about the world around them. On the negative side, however, it has also become a place where shaming and bullying occur, sometimes out in the open and other times behind a cloak of anonymity. The most famous instance of public shaming by social media might have been the firing of Justine Sacco, a corporate communications director who tweeted during layovers en route from New York to South Africa. The worst of her tweets, "Going to Africa. Hope I don't get AIDS. Just Kidding. I'm White!" was posted moments before the last leg of her journey from London to Cape Town. While she slept on the flight, the tweet went viral and more than 10,000 people responded. Those watching live on Twitter knew she'd been fired before her plane landed.[1]

In June 2016, the United Kingdom voted to leave the European Union. Those for and against campaigned vigorously on social media and given that most of us see views similar to our own across our social media feeds, it was easy to believe one's own side held a large majority when in fact it was a very close vote. It turns out that those who wanted to leave the EU were more engaged on social media and had more money behind their campaign.[2] The influence of social media on political discourse seems to be increasing worldwide. In the first US presidential debate between the two major candidates in 2016, Twitter provided real-time fact checking for those watching (and not watching) the television broadcast.[3]

The ability to communicate instantly has led to a proliferation of news sources both formal and informal. Gone are the days when there was an official version of events. Today anyone can be a publisher. News is reported almost instantly on any number of social media platforms in addition to posts by traditional media outlets. By the time, the nightly news is aired on a late weekday afternoon, most of what is shared is a rehashing of information that could have been obtained any number of other ways as it was unfolding live throughout the day.

In 2016, 62% of US adults surveyed by the Pew Research Center reported obtaining news on social media. While this did

[1] http://www.nytimes.com/2015/02/15/magazine/how-one-stupid-tweet-ruined-justine-saccos-life.html?_r=0
[2] http://marcom2.com/blog/brexit-and-social-media-6-things-you-should-know/
[3] http://www.vanityfair.com/news/2016/09/when-moderators-wont-fact-check-the-debate-twitter-users-will?mbid=social_twitter

not exclude news from other sources, only 46% reported receiving news from local TV and only 20% from print newspapers.[4] As social media becomes a primary news source, traditional journalism is struggling to keep up.

Some questions to consider in this unit:

- How does social media impact our sense of community and shared identity?

- How much does the structure of a social media platform influence discourse?
- Who decides what is newsworthy?

[4]http://www.journalism.org/2016/05/26/news-use-across-social-media-platforms-2016/#fn-55250-1

Article

Prepared by: Liz Friedman, *DePaul University* and
Daniel Mittleman, *DePaul University*

What Will Social Media Look Like in the Future?

In 2004, a Harvard student sought revenge on an ex-girlfriend. 10 years on, and Facebook is a household name that reaches an estimated 1 billion users across the globe.

GINA LEDNYAK

Learning Outcomes

After reading this article, you will be able to:

- Enumerate Gina Lednyak's five predictions regarding the future of social media.

- Identify some of Mark Zuckerberg's recent start-up acquisitions.

- Discuss Zuckerberg's characterization of virtual reality as "the platform of tomorrow."

In 2005, a man named Karim realized he couldn't find a copy of the infamous Janet Jackson "wardrobe malfunction" at the Super Bowl, and YouTube was born. Not much grander in conception, Twitter's creators serendipitously plucked a word from the dictionary meaning "a short burst of inconsequential information," which inspired a platform so powerful it has been used to coordinate the revolution of countries.

If the origin stories of today's power players are anything to go by, social media has come a long way since its humble beginnings. So what new and incredible transformations can we expect to see in the coming years?

Long before we were taking selfies, Gina Lednyak (founder of one of the country's leading agencies L&A Social Media) was involved in the first-ever test group for Facebook. Since then she has watched the evolution of social media from a simple idea to the architect of vast fortunes and media empires that are literally reshaping how we engage with one another.

Gina says, "Looking at the advancement of social media in the current landscape, we can get a good sense of the trajectory of big themes that will emerge over the coming years."

These are Gina's five predictions that we can anticipate for the future of social media:

All of Gen-Y will be famous for 15 seconds

Warhol might have been on the money when he said, "In the future, everyone will be world-famous for 15 minutes."

Although, it will be more like 15 seconds. It seems as though every person is under the guise that they're just one viral video away from becoming famous. And it's kind of true. From YouTube sensations to Vine megastars, there's no question that an increasing number are enjoying their 15 seconds. As society's attention span continues to shrink and the value we place on digital things with minimal substance grows, we can expect to see the wave of 15-second-celebrity continue to rise to new and incredible levels.

Dawn of the technosexual age

Tinder is creating an entirely new set of social patterns that are changing the way we engage. The app has not only gamified dating; but by eliminating time lag and distance, Tinder has closed the gap between digital and physical courtship.

What does this mean? While social media will never replace face-to-face relationships, the rise of mobile dating will see social serendipity continue to plunge. The dating market will become more and more defined by efficiency, instant gratification and by our growing curiosity; to not only know about other people's interests and personality without delay, but what they think of ours.

Love it or hate it, Facebook is here to stay

Since Mark Zuckerberg launched "The Facebook" into the world from his dorm room, it's grown into one of the most valuable companies in history, worth $135 billion. Despite this, recent times have seen endless questions around the future of Facebook. But while commentators continue to debate, Zuckerberg has been cleverly collecting start-up acquisitions, from WhatsApp to Britain's Ascenta; and over the coming decade Facebook will continue its transition from the world's largest social network to a bona fide tech giant.

Virtual reality meets social networks

One of these clever acquisitions includes an unexpected multi-million dollar deal to acquire Oculus, the company behind the Oculus Rift virtual reality headset. And our guess is Facebook has a little more planned for Oculus than a virtual reality Farmville. The Zuck himself has called virtual reality "the platform of tomorrow" with the chance to "change the way we work, play and communicate." It has left a lot of us wondering what in the world a Social-Media-Alternate-Universe looks like. This, we can't predict. But we can tell you that big changes to online social experiences are on the way.

The form that wearable technology will take in the future is also up for debate. Much bigger than smart watches and fitness bands, you can expect to see entirely different products emerge. Think helmets with built-in navigation systems, wearables for pets and smart buttons that could be pressed to change the colour of your clothes.

Social media will infiltrate our lives even more in the future. *Source: ThinkStock*

Will there be another MySpace tragedy?

People often dispute when the next "MySpace Situation" will happen.

Unfortunately, one small change in user habit or perception has the potential to steamroll a social media network overnight. It's hard to predict if one of today's power players will suffer a glorious fall from grace akin to MySpace's; but what MySpace didn't have is access to deep analytics, big data and the ability to learn from other networks. In essence, MySpace didn't evolve to meet consumer needs.

We predict the only way the bubble will burst for one of today's social media giants is if it ignores user demand, much like MySpace did.

Critical Thinking

1. By the year 2025, will the "technosexual age" be a thing of the past, or will social media be even more integral to dating than it now is? Explain.
2. Describe a form of wearable technology that is likely to be among the first in common, everyday use.
3. In what ways could MySpace have better evolved to meet consumer needs?

Internet References

MIT Technology Review: "Virtual Reality Aims for the Mobile Phone"
   www.technologyreview.com/news/532351/virtual-reality-aims-for-the-mobile-phone

PC Magazine: "Facebook Looks to Drones to Boost Internet Access"
   www.pcmag.com/article2/0,2817,2455585,00.asp

Tufts Observer: "Technosexual: Identity in the Age of Dating Apps"
   http://tuftsobserver.org/technosexual-identity-in-the-age-of-dating-apps

---

GINA LEDNYAK is the founder of one of the country's leading social media agencies.

Prepared by: Liz Friedman, *DePaul University* and
Daniel Mittleman, *DePaul University*

Article

Activism Moves to Facebook: Why What's Good for Social Media Might Not Be So Good for Democracy

The recorded shooting of Philando Castile is just one example of how social media is changing the face of activism.

Sarah Jaffe

Learning Outcomes

After reading this article, you will be able to:

- Explain how social media might be used to advance a message.
- Evaluate the influence of Facebook's algorithm.
- Identify consequences of Facebook's push to sponsored content.

A round the country, thousands have returned to the streets again to protest the deaths of black people at the hands of the police. One of those deaths, the shooting of 32-year-old Philando Castile in Minnesota was broadcast on Facebook Live by Castile's girlfriend, Diamond Reynolds, spurring the outrage that prompted people around the country to act.

The fact that an extraordinarily self-possessed user managed to deploy Facebook's live tool to broadcast a police killing seemed inevitable once it had happened. Videos of other such killings, spread by social media, have been a key driver of the Black Lives Matter movement. While Facebook's decision to privilege video, particularly video hosted on Facebook itself, in its ever-changing algorithms likely helped Reynolds's video go viral, but it also raises questions about how much power social networking sites have over politics and activism.

While social media has become integral to the work of political organizing, activists are victims of the success they've helped create for the social networks. As social networking companies become the new media giants, they've become less welcoming to the grass roots. Algorithm tweaks leave some scrambling to adapt their strategies. Harassment and trolling—particularly targeting the marginalized—drive others away. And then there is the question of whether progressive activists can trust the motives of those who control the media they use.

For activists, this presents challenges. As Malaya Davis of the Ohio Student Association notes, social media remains a particularly potent tool in "high-intensity movement moments" like now, as well as for community-building in quieter times. Yet problems emerging around the use of social media have led organizers like herself to examine their strategy.

Algorithm troubles

Online organizing persists, despite the fact that Facebook sometimes seems determined to kill it. With some 1.65 billion active users, Facebook is easily the world's largest social network, and that means that every tweak in the algorithms that decide which information its users will see can have a massive effect.

Jenni Dye, who first made her Twitter account public during the Wisconsin protests against Gov. Scott Walker's 2011 anti-union law, considers that moment a "sweet spot in the emergence of social media."

"More and more people were joining Twitter and Facebook, so it was the perfect opportunity to reach a bunch of people but not so many people that your message got drowned out," she says. Now, as an elected member of the Dane County Board of Supervisors and the research director for the nonprofit One Wisconsin Now, she finds that on social media "we've reached a point where there are so many voices that it's harder to break through that noise." Even reaching people who have already "liked" her organization's page has become a challenge.

"You have to have a lot of time to keep up with the algorithm," she adds. "If you aren't going to buy into their just-pay-to-have-your-content-seen service strategy, you have to have time then to come up with a strategy of how to work within the algorithm to still be seen." That makes it harder for new voices and new organizations to break in, Dye notes. Groups or individual users who already have a lot of friends or likes will be more likely to show up in users' news feed, generating even more clicks for them.

The recent changes in the site seem aimed at producing more revenue for Facebook—users who can't afford to pay to promote their pages often find their content hidden with only a few lonely "likes." (Facebook did not respond to multiple requests for an interview for this piece.)

"Their pushing of sponsored content has become much more aggressive over the past six months or so," says Cayden Mak, chief technology officer of 18 Million Rising, a group founded to promote civic engagement and movements within the Asian-American and Pacific Islander community. "It is really tempting, because they're like, 'For a very small amount of money you can promote your thing!' and it's in everything. When I look at Facebook on my phone during off hours it's like 'Don't you want to promote 18 Million Rising?'" Other organizers complain of event invitations being limited in an attempt, perhaps, to push them toward paid advertising.

Of particular concern to political organizers lately has been the question of whether Facebook is intentionally stifling certain topics. The site launched a new tagging system in January to help organizations better target their desired audiences, but the news broke that Black Lives Matter was not an available tag in the system. That followed on the heels of a report, citing a former Facebook "news curator," that the curators regularly suppressed conservative news, and led Facebook users once again to wonder how much control they had over their experience on the site. Facebook curators also said that they were told to "inject" selected stories into the site's trending topics.

"It does raise the question of how much of this is human control," Mak says. "It's impossible to say where humans come into the process and who those humans are, what their perspectives, understandings and biases are." Those perspectives can come into play with trending topic curation or even content moderation. "If you're reporting content to content moderators in multiple countries who don't necessarily understand, especially when we talk about the ways that we talk about race and racism in the U.S. context, it opens up this door for basically naive censorship." Posts that use certain words or imagery often get pulled, he explains, even if the words were used to describe something that happened rather than to insult, or an image had news or historical value. More questions arose when Diamond Reynolds's video of the Castile shooting disappeared from Facebook. The company originally blamed its disappearance on a "glitch," but an unconfirmed report later surfaced blaming the police.

Because it's not an arm of the government or a public utility, Facebook is under no First Amendment obligations. Under the company's Terms of Service, it can block any content it wants, but its users would like some transparency in how those choices are made. Michelle Gunderson, a teacher and member of the Chicago Teachers Union and the Caucus of Rank-and-File Educators says that she's been put in "Facebook jail" (had her account blocked from posting) after a post she wrote about the education reform group Teach for America was reported.

Even so, Gunderson and the CTU teachers continue to use Facebook and have found ways to work within its algorithms. They shot one-minute videos around their April strike vote, explaining their reasons for voting to walk off the job, which were particularly successful.

Facebook has been central to the work of OUR Walmart, a group of Walmart workers who have been organizing for better working conditions at the retail giant since 2012. But they spend less time these days on their main page, using a small bit of paid promotion as a supplement to it. Unlike most of the labor movement, which still uses social mainly to push one-way messages, OUR Walmart uses Facebook groups to connect to new recruits and let workers connect with each other and realize the problems that are common across multiple stores. On the Facebook groups, "people find other people in their stores," says Cynthia Murray, one of the group's founding members. "They had no idea that they were in one of our groups."

Social media, says Andrea Dehlendorf, co-director of OUR Walmart, is "such an opportunity for workers to build power for themselves, and it requires organizations to be really open and to not fear the dialogue." The workers, not staff members, are the most effective organizers.

Ultimately, whether it makes sense for organizers to spend a lot of energy (or money) on Facebook depends on which audience they are trying to reach. Social media was an effective part of the Ohio Student Association's successful campaign against Cuyahoga County Prosecutor Timothy McGinty after the failure to prosecute the police officer who killed 12-year-old Tamir Rice and the botched prosecutions of other officers who killed black Cleveland residents.

Critical Thinking

1. How much power should social media sites have over politics and activism?

2. How do tweaks in the algorithm Facebook uses influence an organizer's ability to promote their cause?

3. Should Facebook be able to stifle certain topics? Defend your position.

Internet References

Facebook Employees Asked Mark Zuckerberg if They Should Try to Stop a Donald Trump Presidency
https://goo.gl/hdRlBf

Facebook Outreach Tool Ignores Black Lives Matter
https://goo.gl/GbvAUr

Mark Zuckerberg's Dilemma with Conservatives
https://goo.gl/fu7rN6

Jaffe, Sarah. "Activism Moves to Facebook: Why What's Good for Social Media Might Not Be So Good for Democracy," *Salon*, July 2016. Copyright © 2016 by Salon Media Group. Used with permission.

Article

Prepared by: Liz Friedman, *DePaul University* and
Daniel Mittleman, *DePaul University*

How Technology Disrupted the Truth

Social media has swallowed the news—threatening the funding of public-interest reporting and ushering in an era when everyone has their own facts. But the consequences go far beyond journalism

Katharine Viner

Learning Outcomes

After reading this article, you will be able to:

- Explain how the 'filter bubble' works.
- Describe the consumerist shift in the values of journalism.
- Identify the prevailing business model of digital news organisations today.

One Monday morning last September, Britain woke to a depraved news story. The prime minister, David Cameron, had committed an 'obscene act with a dead pig's head', according to the Daily Mail. 'A distinguished Oxford contemporary claims Cameron once took part in an outrageous initiation ceremony at a Piers Gaveston event, involving a dead pig', the paper reported. Piers Gaveston is the name of a riotous Oxford university dining society; the authors of the story claimed their source was an MP, who said he had seen photographic evidence: 'His extraordinary suggestion is that the future PM inserted a private part of his anatomy into the animal'.

The story, extracted from a new biography of Cameron, sparked an immediate furore. It was gross, it was a great opportunity to humiliate an elitist prime minister, and many felt it rang true for a former member of the notorious Bullingdon Club. Within minutes, #Piggate and #Hameron were trending on Twitter, and even senior politicians joined the fun: Nicola

Sturgeon said the allegations had 'entertained the whole country', while Paddy Ashdown joked that Cameron was 'hogging the headlines'. At first, the BBC refused to mention the allegations, and 10 Downing Street said it would not 'dignify' the story with a response—but soon it was forced to issue a denial. And so a powerful man was sexually shamed, in a way that had nothing to do with his divisive politics, and in a way he could never really respond to. But who cares? He could take it.

Then, after a full day of online merriment, something shocking happened. Isabel Oakeshott, the Daily Mail journalist who had co-written the biography with Lord Ashcroft, a billionaire businessman, went on TV and admitted that she did not know whether her huge, scandalous scoop was even true. Pressed to provide evidence for the sensational claim, Oakeshott admitted she had none.

'We couldn't get to the bottom of that source's allegations', she said on Channel 4 News. 'So we merely reported the account that the source gave us . . . We don't say whether we believe it to be true'. In other words, there was no evidence that the prime minister of the United Kingdom had once 'inserted a private part of his anatomy' into the mouth of a dead pig—a story reported in dozens of newspapers and repeated in millions of tweets and Facebook updates, which many people presumably still believe to be true today.

Oakeshott went even further to absolve herself of any journalistic responsibility: 'It's up to other people to decide whether they give it any credibility or not', she concluded. This was not, of course, the first time that outlandish claims were published on the basis of flimsy evidence, but this was an unusually brazen defence. It seemed that journalists were no longer required to believe their own stories to be true, nor, apparently, did they need to provide evidence. Instead it was up to the reader—who does not even know the identity of the source—to make up their own mind. But based on what? Gut instinct, intuition, mood?

Does the truth matter any more?

Nine months after Britain woke up giggling at Cameron's hypothetical porcine intimacies, the country arose on the morning of 24 June to the very real sight of the prime minister standing outside Downing Street at 8am, announcing his own resignation.

'The British people have voted to leave the European Union and their will must be respected', Cameron declared. 'It was not a decision that was taken lightly, not least because so many things were said by so many different organisations about the significance of this decision. So there can be no doubt about the result'.

But what soon became clear was that almost everything was still in doubt. At the end of a campaign that dominated the news for months, it was suddenly obvious that the winning side had no plan for how or when the United Kingdom would leave the EU—while the deceptive claims that carried the leave campaign to victory suddenly crumbled. At 6.31am on Friday 24 June, just over an hour after the result of the EU referendum had become clear, Ukip leader Nigel Farage conceded that a post-Brexit UK would not in fact have £350m a week spare to spend on the NHS—a key claim of Brexiteers that was even emblazoned on the Vote Leave campaign bus. A few hours later, the Tory MEP Daniel Hannan stated that immigration was not likely to be reduced—another key claim.

It was hardly the first time that politicians had failed to deliver what they promised, but it might have been the first time they admitted on the morning after victory that the promises had been false all along. This was the first major vote in the era of post-truth politics: the listless remain campaign attempted to fight fantasy with facts, but quickly found that the currency of fact had been badly debased.

The remain side's worrying facts and worried experts were dismissed as 'Project Fear'—and quickly neutralised by opposing 'facts:' if 99 experts said the economy would crash and one disagreed, the BBC told us that each side had a different view of the situation. (This is a disastrous mistake that ends up obscuring truth, and echoes how some report climate change.) Michael Gove declared that 'people in this country have had enough of experts' on Sky News. He also compared 10 Nobel prize-winning economists who signed an anti-Brexit letter to Nazi scientists loyal to Hitler.

For months, the Eurosceptic press trumpeted every dubious claim and rubbished every expert warning, filling the front pages with too many confected anti-migrant headlines to count—many of them later quietly corrected in very small print. A week before the vote—on the same day Nigel Farage unveiled his inflammatory 'Breaking Point' poster, and the Labour MP Jo Cox, who had campaigned tirelessly for refugees, was shot dead—the cover of the Daily Mail featured a picture of migrants in the back of a lorry entering the UK, with the headline 'We are from Europe—let us in!' The next day, the Mail and the Sun, which also carried the story, were forced to admit that the stowaways were actually from Iraq and Kuwait.

The brazen disregard for facts did not stop after the referendum: just this weekend, the short-lived Conservative leadership candidate Andrea Leadsom, fresh from a starring role in the leave campaign, demonstrated the waning power of evidence. After telling the Times that being a mother would make her a better PM than her rival Theresa May, she cried 'gutter journalism!' and accused the newspaper of misrepresenting her remarks—even though she said exactly that, clearly and definitively and on tape. Leadsom is a post-truth politician even about her own truths.

When a fact begins to resemble whatever you feel is true, it becomes very difficult for anyone to tell the difference between facts that are true and 'facts' that are not. The leave campaign was well aware of this—and took full advantage, safe in the knowledge that the Advertising Standards Authority has no power to police political claims. A few days after the vote, Arron Banks, Ukip's largest donor and the main funder of the Leave. EU campaign, told the Guardian that his side knew all along that facts would not win the day. 'It was taking an American-style media approach', said Banks. 'What they said early on was 'Facts don't work', and that's it. The remain campaign featured fact, fact, fact, fact, fact. It just doesn't work. You have got to connect with people emotionally. It's the Trump success'.

It was little surprise that some people were shocked after the result to discover that Brexit might have serious consequences and few of the promised benefits. When 'facts don't work' and voters don't trust the media, everyone believes in their own 'truth'—and the results, as we have just seen, can be devastating.

How did we end up here? And how do we fix it?

Twenty-five years after the first website went online, it is clear that we are living through a period of dizzying transition. For 500 years after Gutenberg, the dominant form of information was the printed page: knowledge was primarily delivered in a fixed format, one that encouraged readers to believe in stable and settled truths.

Now, we are caught in a series of confusing battles between opposing forces: between truth and falsehood, fact and rumour, and kindness and cruelty; between the few and the many, the connected and the alienated; between the open platform of the web as its architects envisioned it and the gated enclosures of Facebook and other social networks; and between an informed public and a misguided mob.

What is common to these struggles—and what makes their resolution an urgent matter—is that they all involve the diminishing status of truth. This does not mean that there are no truths. It simply means, as this year has made very clear, that we cannot agree on what those truths are, and when there is no consensus about the truth and no way to achieve it, chaos soon follows.

Increasingly, what counts as a fact is merely a view that someone feels to be true—and technology has made it very easy for these 'facts' to circulate with a speed and reach that was unimaginable in the Gutenberg era (or even a decade ago). A dubious story about Cameron and a pig appears in a tabloid one morning, and by noon, it has flown around the world on social media and turned up in trusted news sources everywhere. This may seem like a small matter, but its consequences are enormous.

'The Truth', as Peter Chippindale and Chris Horrie wrote in Stick It Up Your Punter! their history of the Sun newspaper, is a 'bald statement which every newspaper prints at its peril'. There are usually several conflicting truths on any given subject, but in the era of the printing press, words on a page nailed things down, whether they turned out to be true or not. The information felt like the truth, at least until the next day brought another update or a correction, and we all shared a common set of facts.

This settled 'truth' was usually handed down from above: an established truth, often fixed in place by an establishment. This arrangement was not without flaws: too much of the press often exhibited a bias towards the status quo and a deference to authority, and it was prohibitively difficult for ordinary people to challenge the power of the press. Now, people distrust much of what is presented as fact—particularly if the facts in question are uncomfortable, or out of sync with their own views—and while some of that distrust is misplaced, some of it is not.

In the digital age, it is easier than ever to publish false information, which is quickly shared and taken to be true—as we often see in emergency situations, when news is breaking in real time. To pick one example among many, during the November 2015 Paris terror attacks, rumours quickly spread on social media that the Louvre and Pompidou Centre had been hit, and that François Hollande had suffered a stroke. Trusted news organisations are needed to debunk such tall tales.

Sometimes rumours like these spread out of panic, sometimes out of malice, and sometimes deliberate manipulation, in which a corporation or regime pays people to convey their message. Whatever the motive, falsehoods and facts now spread the same way, through what academics call an 'information cascade'. As the legal scholar and online-harassment expert Danielle Citron describes it, 'people forward on what others think, even if the information is false, misleading or incomplete, because they think they have learned something valuable'. This cycle repeats itself, and before you know it, the cascade has unstoppable momentum. You share a friend's post on Facebook, perhaps to show kinship or agreement or that you're 'in the know', and thus you increase the visibility of their post to others.

Algorithms such as the one that powers Facebook's news feed are designed to give us more of what they think we want—which means that the version of the world we encounter every day in our own personal stream has been invisibly curated to reinforce our pre-existing beliefs. When Eli Pariser, the co-founder of Upworthy, coined the term 'filter bubble' in 2011, he was talking about how the personalised web—and in particular Google's personalised search function, which means that no two people's Google searches are the same—means that we are less likely to be exposed to information that challenges us or broadens our worldview, and less likely to encounter facts that disprove false information that others have shared.

Pariser's plea, at the time, was that those running social media platforms should ensure that 'their algorithms prioritise countervailing views and news that's important, not just the stuff that's most popular or most self-validating'. But in less than five years, thanks to the incredible power of a few social platforms, the filter bubble that Pariser described has become much more extreme.

On the day after the EU referendum, in a Facebook post, the British internet activist and mySociety founder, Tom Steinberg, provided a vivid illustration of the power of the filter bubble—and the serious civic consequences for a world where information flows largely through social networks:

I am actively searching through Facebook for people celebrating the Brexit leave victory, but the filter bubble is SO strong, and extends SO far into things like Facebook's custom search that I can't find anyone who is happy *despite the fact that over half the country is clearly jubilant today* and despite the fact that I'm *actively* looking to hear what they are saying.

This echo-chamber problem is now SO severe and SO chronic that I can only beg any friends I have who actually work for Facebook and other major social media and technology to urgently tell their leaders that to not act on this problem now is tantamount to actively supporting and funding the tearing apart of the fabric of our societies . . . We're getting countries where one half just doesn't know anything at all about the other.

But asking technology companies to 'do something' about the filter bubble presumes that this is a problem that can be easily fixed—rather than one baked into the very idea of social networks that are designed to give you what you and your friends want to see.

Facebook, which launched only in 2004, now has 1.6bn users worldwide. It has become the dominant way for people to find news on the internet—and in fact it is dominant in ways that would have been impossible to imagine in the newspaper era. As Emily Bell has written: 'Social media hasn't just swallowed journalism, it has swallowed everything. It has swallowed political campaigns, banking systems, personal histories, the leisure industry, retail, even government and security'.

Bell, the director of the Tow Centre for Digital Journalism at Columbia University—and a board member of the Scott Trust, which owns the Guardian—has outlined the seismic impact of social media for journalism. 'Our news ecosystem has changed more dramatically in the past five years', she wrote in March, 'than perhaps at any time in the past 500'. The future of publishing is being put into the 'hands of the few, who now control the destiny of the many'. News publishers have lost control over the distribution of their journalism, which for many readers is now 'filtered through algorithms and platforms which are opaque and unpredictable'. This means that social media companies have become overwhelmingly powerful in determining what we read—and enormously profitable from the monetisation of other people's work. As Bell notes: 'There is a far greater concentration of power in this respect than there has ever been in the past'.

Publications curated by editors have in many cases been replaced by a stream of information chosen by friends, contacts and family, processed by secret algorithms. The old idea of a wide-open web—where hyperlinks from site to site created a non-hierarchical and decentralised network of information—has been largely supplanted by platforms designed to maximise your time within their walls, some of which (such as Instagram and Snapchat) do not allow outward links at all.

Many people, in fact, especially teenagers, now spend more and more of their time on closed chat apps, which allow users to create groups to share messages privately—perhaps because young people, who are most likely to have faced harassment online, are seeking more carefully protected social spaces. But the closed space of a chat app is an even more restrictive silo than the walled garden of Facebook or other social networks.

As the pioneering Iranian blogger Hossein Derakhshan, who was imprisoned in Tehran for six years for his online activity, wrote in the Guardian earlier this year, the 'diversity that the world wide web had originally envisioned' has given way to 'the centralisation of information' inside a select few social networks—and the end result is 'making us all less powerful in relation to government and corporations'.

Of course, Facebook does not decide what you read—at least not in the traditional sense of making decisions—and nor does it dictate what news organisations produce. But when one platform becomes the dominant source for accessing information, news organisations will often tailor their own work to the demands of this new medium. (The most visible evidence of Facebook's influence on journalism is the panic that accompanies any change in the news feed algorithm that threatens to reduce the page views sent to publishers.)

In the last few years, many news organisations have steered themselves away from public-interest journalism and towards junk-food news, chasing page views in the vain hope of attracting clicks and advertising (or investment)—but like junk food, you hate yourself when you've gorged on it. The most extreme manifestation of this phenomenon has been the creation of fake news farms, which attract traffic with false reports that are designed to look like real news, and are therefore widely shared on social networks. But the same principle applies to news that is misleading or sensationally dishonest, even if it wasn't created to deceive: the new measure of value for too many news organisations is virality rather than truth or quality.

Of course, journalists have got things wrong in the past—either by mistake or prejudice or sometimes by intent. (Freddie Starr probably didn't eat a hamster.) So it would be a mistake to think this is a new phenomenon of the digital age. But what is new and significant is that today, rumours and lies are read just as widely as copper-bottomed facts—and often more widely, because they are wilder than reality and more exciting to share. The cynicism of this approach was expressed most nakedly by Neetzan Zimmerman, formerly employed by Gawker as a specialist in high-traffic viral stories. 'Nowadays it's not important if a story's real', he said in 2014. 'The only thing that really matters is whether people click on it'. Facts, he suggested, are over; they are a relic from the age of the printing press, when readers had no choice. He continued: 'If a person is not sharing a news story, it is, at its core, not news'.

The increasing prevalence of this approach suggests that we are in the midst of a fundamental change in the values of journalism—a consumerist shift. Instead of strengthening social bonds, or creating an informed public, or the idea of news as a civic good, a democratic necessity, it creates gangs, which spread instant falsehoods that fit their views, reinforcing each other's beliefs, driving each other deeper into shared opinions, rather than established facts.

But the trouble is that the business model of most digital news organisations is based around clicks. News media around the world has reached a fever-pitch of frenzied binge-publishing, in order to scrape up digital advertising's pennies and cents. (And there's not much advertising to be got: in the first quarter of

2016, 85 cents of every new dollar spent in the United States on online advertising went to Google and Facebook. That used to go to news publishers.)

In the news feed on your phone, all stories look the same—whether they come from a credible source or not. And, increasingly, otherwise-credible sources are also publishing false, misleading, or deliberately outrageous stories. 'Clickbait is king, so newsrooms will uncritically print some of the worst stuff out there, which lends legitimacy to bullshit', said Brooke Binkowski, an editor at the debunking website Snopes, in an interview with the Guardian in April. 'Not all newsrooms are like this, but a lot of them are'.

We should be careful not to dismiss anything with an appealing digital headline as clickbait—appealing headlines are a good thing, if they lead the reader to quality journalism, both serious and not. My belief is that what distinguishes good journalism from poor journalism is labour: the journalism that people value the most is that for which they can tell someone has put in a lot of work—where they can feel the effort that has been expended on their behalf, over tasks big or small, important or entertaining. It is the reverse of so-called 'churnalism', the endless recycling of other people's stories for clicks.

The digital advertising model doesn't currently discriminate between true or not true, just big or small. As the American political reporter Dave Weigel wrote in the wake of a hoax story that became a viral hit all the way back in 2013: ''Too good to check' used to be a warning to newspaper editors not to jump on bullshit stories. Now it's a business model'.

A news-publishing industry desperately chasing down every cheap click doesn't sound like an industry in a position of strength, and indeed, news publishing as a business is in trouble. The shift to digital publishing has been a thrilling development for journalism—as I said in my 2013 AN Smith lecture at the University of Melbourne, 'The Rise of the Reader', it has induced 'a fundamental redrawing of journalists' relationship with our audience, how we think about our readers, our perception of our role in society, our status'. It has meant we have found new ways to get stories—from our audience, from data, from social media. It has given us new ways to tell stories—with interactive technologies and now with virtual reality. It has given us new ways to distribute our journalism, to find new readers in surprising places; and it has given us new ways to engage with our audiences, opening ourselves up to challenge and debate.

But while the possibilities for journalism have been strengthened by the digital developments of the last few years, the business model is under grave threat, because no matter how many clicks you get, it will never be enough. And if you charge readers to access your journalism you have a big challenge to persuade the digital consumer who is used to getting information for free to part with their cash.

News publishers everywhere are seeing profits and revenue drop dramatically. If you want a stark illustration of the new realities of digital media, consider the first-quarter financial results announced by the New York Times and Facebook within a week of one another earlier this year. The New York Times announced that its operating profits had fallen by 13%, to $51.5m—healthier than most of the rest of the publishing industry, but quite a drop. Facebook, meanwhile, revealed that its net income had tripled in the same period—to a quite staggering $1.51bn.

Many journalists have lost their jobs in the past decade. The number of journalists in the United Kingdom shrank by up to one-third between 2001 and 2010; US newsrooms declined by a similar amount between 2006 and 2013. In Australia, there was a 20% cut in the journalistic workforce between 2012 and 2014 alone. Earlier this year, at the Guardian we announced that we would need to lose 100 journalistic positions. In March, the Independent ceased existing as a print newspaper. Since 2005, according to research by Press Gazette, the number of local newspapers in the United Kingdom has fallen by 181—again, not because of a problem with journalism, but because of a problem with funding it.

But journalists losing their jobs is not simply a problem for journalists: it has a damaging impact on the entire culture. As the German philosopher Jürgen Habermas warned, back in 2007: 'When reorganisation and cost-cutting in this core area jeopardise accustomed journalistic standards, it hits at the very heart of the political public sphere. Because, without the flow of information gained through extensive research, and without the stimulation of arguments based on an expertise that doesn't come cheap, public communication loses its discursive vitality. The public media would then cease to resist populist tendencies, and could no longer fulfil the function it should in the context of a democratic constitutional state'.

Perhaps, then, the focus of the news industry needs to turn to commercial innovation: how to rescue the funding of journalism, which is what is under threat. Journalism has seen dramatic innovation in the last two digital decades, but business models have not. In the words of my colleague Mary Hamilton, the Guardian's executive editor for audience: 'We've transformed everything about our journalism and not enough about our businesses'.

The impact on journalism of the crisis in the business model is that, in chasing down cheap clicks at the expense of accuracy and veracity, news organisations undermine the very reason they exist: to find things out and tell readers the truth—to report, report, report.

Many newsrooms are in danger of losing what matters most about journalism: the valuable, civic, pounding-the-streets, sifting-the-database, asking-challenging-questions hard graft of uncovering things that someone doesn't want you to know. Serious, public-interest journalism is demanding, and there is more of a need for it than ever. It helps keep the powerful honest; it helps people make sense of the world and their place in it. Facts and reliable information are essential for the functioning of democracy—and the digital era has made that even more obvious.

But we must not allow the chaos of the present to cast the past in a rosy light—as can be seen from the recent resolution to a tragedy that became one of the darkest moments in the history of British journalism. At the end of April, a two-year-long inquest ruled that the 96 people who died in the Hillsborough disaster in 1989 had been unlawfully killed and had not contributed to the dangerous situation at the football ground. The verdict was the culmination of an indefatigable 27-year-campaign by the victims' families, whose case was reported for two decades with great detail and sensitivity by Guardian journalist David Conn. His journalism helped uncover the real truth about what happened at Hillsborough, and the subsequent cover-up by the police—a classic example of a reporter holding the powerful to account on behalf of the less powerful.

What the families had been campaigning against for nearly three decades was a lie put into circulation by the Sun. The tabloid's aggressive rightwing editor, Kelvin MacKenzie, blamed the fans for the disaster, suggesting that they had forced their way into the ground without tickets—a claim later revealed to be false. According to Horrie and Chippindale's history of The Sun, MacKenzie overruled his own reporter and put the words 'THE TRUTH' on the front page, alleging that Liverpool fans were drunk, that they picked the pockets of victims, that they punched, kicked and urinated on police officers, and that they shouted that they wanted sex with a dead female victim. The fans, said a 'high-ranking police officer', were 'acting like animals'. The story, as Chippindale and Horrie write, is a 'classic smear', free of any attributable evidence and 'precisely fitting MacKenzie's formula by publicising the half-baked ignorant prejudice being voiced all over the country'.

It is hard to imagine that Hillsborough could happen now: if 96 people were crushed to death in front of 53,000 smartphones, with photographs and eyewitness accounts all posted to social media, would it have taken so long for the truth to come out? Today, the police—or Kelvin MacKenzie—would not have been able to lie so blatantly and for so long.

The truth is a struggle. It takes hard graft. But the struggle is worth it: traditional news values are important and they matter and they are worth defending. The digital revolution has meant that journalists—rightly, in my view—are more accountable to their audience. And as the Hillsborough story shows, the old media were certainly capable of perpetrating appalling falsehoods, which could take years to unravel. Some of the old hierarchies have been decisively undermined, which has led to a more open debate and a more substantial challenge to the old elites whose interests often dominated the media. But the age of relentless and instant information—and uncertain truths—can be overwhelming. We career from outrage to outrage, but forget each one very quickly: it's doomsday every afternoon.

At the same time, the levelling of the information landscape has unleashed new torrents of racism and sexism and new means of shaming and harassment, suggesting a world in which the loudest and crudest arguments will prevail. It is an atmosphere that has proved particularly hostile to women and people of colour, revealing that the inequalities of the physical world are reproduced all too easily in online spaces. The Guardian is not immune—which is why one of my first initiatives as editor-in-chief was to launch the Web We Want project, in order to combat a general culture of online abuse and ask how we as an institution can foster better and more civil conversations on the web.

Above all, the challenge for journalism today is not simply technological innovation or the creation of new business models. It is to establish what role journalistic organisations still play in a public discourse that has become impossibly fragmented and radically destabilised. The stunning political developments of the past year—including the vote for Brexit and the emergence of Donald Trump as the Republican candidate for the US presidency—are not simply the byproducts of a resurgent populism or the revolt of those left behind by global capitalism.

As the academic Zeynep Tufekci argued in an essay earlier this year, the rise of Trump 'is actually a symptom of the mass media's growing weakness, especially in controlling the limits of what it is acceptable to say'. (A similar case could be made for the Brexit campaign.) 'For decades, journalists at major media organisations acted as gatekeepers who passed judgment on what ideas could be publicly discussed, and what was considered too radical', Tufekci wrote. The weakening of these gatekeepers is both positive and negative; there are opportunities and there are dangers.

As we can see from the past, the old gatekeepers were also capable of great harm, and they were often imperious in refusing space to arguments they deemed outside the mainstream political consensus. But without some form of consensus, it is hard for any truth to take hold. The decline of the gatekeepers has given Trump space to raise formerly taboo subjects, such as the cost of a global free-trade regime that benefits corporations rather than workers, an issue that American elites and much of the media had long dismissed—as well as, more obviously, allowing his outrageous lies to flourish.

When the prevailing mood is anti-elite and anti-authority, trust in big institutions, including the media, begins to crumble.

I believe that a strong journalistic culture is worth fighting for. So is a business model that serves and rewards media organisations that put the search for truth at the heart of everything—building an informed, active public that scrutinises the powerful, not an ill-informed, reactionary gang that attacks the vulnerable. Traditional news values must be embraced and celebrated: reporting, verifying, gathering together eyewitness statements, making a serious attempt to discover what really happened.

We are privileged to live in an era when we can use many new technologies—and the help of our audience—to do that. But we must also grapple with the issues underpinning digital culture, and realise that the shift from print to digital media was never just about technology. We must also address the new power dynamics that these changes have created. Technology and media do not exist in isolation—they help shape society, just as they are shaped by it in turn. That means engaging with people as civic actors, citizens, equals. It is about holding power to account, fighting for a public space, and taking responsibility for creating the kind of world we want to live in.

Critical Thinking

1. What does the author mean by 'diminishing status of truth' and how has technology, and in particular social media, influenced it?

2. Who curates the news today?

3. What is the impact of the declining journalist workforce?

Internet References

How the Media's Reliance on Social Media Made Us All Angrier—and Dumber
https://goo.gl/QrlhLg

News Use Across Social Media Platforms 2016
https://goo.gl/KM3YNV

Who Owns the News Consumer: Social Media Platforms or Publishers?
https://goo.gl/Ry9zX8

KATHARINE VINER is editor-in-chief of Guardian News & Media.

Article

Prepared by: Liz Friedman, *DePaul University* and
Daniel Mittleman, *DePaul University*

Could Social Media Be Tearing Us Apart?

While social networks have allowed the sharing of controversial opinions there remains a worry that they are helping to fuel such views.

JERRY DAYKIN

Learning Outcomes

After reading this article, you will be able to:

- Identify how social media divides us.
- Discuss how free speech fuels the development of controversial opinions.
- Summarise the consequences of 'context collapse'.

There's nothing new about swings in political ideology but there is something different about the way these debates are playing out across the world. While social media channels were hailed as great unifiers that would connect and bring people together, now they seem to be making us more divisive than ever before. Can the internet giants really be to blame for our eccentric political scene and, if so, do they have a responsibility to do anything about?

Thousands of years of democracy have been marked by striking changes in the dominant political opinion—driven by economics, immigration, charismatic leaders, emergency crises, other hot issues and at times even good marketing. The majorities commanded by many modern governments don't equate to a true majority of the popular vote but, for better or worse, the system seems to have held together far longer than its Greek creators would ever have expected. Yet in the aftermath of Britain's own Brexit vote, and as the United States gears up

for a debate just as divisive, the strength of opinions on all sides of the argument seems to be being hugely amplified.

Social media channels have been inescapably linked to political debate since their conception. Indeed they have played a public role in giving persecuted minorities voices to be heard and even in catalysing entire revolutions. Of course by the definition of free speech you cannot pick and choose who you give it to, so such platforms have also bred new types of trolls and enabled terrorist organisations to spread their rhetoric and recruit. Yet it isn't just that they allow the sharing of controversial opinions—there's a real worry they may be fuelling the development of them too.

One increasingly discussed issue is that social media naturally organises us into bubbles of people with the same opinions. Far from breaking down global barriers and exposing us to challenging new opinions, these platforms simply make it easier to find like-minded people in whatever corner of the world they were hiding before.

It's the opposite effect of real life where all sorts of social and political differences can be swept aside when you happen to live next to someone, work in the same building as someone or meet with a mutual group of friends. If you've got a passion for an obscure type of traditional tapestry, it's of course wonderful to connect with others who share the same interest – but such connections can also radicalise darker debates.

In person, we're well adapted to conversational debate – or polite avoidance of it if it's really unresolvable – and are able to build relationships on the overwhelming common ground that we do share. Through the flat reality of a computer screen, it's far harder to get to that place: any sort of written debate comes across as a much more direct challenge; we share a lot less so don't get to see the breadth of commonality; when people share opposing opinions it's a natural behaviour to simply want to unfollow, or even block them; and ultimately there's something inherently disarming about face-to-face contact which doesn't seem to apply online.

This leads rapidly to a context collapse where your news and information is no longer shared alongside a representative range of opinions, but filtered to reinforce your own beliefs. It's very hard to judge the mood of the entire country by looking at your Facebook feed, because unless you've done a very good job of building a diverse network, it's probably filled with many people saying the same thing. In the context of recent polls which suggest social media is overtaking traditional channels as the preferred source of news, this isn't merely a biased side conversation, it's a complete whitewashing of your main news channel.

A bad workman blames his tools but it does seem these tools are also colluding against us more than people realise. If you think the trending section of Twitter is your window to the wider world, then you may be surprised to learn that by default that too is showing you personalised trends most likely to interest you. The algorithms which all major social platforms use to control which content you see optimise automatically around the content you best respond to, almost certainly again further filtering out opposing opinion.

This doesn't just mute opposing opinions, it begins to have the effect of amplifying your own side of the argument too. These echo chambers of opinion can slowly reinforce specific angles of an argument and even encourage the public sharing of more controversial suggestions which you might be hesitant to do with a greater chance that they would be challenged.

The short attention spans encouraged by ever-updating feeds no doubt play a role here, too, elevating headlines and pithy tweets to have more importance than deep articles, fleshed out policies or manifestos. It moves the news agenda into emotive issues where headlines are shaped to be heart-grabbing clickbait, which people are more likely to share than a measured take on a complex issue.

Beyond the algorithms there's also a wider trend in social content actually being curated by humans – Snapchat's public stories, Twitter's moments and Facebook's trends are put together by hands, not pure algorithms. Facebook went through a recent scandal when it was accused of actively hiding right-wing stories from the feed and, while investigations have shown no evidence, the worry remains.

In fact there's really no reason why platforms couldn't have a bias, traditional media has done so for years and companies such as Buzzfeed have been outspoken in not receiving ad dollars from politicians they disagree with. The difference here is that social platforms present themselves, and are perceived to be, neutral pipes through which content and thoughts can flow. If they wish to exert a bias they should probably find a way of being more open about that.

Ultimately, it's easy for animosity and hatred to develop against people you don't see. You see it in offices every day when strings of annoyed emails melt away into collaboration when colleagues finally talk things through face to face. It's easy to hate an abstract concept but much harder when that person materialises as a friend, as a neighbour, as a colleague or as a relative.

Negative views of immigration tend to be weaker in areas with very high levels of immigration, where you are more likely to be friends with a diverse group, than those with lower levels – it's easier to blame a group when you're not personally engaging with them.

There are always going to be big political issues to discuss but, if recent events have shown us anything, it's that we need to be careful about how radically the nature of that debate is unconsciously changing and playing by new rules. Increased availability of information and freedom of speech a good thing, and breadth of opinion is essential to agitate and move us forwards.

My day job is convincing marketers to spend more time and money advertising through social platforms. For a change, it's worth acknowledging when we need to put our phones down.

Critical Thinking

1. How does social media organise us 'into bubbles of people with the same opinions'?

2. To what extent does social media amplify your own side of an argument?

3. How is social media influenced by bias?

Internet References

Facebook and Twitter Join Coalition to Improve Social Newsgathering
   https://goo.gl/cdhzzu

Fake Story in Facebook's 'Trending' News Section Highlights Social Media's Curation Challenges
   https://goo.gl/I1SkZS

Will Facebook Replace the News Media?
   https://goo.gl/h948K7

Unit 3

UNIT

Prepared by: Liz Friedman, *DePaul University* and
Daniel Mittleman, *DePaul University*

Social Media and Marketing

On average in 2016, Facebook users spend 50 minutes on the platform each day, up from 40 minutes in 2014. As a leisure activity, that is more time than any other pursuit outside of TV and movies. More than reading, exercise, and almost as much as eating and drinking. Your time is their money. Facebook's net income in the first quarter of 2016 was $1.5 billion.[1]

Facebook has more than 1.7 billion monthly active users worldwide.[2] It is no surprise advertisers are looking for ways to capture that audience. In fact advertisers on Facebook grew 33% from 3,000,000 in March 2016 to 4,000,000 in September 2016.[3] As more and more users access technology via smartphones and tablets, the advertising industry has shifted to digital, spending more than $64 billion in 2015, up nearly 60% from 2014.[4]

The information age (mid-20th century to perhaps the beginning of the 21st century) was brought about by mass adoption of computing technologies. It became possible to accumulate vast wealth by building software tools and databases to access and organize information better than others. The scarce resource that drove this economy was information, and the knowledge to use it effectively.

Several commentators have suggested that the information age was short lived; that we are moving into a new age already. But few have captured just what differentiates this new age from the information age. Clearly information is no longer a scarce resource. All of us can Google almost any information we need. Most of us are bombarded with way too much information on a daily basis in the form of e-mail, text messages, tweets, and Facebook status updates. A few of us are able to find the time to consume more than a small fraction of the information we would find interesting or useful. So, if information is no longer scare, what is it that is scarce?

Google's value propositions may provide a clue. Yes, Google provides us with information. But so do Microsoft, Apple, and others. What Google does is provide us with this information within a user experience intended to minimize our attention resources. That is, it is not the information that is scarce; rather is our time and our ability to focus on, parse through, and prioritize all the information being pushed our way. When Google helps us with that, we come back for more. And most of us will happily accept their ads on the page if we perceive real value from their services.

Google's search engine prioritizes results of our searches guessing at which pages will be most useful. Google's Gmail filters our incoming e-mail messages guessing at which ones are important. Google Maps and Earth help us navigate the physical world—and even make shopping recommendations if we request them. Google Docs, Pixlr, and YouTube (all Google products) help us organize multimedia resources in the cloud. In each case, the tool provides information, but more importantly, it organizes, filters, and prioritizes to permit us to consume information using less attention resources.

Amazon.com's growth into a retail giant can be characterized by excellence on multiple dimensions. One, they have taken a long view of a supply chain, running at a loss over their first six years of operations, not because of poor sales or management, but because they reinvested would-be profits into supply-chain infrastructure. They built large automated warehouse and distribution facilities, with far greater capacity than the needed at the time. Because of this long-term investment they can now deliver product faster, cheaper, and more reliably than almost anyone else. Faster, better, and cheaper is hard to beat.

Two, they have focused on customer personalization. Amazon has invested in ecommerce technology in the same manner they invested in supply-chain technology. By doing so, they have crafted a site effectively individualized to every shopper. Unless you have taken action (such as blocking cookies) to mask your identity from Amazon, their website will build you a customized homepage based on their knowledge of your past purchase and borrowing behaviors. They constantly strive to improve their algorithms to provide a better shopping experience (better for both Amazon and you in the sense you see products you are interested in).

And, three, they have been ambitious in moving into new retail markets while not locking into any particular business acquisition strategy. They have bought retailers and folded the stores into

[1] http://www.nytimes.com/2016/05/06/business/facebook-bends-the-rules-of-audience-engagement-to-its-advantage.html?_r=0
[2] https://zephoria.com/top-15-valuable-facebook-statistics/
[3] http://www.nbcnews.com/tech/social-media/facebook-added-1-million-advertisers-last-six-months-n655516
[4] http://www.gmrsalesandservice.com/advertising-trends-for-2016-a-shift-from-traditional-to-online/

Amazon's brand; they have partnered with established retailers serving as storefront and/or distribution channel for the partnership. Each model has been employed when deemed optimal. And this has enabled Amazon to grow inventory well beyond books and digital media, where they got their start.

Some questions to consider in this unit:

- How does data gathered from social media influence marketing?
- How effective is social media as an advertising platform?

Article

Prepared by: Liz Friedman, *DePaul University* and
Daniel Mittleman, *DePaul University*

How Psychology Will Shape the Future of Social Media Marketing

Jayson DeMers

Learning Outcomes

After reading this article, you will be able to:

- Identify, from a marketing perspective, some of the major shortcomings of current technology.

- Discuss how the degree of sophistication in an algorithm can affect its usefulness in brand promotion.

- Enumerate what DeMers calls the "four elements of any action."

- Recognize that basic psychological concepts are always applicable to social media marketing.

With marketing analytics software so pervasive, marketing professionals have the power to monitor everything on a business's social media accounts. How many retweets did a post get? Did customers favorite or reply to it? Thanks to automatic alerts, like Google Alerts, staff can also know immediately when their business gets mentioned, allowing them to take action if necessary.

One major shortcoming with current technology, however, is its inability to accurately detect context in human behavior. As the *Washington Post* recently pointed out, some businesses are relying on natural language processing software to sift through millions of social media posts being generated each day. While this technology is effective in pinpointing mentions of keywords specified by a user, it lacks the human touch. To correct this, developers are now relying on psychological principles to develop more sophisticated algorithms.

The Human Touch

If your business relies on technology like alerts, the *Washington Post* article points out the weakness in depending on software to find instances of a brand's mention. You may be notified every time your brand name is mentioned online, but will you know when someone misspells your name or uses the abbreviated version of your name?

Technology will never replace the human ability to extract meaningful data from volumes of information. If a human were to sift through each post and identify only those items that pertain to him, he'd likely pull out more than he'd originally thought. The same applies to brands and social media. A brand might think it only needs to be alerted when someone mentions it or a competitor by name, but what about a local eatery that misses a post along the lines of, "Looking for a great place to eat tonight. Any suggestions?" As technology advances, brands can expect more sophisticated algorithms to attack these challenges.

Contextual Sifting

Another shortfall for technology-based searches is context. A complaint from a social media user who is constantly complaining about companies online carries less weight than a complaint from a social media user whose posts are generally positive or neutral. Companies are often required to dig deeper into a user's profile to determine if a post will be taken more seriously by the poster's followers.

Current technology also lacks the ability to detect human personality traits like sarcasm; posts tend to be taken literally. Because of this, if an algorithm is set to extract any negative posts on a company, it may miss a post stating that someone "Really loved the experience" at a particular establishment, followed by a hashtag stating that the company sucks. Over time, developers will be required to enhance software to address that, as well.

Different Platforms

Another area of context that poses problems for current technology is the context surrounding the platform through which posts are made. As I pointed out in my post Twitter vs. Facebook: How Do They Compare?, each social media site has its own unique uses. Facebook tends to connect users with people they know personally, while Twitter allows more anonymity. Facebook also tends to be more of a way to capture snippets of people's lives, while Twitter is a great way to keep up with news and celebrities outside of a person's life.

These major differences have an impact on how users respond to marketing messages. A Twitter user will likely have completely different expectations for his newsfeed than a Facebook user. When your marketing message is scattered among family vacation photos and forwarded recipes on Facebook, it might be perceived differently than it would on Twitter, where it's more likely to be surrounded by links to articles of interest and photos of celebrities.

Algorithms vs. People

What algorithms miss today will likely be solved in the near future. Still, the human ability to reason is difficult to duplicate. Many users don't even realize that they filter their perceptions based on the medium through which they receive communication. Even a savvy marketer may recognize and address the differences between Facebook and Twitter without putting those differences into words. Posts are simply tweaked to address the separate audiences and adjusted as responses are calculated.

Even if algorithms are tweaked to directly address these issues, professionals need to tweak their own thinking. Whether reaching out to users on Facebook, Twitter, Instagram, Pinterest, Vine, or one of the other many social media outlets, businesses must consider the platform and its users, adjusting messages to ensure users will respond to them.

Understanding Customer Motivations

One way businesses can better reach customers is to develop an understanding of why customers interact the way they do. As I wrote in my article "The Four Elements of Any Action, And How To Use Them In Your Online Marketing Initiative," there are four elements that define any action a person takes, and those elements apply to social media. They are

- Opportunity
- Ability
- Incentive
- Willpower

When a business initiates a social media marketing campaign, it immediately addresses the first of those four elements, opportunity. If a customer isn't first aware of a business's existence, that customer can't take action. Ability is a little more challenging for businesses, since social media sites don't make it easy for users to click to purchase an item or service. ClickMeeting blogger Agnes Jozwiac suggests providing an array of access points that "involves a mash-up of the three basic learning styles: visual, audio, and kinesthetic."

Once a customer is aware of your business and able to easily order from you, that customer must have an incentive to take action. What will have the power to lure social media users away from their newsfeeds, ideally to make a purchase? Once a customer has been lured away, it's important to feed into the fourth element, willpower, which prompts a person to overcome barriers to completing a task. In the social media marketing world, this means your shopping and checkout process should be so straightforward and challenge-free, your customers carry through until the end.

A Call to Action

Underneath all of these psychological factors is the fact that businesses must incite a call to action from customers to be successful. Simply posting about your great product may build awareness, but it won't result in any ROI. Customers should feel compelled to click on links within your photos and text and, once they've clicked, to take the action you're requesting, whether it's enjoying savings using a coupon or signing up for an e-mail newsletter.

If you want something, don't be afraid to ask. Small things like asking customers to like, share, or retweet an item can make a difference in your results. In fact, an independent study by SocialBakers found that simply asking followers to retweet led to a greater response rate than when a post didn't request that action. If you provide an incentive for sharing like an entry in a contest, you'll see even better results.

Social media marketing is still a relatively new field, but basic psychological concepts still apply. The best way to succeed in reaching your customer base is to begin to see things as they do. Study your online results and make notes on which behaviors get the best response and soon, you'll have a roadmap for getting better results.

Critical Thinking

1. Is it a valid assumption that technology will never replace the human ability to extract meaningful data from volumes of information? Explain.
2. Why is the inability to detect such human personality traits as sarcasm considered a drawback of current technology?
3. How do the differences between Twitter and Facebook affect how their users respond to marketing messages?

Internet References

CompuKol: "The Psychology Behind Social Media"
www.compukol.com/blog/the-psychology-behind-social-media

Huffington Post: "7 Social Media Psychology Studies That Will Make Your Marketing Smarter"
www.huffingtonpost.com/courtney-seiter/7-social-media-psychology_b_5697909.html

Marketing Land: "The Science & Psychology of Social Media"
http://marketingland.com/the-science-psychology-of-social-media-66093

Social Media Examiner: "How to Use Social Psychology to Improve Your Marketing"
www.socialmediaexaminer.com/social-psychologyto-improve-marketing

Customized Or Creepy? Websites and Your Data, a Guide by Steven Melendez

55

Prepared by: Liz Friedman, *DePaul University* and
Daniel Mittleman, *DePaul University*

Article

Customized Or Creepy? Websites and Your Data, a Guide

A Princeton "web census" sheds new light on how websites are customizing and testing content for different users and audience segments.

Steven Melendez

Learning Outcomes

After reading this article, you will be able to:

- Identify pros and cons to customization of Internet content.

- Distinguish between first- and third-party cookies.

- Discuss Facebook and Cornell University's manipulation of users' news feeds.

Two visitors to the same news site see different headlines on the same article. Two potential donors see different suggested giving amounts on a charity website. A software vendor with free and premium versions keeps a list of "countries that are likely to pay."

Those are some recent findings from the Princeton University Center for Information Technology Policy's Web Transparency and Accountability Project, which conducts a monthly "web census," tracking privacy-related practices across the Internet. Essentially, the project team sends an automated web-crawling bot to visit about 1 million websites and monitor how they, in turn, monitor their visitors.

Showing different versions of a site to different people isn't inherently creepy, nor is monitoring what they do while visiting a website—without some basic monitoring and user segmentation, there would be no recommended products on Amazon or Netflix and no way for international websites to figure out which language users prefer.

And yet, some types of customization just make Internet users uncomfortable, and some may even risk crossing ethical boundaries. And so, without further ado, here's a mostly unscientific guide to web-tracking practices in the wild, on a scale of 1 (not particularly creepy) to 5 (pretty creepy).

First-Party Cookies

If you've visited any European websites in the past few years, you've probably seen a little pop-up warning explaining that the sites use cookies—small text files stored by your browser with information about your activity on the site.

Under EU regulations, sites are required to let you know if they use cookies and allow you to opt out of having your browser store the files.

But despite the ubiquitous warnings, basic, first-party cookies, which are stored by a particular website you're visiting and served back with each page on the site you load, really aren't all that creepy.

First, sites are generally out in the open about their use of cookies—if there's no European-style pop up, they're often disclosed in reasonably plain English in privacy policies—and it's easy to find instructions on viewing and deleting stored cookies in any major browser or on using private browsing modes to avoid storing them from browsing session to browsing session.

More importantly, first-party cookies are by definition tied to a particular website. They're just a convenient way for programmers to keep track of information, like your user name or what's in your shopping cart, that you've already provided to the site, often with the assumption that they'd store it.

A/B Testing

One reason different users see different editions of the same site or app is A/B testing—a practice where different users are purposely shown different versions of a site in order to measure which one is more effective.

The practice is a cornerstone of many modern, agile development practices, and of data-oriented business philosophies like Eric Ries's "Lean Startup" methodology. It's used by websites to test everything from quick color scheme tweaks to radically revamped algorithms for ordering social networking feeds. And modern Internet users are often accustomed to sites varying slightly from user to user, says Pete Koomen, cofounder and CTO of Optimizely, Optimizely, a San Francisco company that provides tools for customer segmentation and A/B testing.

"I actually think that at this point this is part and parcel of most users' expectation of how the web works," he says.

And yet, for particular sites, even sophisticated users can be unaware that there are multiple versions of the user experience, says Lisa Barnard, an assistant professor of strategic communication at Ithaca College who's studied online marketing. And they can be disturbed to learn that even seemingly static content like news headlines can vary from user to user as part of an experiment.

"I teach students who are digital natives, they understand how this stuff works, and every time I tell them about A/B testing, they're shocked," Barnard says. "They realize that something's happening [with targeted ads] because they know that they're seeing something they were looking at before, but with something like A/B testing of headlines on a news site, there's no tip off."

And once they find out it's been happening without their knowledge, they're not always happy, she says.

Among the information the Princeton researchers gather in their web census is the complete set of JavaScript code embedded in each page, explains project research engineer Dillon Reisman in a recent blog post. And on many sites, that includes code from Optimizely to implement A/B tests.

The team even built a Google Chrome extension—cheekily called Pessimizely—that can, depending on a website's configuration, make it possible to see which segments of a particular web page are being tested and tweaked with Optimizely and how the page's audience is being segmented.

Reisman emphasizes that there's absolutely nothing wrong with using Optimizely, which boasts more than 6,000 corporate customers. But, he says, the findings still point to general unresolved questions about how transparent Internet companies ought to be about how they're tracking visitor data and conducting user experiments, even if the practices themselves aren't inherently negative.

To be clear, Optimizely doesn't track users from website to website, explains Koomen.

"When a customer uses Optimizely to run experiments on their site, they only see the results of those experiments for their site alone," he says.

For researchers and the public at large, Optimizely actually provides an unusually good look at how websites can vary from visitor to visitor, says Reisman. Customers can configure it to make testing variations and customer segment names visible for better integration with third-party tools, and the web census project and Pessimizely extension are able to access that data as well.

Reisman says he'd generally like to see companies more explicitly spell out all of the tracking, testing, and personalized tweaking they do, perhaps in their privacy policies.

"I'm grateful that data's there, because it's so rare that you get to see what websites are doing when they're A/B testing, and this actually is a very unique opportunity," he says.

Third-Party Tracking Cookies

A little more off-putting are third-party cookies: cookies set by a website other than the site you're visiting, which can help advertising companies and others track your behavior across the Internet.

Advertisers say these and other more complex tools for tracking users from site to site allow for better targeting of ads based on your browser history, but several studies have found consumers can find this more stalkerish than helpful.

A study by Barnard, the Ithaca College professor, found last year that ads that track users across websites can be perceived as "creepy" and sometimes make customers less likely to buy.

"They feel like companies know too much about them, and that they're tracking them around the Internet," Barnard says. "There's something about that tracking that makes people uncomfortable, and, kind of, the uncertainty of how much these companies know about them and how they're using it."

And a Consumer Reports survey found most consumers unwilling to trade personal information for targeted ads and unconvinced such ads brought them more value. For those users, many popular browsers now contain built-in features to block third-party cookies.

Customized Or Creepy? Websites and Your Data, a Guide by Steven Melendez

57

Consumer Data Collection Tools

Cookies are data files stored by your browser, which means that if you're aware of them and willing to do a little legwork, you can control if and when they're stored.

But they're not the only way for advertisers and website owners to track visitors from site to site. Clever—or creepy—programmers have found other ways to monitor your travels around the web that can be harder to detect and control.

The researchers behind the Princeton web census found websites using a variety of "device fingerprinting" techniques that allow them to identify visitors based on characteristics of their computers or phones, without having to store any data. For instance, websites—and advertisers—can examine the list of fonts installed on a computer or the exact output produced by a system's audio or image processing software, which can vary from system to system.

It's hard not to view these techniques, which are generally designed to circumvent users' desired tracking restrictions, as intrusive. Luckily, at least one of the techniques, using characteristics of HTML graphics canvas elements to track users, appears to be on the decline after some public backlash, the researchers report.

"First, the most prominent trackers have by and large stopped using it, suggesting that the public backlash following that study was effective," they write. "Second, the overall number of domains employing it has increased considerably, indicating that knowledge of the technique has spread and that more obscure trackers are less concerned about public perception."

Still, while more legitimate websites may shy away from these techniques, it's likely there will be a cat-and-mouse game for some time between shadier trackers and researchers who reveal their techniques.

Psychological Experiments

In 2012, researchers at Facebook and Cornell University tweaked a selection of users' news feeds, showing them either a week of all positive stories or all negative stories. The immediate result? People who saw positive posts created more positive content of their own; people who saw negative stories posted more negative messages.

But the broader result was widespread condemnation of the project from across the Internet, including from the scientific community. Doing experiments with vague-at-best consent through website terms of service, with an eye toward influencing people's emotional state, was widely denounced as unsavory, unethical, and potentially even dangerous.

"Deception and emotional manipulation are common tools in psychological research, but when they're done in an academic setting they are heavily reviewed and participants have to give consent," says data ethicist Jake Metcalf, a founding partner at ethics consultancy Ethical Resolve.

The company has since adopted and published new research vetting guidelines, influenced by those used in academic studies, and says it hopes they can be informative to other companies doing similar work.

"It is clear now that there are things we should have done differently," Facebook CTO Mike Schroepfer acknowledged in a statement after the study came to light.

Surprising Price Variations

Last year, investigative journalism site ProPublica reported that prices of online test prep services booked through the *Princeton Review*'s website could vary by more than $1,000 dollars based on users' zip codes. One result, according to the report, was that Asian users were more likely to be offered higher prices for tutoring services than non-Asians. The Princeton Review emphasized in a statement this was not its intent and that prices were based on "differential costs" and "competitive attributes" of different regional markets.

And in 2012, the *Wall Street Journal* reported that office supply chain Staples offered different prices to users in different zip codes and pointed out numerous other examples of online stores offering different prices, or discount offers, based on users' location, device type, or other information, often to users' frustration.

Also that year, the paper famously reported that travel booking site Orbitz was showing different lists of hotels on the first page of search results to Mac and Windows users, specifically showing higher-priced options for Apple users, who were found to be bigger spenders (though the company has emphasized particular hotels were priced the same for all users).

While differential pricing isn't generally illegal, as long as there's no discrimination against a protected class like a racial or religious group, it still often makes customers uncomfortable and anxious about whether they've truly gotten the best deal available.

"When that type of story comes out, people get upset," says Barnard. "It's that uncertainty that, I think, makes people really uncomfortable."

Critical Thinking

1. How transparent should companies be about the ways in which they track you online or experiment with customization?

2. Why would a company use A/B testing and how does it work?

3. Make a case for which is worse: emotional manipulation or differential pricing.

Internet References

How Marketers Are Driving Growth Through Personalized Content
https://goo.gl/F6JiCd

Why a Personalized Web Robs Us of the Internet's Rich Diversity
https://goo.gl/41dv1n

What Does Netflix's Algorithm Want?
https://goo.gl/UghwRK

STEVEN MELENDEZ is an independent journalist living in New Orleans.

Article

Prepared by: Liz Friedman, *DePaul University* and
Daniel Mittleman, *DePaul University*

Essena O'Neill Quits Instagram Claiming Social Media 'Is Not Real Life'

Australian teenager with more than 612,000 Instagram followers radically rewrites her "self-promoting" history on social media (and launches new website).

ELLE HUNT

Learning Outcomes

After reading this article, you will be able to:

- Describe O'Neill's "crisis of conscience."
- Define social media validation.

An Australian teenager with more than half a million followers on Instagram has quit the platform, describing it as "contrived perfection made to get attention," and called for others to quit social media—perhaps with help from her new website.

Essena O'Neill, 18, said she was able to make an income from marketing products to her 612,000 followers on Instagram—"$2000AUD a post EASY." But her dramatic rejection of social media celebrity has won her praise.

On 27 October she deleted more than 2,000 pictures "that served no real purpose other than self-promotion" and dramatically edited the captions to the remaining 96 posts in a bid to reveal the manipulation, mundanity, and even insecurity behind them. O'Neill did not respond to requests for an interview.

A photo of her wearing a bikini, once captioned "Things are getting pretty wild at my house. Maths B and English in the sun," has been edited: "see how relatable my captions were—stomach sucked in, strategic pose, pushed up boobs. I just want

younger girls to know this isn't candid life, or cool or inspirational. It's contrived perfection made to get attention."

"Why would you tell your followers that you're paid a lot to promote what you promote? Why would you tell your followers that you literally just do shoots every day to take pictures for Instagram?" she said in a 22-minute vlog posted to YouTube, titled "HOW PEOPLE MAKE 1000's ON SOCIAL MEDIA." "Like, it's not cool. No one thinks that's radical, or revolutionary."

"Yet I, myself, was consumed by it. This was the reason why I quit social media: for me, personally, it consumed me. I wasn't living in a 3D world."

"I remember I obsessively checked the like count for a full week since uploading it," she wrote of her first-ever post, a selfie that now has close to 2,500 likes. "It got 5 likes. This was when I was so hungry for social media validation . . . Now marks the day I quit all social media and focus on real life projects."

This includes letsbegamechangers.com, O'Neill's new site "aimed to inspire constant QUESTIONING," where there's "no likes or views or followers . . . just my content as raw as I want." In her first post, dated 31 October, she challenged her followers to go a week without social media and recommended Eckhart Tolle's book The Power of Now.

The site will cover "veganism, creative imagery with purpose, poems, writing, interviews with people that inspire me, and of course the finical reality behind deluding people off Instagram" [sic]. She will continue to post videos about vegan eating to YouTube, but Vimeo ("made to help not to get views or $$$") will "host all the new quality content."

But O'Neill's "crisis of conscience," as it was described by US Magazine, seems to be extending to more than just the manipulation of social media. O'Neill, whose veganism has long been a cornerstone of her online presence, edited the caption of a photograph of scrambled eggs and bacon pre-dating her change in diet to read "Chicken periods scrambled up with pig flesh ."

A snapshot of her fishing now refers to "how fun . . . to put a hook through an innocent beings mouth"; one of a pile of chocolate bars is described as "Poison and Violence." "I wish I would have been more conscious to see how white privileged I was," she writes of her time spent volunteering in Laos.

The one image to survive with O'Neill's ringing endorsement is of a smiling quokka.

O'Neill's debunking of online celebrity was widely discussed on social media.

A fellow vegan, Australian Instagram star Bonny Rebecca—a friend of O'Neill's—said at first she "may have been confused" by the rebrand, because her own experiences of social media have been "very positive."

Rebecca commented to a follower on Tumblr: "Obviously it's been super hard for me because Essena has put out all this information about what SOME instagramers are like, then left social media and of course I have been left with everyone comparing us and thinking that she is implying those concepts are relevant to my account. And man that is not fair, because thats NEVER what I have been about."

But she was supportive of O'Neill's decision.

"So many people strive to be 'popular' online to validate themselves, manipulating photos and captions to give the idea they are happy just to get 'followers' . . . And be 'idolised'. . . When NONE of that truly matters and that's what can be wrong with social media! Essena is exposing that(!!!) and that is a big game changer," she captioned a photo of the two of them together that had attracted 13,800 likes.

O'Neill would "still be creating awesome content," concluded Rebecca—and in the meantime, she had uploaded her own vlog about the drama, "where I try to shed some light on the situation and my thoughts."

Critical Thinking

1. How did O'Neill make money from her social media posts?
2. Describe O'Neill's struggle with social media validation.
3. How well do you think O"enill debunked her online celebrity?

Internet References

Essena O'Neill-Why I Really Am Quitting Social Media (Original Video)
   https://goo.gl/ECdDHi

Essena O'Neill: The Girl Using Social Media to Tell You Social Media Is Evil
   https://goo.gl./EaXTth

Instagram Star Essena O'Neill Breaks Her Silence on Quitting Social Media
   https://goo.gl/zaatt1s

When Online Shaming Spins Out of Control (TED Talk)
   https://goo.gl/jOCSgx

Article

Prepared by: Liz Friedman, *DePaul University* and
Daniel Mittleman, *DePaul University*

The Rising Influence of Social Media, as Reflected by Data

ANDREW HUTCHINSON

Learning Outcomes

After reading this article, you will be able to:

- See the marketing relevance of a generation that has grown up with social media as a customary mode of interaction.
- Discern the value in looking to industry leaders for models of marketing strategies.
- Discuss how the modern configuration of "social" is being approached by leaders in the business world.

A recent study found that in 2013, 75% of higher education students used social media in their process of deciding where to enroll. There were several articles on this, most highlighting the growing use of social media in the higher ed sector, but the point missed by many is that this stat is more indicative of demographics than sector. Yes, social media has had a huge impact on higher education process, providing new ways for institutions to connect and engage with current and prospective students, but it makes perfect sense that this age group, for whom social media has existed for as long as they can remember, would be most likely to conduct their research via social platforms. But it isn't just their future education this relates to. It's everything. The shoes they're going to buy, the movies they're going to watch, places they're going to visit—social media is where the next generation do their research, on all decisions. And this reliance on social as their go-to resource is only going to grow.

This Is What They've Learned

The increasing reliance on social media can sometimes be missed when looking at the effectiveness of social as a business platform. Many still see it as fun, as a platform for kids to share updates about what they had for dinner or pictures of themselves pouting in the sun. But amidst those interactions, habits develop, learned processes, and those actions become part of what they do, of how they live, in a wider sense. The best comparison is the Internet–twenty-five years ago, the Internet was a slow, clunky, dial-up service. At that time, many of us were using DOS prompts to navigate our own PCs, let alone have any sort of rational functionality on the web. But as the Internet developed, people started to use it more—you'd check for something on Yahoo!, you created a Hotmail account, maybe you even used a message board to voice your thoughts. Over time, these things become part of your normal process till eventually you can't imagine how you ever got by without them. You don't send letters anymore, right? Young people these days don't make phone calls at anywhere near the same rate. For the next generation, social media has always been—it's a part of how they've grown, how they've learned to interact. Seeing stats like 75% of students are using social media for research is not only expected, it underlines the baseline trends highlighted by every study and every research paper looking at the impact of social on the global communications landscape.

Slower Growth Is Still Growth

This is also what's interesting about seeing reports of Facebook's slowdown in youth demographics or Twitter's issues with attracting new users (somewhat alleviated by their latest results). While youth take-up has slowed, the fastest growing user-bases are in older demographic groups. This makes sense—five years ago, a large proportion of the 25–34 demographic were in the 18–24 category. Logically, as generations move through, you'd expect those high adoption rates from the younger brackets to continue to spread through into the older tiers, as those people continue using the platforms they've become aligned to. Slowing growth rates in youth categories generally reflect that they're hitting peak take-up, its the increases among older demographics that represent the more important aspect for the future of social business. More generations active on social means more businesses heading there to reach them—and more businesses utilising social, leads to more of their competition doing the same. Rolling increases in user growth rates underline the need to take social seriously, and to initiate yourself and your business to the opportunities in the wider social space.

Look to Industry Leaders

While the numbers all indicate that social media isn't a fad and that social business is going to become a crucial part of all marketing strategies moving forward, there are still many businesses who aren't yet ready to allocate the time or money to undertake the necessary learning and monitoring of social platforms. Yes, it takes some time to understand, and yes, there will be additional requirements, in terms of posting, interacting and listening. But if the trends aren't enough to sway you, maybe you should look to how social is being approached by leaders in the business world. As of 2013, 77% of Fortune 500 companies maintain an active Twitter presence. 70% have Facebook profiles, 69% have YouTube accounts. That is a huge amount, and while you could surmise that a Fortune 500 business would have more money to allocate to new media, you can also be assured that they wouldn't do so without good reason. ROI remains a contentious point, one which marketers are still trying to clearly define, but one aspect that cannot be ignored is the numbers—the data suggests social business is only going to become more important. It's not going to go away, you're not going to see social media switch off and people revert back to phones and faxes. Do you think the Internet's going away?

Imagine what it would do to your business if it did? In a few years' time, you'll likely to be looking at social in the exact same way.

Critical Thinking

1. If we can trust the overwhelming indications that social media is not a fad, why are so many businesses reluctant to allocate time and money to learn how to exploit it?
2. What demographic considerations are most important for the future of social business, and why?

Create Central

www.mhhe.com/createcentral

Internet References

CIO: "How Social Media Can Influence High-Stakes Business Decisions"
www.cio.com/article/2686973/social-media/how-social-media-can-influence-high-stakes-business-decisions.html

Inc.: "Why Social Influence Matters to Businesses"
www.inc.com/guides/201103/why-social-influence-matters-to-businesses.html

Social Media Examiner: "16 Social Media Marketing Tips From the Pros"
www.socialmediaexaminer.com/16-social-media-marketing-tips-from-the-pros

ANDREW HUTCHINSON is an internationally published author, award-winning blogger and social media consultant from Melbourne, Australia. He has more than 12 years experience working in media monitoring, helping clients locate, evaluate, and action keyword occurrences in all forms of traditional and digital media. He's also a Hootsuite Ambassador for the APAC regioin and one of the "Best Thinkers" on leading social media news website Social Media Today.

Unit 4

UNIT

Prepared by: Liz Friedman, *DePaul University* and
Daniel Mittleman, *DePaul University*

Privacy in a Digital World

Privacy is the yin to security's yang. They are two sides of the same dilemma we face in America today. We want our government to keep us secure. And to do so, they require the ability to conduct surveillance. But we also value our privacy and the constitutional protections designed to preserve that privacy. And some of us do not trust the government. Policies that make for more effective security often seem to erode our privacy. And policies that preserve our privacy hinder our government's ability to protect.

Privacy concerns exist not just in the realm of our collective relationships with government. Large corporations have as much—perhaps more—information about us. Google's vast database of our web browsing and related history contains far more detailed personal interests and behaviors than any government could know.[1] And Facebook is aiming to capture every one of everyone's relationships with objects, organizations, and each other.[2] What are the implications of having such personal and complete information about almost all of us sitting in corporate databases?

As the Patriot Act enacted after the 9/11 attacks has shown, a normal response of government during times of threatened public safety is to reduce civil liberties. In theory, a free press, a concerned citizenry, and the normal checks and balances built into our system should prevent the worst abuses. If only the federal government were all we had to worry about. In a world of networked computers, e-commerce, and social networking, we blithely hand over valuable data to providers of services we usually think of as free. To take a simple example, imagine that you are Gmail subscriber. You may well think you have deleted private messages. But they are stored on a server, who knows where for who knows how long, with access by who knows whom.

In June 2013, Edward Snowden, a low-level government contractor, admitted to being the source behind a series of leaks about the government's surveillance programs that spied on many ordinary American citizens. In response, some companies have increased protections for personal privacy but, according to a 2015 Pew Research Center study, only 25% of U.S. adults aware of the government surveillance programs have taken at least one step to change the way they use technology.[3]

Notably in 2016, following a tragic shooting attack the previous December in San Bernardino, California, Apple rejected a request from the FBI to create an application to override the password on the deceased suspect's iPhone. The FBI eventually found another way into the phone, which ended the "historical legal showdown that pitted the demands of law enforcement investigating crimes against the privacy rights of companies to protect their customer's privacy."[4] Though that individual case has been resolved, companies are steadily increasing privacy protections for users. WhatsApp added end-to-end encryption for every form of communication on its popular messaging app shortly after the FBI vs Apple showdown. Not every company is shifting toward protecting its users however, in October 2016, Yahoo revealed that they had built a program in 2015 to aid the FBI and NSA in monitoring the email accounts of its users.[5]

Nothing has yet stopped hackers from doing what they can to get our information anyway. In the summer of 2016, it was revealed that The Democratic National Committee (DNC) was hacked by a Russian in a first-ever effort by a foreign nation to potentially sway US elections. In September of 2016, Yahoo suffered the largest data breach ever when they were forced to reveal that data associated with at least 500,000,000 user accounts had been stolen by a "state-sponsored actor" in late 2014.[6]

Some questions to consider in this unit:

- How important are personal privacy protections to you?
- Under what circumstances are you willing to relinquish privacy protections?
- What are the trade-offs between privacy and security?

[1] http://www.nybooks.com/articles/2011/08/18/how-google-dominates-us/
[2] https://www.technologyreview.com/s/428150/what-facebook-knows/
[3] http://www.pewinternet.org/2015/03/16/Americans-Privacy-Strategies-Post-Snowden/.
[4] http://www.latimes.com/local/lanow/la-me-ln-fbi-drops-fight-to-force-apple-to-unlock-san-bernardino-terrorist-iphone-20160328-story.html
[5] https://www.wired.com/2016/10/yahoo-spy-scandal-shows-encryption-fails-without-backbone/
[6] http://money.cnn.com/2016/09/22/technology/yahoo-data-breach/.

Article

Prepared by: Liz Friedman, *DePaul University* and
Daniel Mittleman, *DePaul University*

The Death of Privacy

ALEX PRESTON

Learning Outcomes

After reading this article, you will be able to:

• Describe the distinction between privacy and secrecy.

• Explain the "right to be forgotten."

• Understand the trade-offs when privacy is relinquished.

We have come to the end of privacy; our private lives, as our grandparents would have recognised them, have been winnowed away to the realm of the shameful and secret. To quote ex-tabloid hack Paul McMullan, "privacy is for paedos." Insidiously, through small concessions that only mounted up over time, we have signed away rights and privileges that other generations fought for, undermining the very cornerstones of our personalities in the process. While outposts of civilisation fight pyrrhic battles, unplugging themselves from the web—"going dark"—the rest of us have come to accept that the majority of our social, financial and even sexual interactions take place over the internet and that someone, somewhere, whether state, press or corporation, is watching.

The past few years have brought an avalanche of news about the extent to which our communications are being monitored: WikiLeaks, the phone-hacking scandal, the Snowden files. Uproar greeted revelations about Facebook's "emotional contagion" experiment (where it tweaked mathematical formulae driving the news feeds of 700,000 of its members in order to prompt different emotional responses). Cesar A Hidalgo of the Massachusetts Institute of Technology described the Facebook news feed as "like a sausage . . . Everyone eats it, even though nobody knows how it is made."

Sitting behind the outrage was a particularly modern form of disquiet—the knowledge that we are being manipulated, surveyed, rendered and that the intelligence behind this is artificial as well as human. Everything we do on the web, from our social media interactions to our shopping on Amazon, to our Netflix selections, is driven by complex mathematical formulae that are invisible and arcane.

Most recently, campaigners' anger has turned upon the so-called Drip (Data Retention and Investigatory Powers) bill in the United Kingdom, which will see internet and telephone companies forced to retain and store their customers' communications (and provide access to this data to police, government and up to 600 public bodies). Every week, it seems, brings a new furore over corporations—Apple, Google, Facebook—sidling into the private sphere. Often, it's unclear whether the companies act brazenly because our governments play so fast and loose with their citizens' privacy ("If you have nothing to hide, you've nothing to fear," William Hague famously intoned); or if governments see corporations feasting upon the private lives of their users and have taken this as a licence to snoop, pry, survey.

We, the public, have looked on, at first horrified, then cynical, then bored by the revelations, by the well-meaning but seemingly useless protests. But what is the personal and psychological impact of this loss of privacy? What legal protection is afforded to those wishing to defend themselves against intrusion? Is it too late to stem the tide now that scenes from science fiction have become part of the fabric of our everyday world?

Novels have long been the province of the great What If?, allowing us to see the ramifications from present events extending into the murky future. As long ago as 1921, Yevgeny Zamyatin imagined One State, the transparent society of his dystopian novel, *We*. For Orwell, Huxley, Bradbury, Atwood and many others, the loss of privacy was one of the establishing nightmares of the totalitarian future. Dave Eggers's 2013 novel *The Circle* paints a portrait of an America without privacy, where a vast, internet-based, multimedia empire surveys and controls the lives of its people, relying on strict adherence to its motto: "Secrets are lies, sharing is caring, and privacy is theft." We watch as the heroine, Mae, disintegrates under the pressure of scrutiny, finally becoming one of the faceless, obedient hordes. A contemporary (and because of this, even more chilling) account of life lived in the glare of the privacy-free internet is Nikesh Shukla's *Meatspace*, which charts the existence of a lonely writer whose only escape is into the shallows of the web. "The first and last thing I do every day," the book begins, "is see what strangers are saying about me."

Our age has seen an almost complete conflation of the previously separate spheres of the private and the secret. A taint of shame has crept over from the secret into the private so that anything that is kept from the public gaze is perceived as suspect. This, I think, is why defecation is so often used as an example of the private sphere. Sex and shitting were the only actions that the authorities in Zamyatin's One State permitted to take place in private, and these remain the battlegrounds of the privacy debate almost a century later. A rather prim leaked memo from a GCHQ operative monitoring Yahoo webcams notes that "a surprising number of people use webcam conversations to show intimate parts of their body to the other person."

It is to the bathroom that Max Mosley turns when we speak about his own campaign for privacy. "The need for a private life is something that is completely subjective," he tells me. "You either would mind somebody publishing a film of you doing your ablutions in the morning or you wouldn't. Personally I would and I think most people would." In 2008, Mosley's "sick Nazi orgy," as the *News of the World* glossed it, featured in photographs published first in the pages of the tabloid and then across the internet. Mosley's defense argued, successfully, that the romp involved nothing more than a "standard S&M prison scenario" and the former president of the FIA won £60,000 damages under Article 8 of the European Convention on Human Rights. Now he has rounded on Google and the continued presence of both photographs and allegations on websites accessed via the company's search engine. If you type "Max Mosley" into Google, the eager autocomplete presents you with "video," "case," "scandal," and "with prostitutes," Half-way down the first page of the search we find a link to a professional-looking YouTube video montage of the *NotW* story, with no acknowledgment that the claims were later disproved. I watch it several times. I feel a bit grubby.

"The moment the Nazi element of the case fell apart," Mosley tells me, "which it did immediately, because it was a lie, any claim for public interest also fell apart."

Here we have a clear example of the blurred lines between secrecy and privacy. Mosley believed that what he chose to do in his private life, even if it included whips and nipple-clamps, should remain just that—private. The *News of the World*, on the other hand, thought it had uncovered a shameful secret that, given Mosley's professional position, justified publication. There is a momentary tremor in Mosley's otherwise fluid

delivery as he speaks about the sense of invasion. "Your privacy or your private life belongs to you. Some of it you may choose to make available, some of it should be made available, because it's in the public interest to make it known. The rest should be yours alone. And if anyone takes it from you, that's theft and it's the same as the theft of property."

Mosley has scored some recent successes, notably in continental Europe, where he has found a culture more suspicious of Google's sweeping powers than in Britain or, particularly, the US. Courts in France and then, interestingly, Germany, ordered Google to remove pictures of the orgy permanently, with far-reaching consequences for the company. Google is appealing against the rulings, seeing it as absurd that "providers are required to monitor even the smallest components of content they transmit or store for their users." But Mosley last week extended his action to the United Kingdom, filing a claim in the high court in London.

Mosley's willingness to continue fighting, even when he knows that it means keeping alive the image of his white, septuagenarian buttocks in the minds (if not on the computers) of the public, seems impressively principled. He has fallen victim to what is known as the Streisand Effect, where his very attempt to hide information about himself has led to its proliferation (in 2003 Barbra Streisand tried to stop people taking pictures of her Malibu home, ensuring photos were posted far and wide). Despite this, he continues to battle—both in court, in the media and by directly confronting the websites that continue to display the pictures. It is as if he is using that initial stab of shame, turning it against those who sought to humiliate him. It is noticeable that, having been accused of fetishising one dark period of German history, he uses another to attack Google. "I think, because of the Stasi," he says, "the Germans can understand that there isn't a huge difference between the state watching everything you do and Google watching everything you do. Except that, in most European countries, the state tends to be an elected body, whereas Google isn't. There's not a lot of difference between the actions of the government of East Germany and the actions of Google."

All this brings us to some fundamental questions about the role of search engines. Is Google the de facto librarian of the internet, given that it is estimated to handle 40% of all traffic? Is it something more than a librarian, since its algorithms carefully (and with increasing use of your personal data) select the sites it wants you to view? To what extent can Google be held responsible for the content it puts before us?

It isn't Mosley who has pushed European courts into giving a definitive answer to these questions, but, rather, an unknown lawyer from northwest Spain. In 2009, Mario Costeja González found that a Google search of his name brought up a 36-word document concerning a case from the late 90s in which banks threatened to seize his home. The information was factually incorrect—he'd actually paid off the debts in question. More than this, it was, he argued, irrelevant. He is now a lawyer with a successful practice and any former money worries ought not to feature on the internet record of his life. Google fought the case within Spain and then all the way to the European Court of Justice. Costeja González won, the article was taken down, the victory labelled "the right to be forgotten."

Google's response to the ruling has been swift and sweeping, with 70,000 requests to remove information processed in the weeks following the judgment. A message now appears at the bottom of every search carried out on Google, warning: "Some results may have been removed under data protection law in Europe." It seems that Google has not been judging the quality of these requests and relying on others to highlight content that has been taken down erroneously. Search results to newspaper articles on Dougie McDonald, a Scottish football referee accused of lying, were taken down. And a Robert Peston piece for the BBC about Merrill Lynch CEO Stan O'Neal's role in the 2008 financial crisis was removed; as of August 2014, it is still missing from Google searches.

To understand how much protection the law offers those wishing to defend their privacy against the triumvirate of state, press and data-harvesting corporations, I turn to one of the country's top privacy lawyers, Ruth Collard at Carter Ruck. We meet in Carter Ruck's offices near St Paul's Cathedral. I sit under the beady gaze of the firm's late founder—the target of much *Private Eye* bile—until Collard, more genial than I'd expected, with short, neat hair, comes to meet me. We stroll to a coffee shop and I ask her about the Costeja González case.

"I think it's a very surprising decision, I really do," she says, "but it was Google's collection of data, the arrangement and prioritisation of it that influenced the judgment, as the court found they were a 'controller' of the information."

I ask about the freedom of speech implications of the judgment—surely every politician will be applying to Google, trying to scrub away the traces of the sordid affair, the expenses scandal? She nods emphatically. "Almost immediately after the judgment, there were reports of a politician trying to clean up his past. We have been contacted by clients who have read about the judgment and are interested. So far, the ones that have contacted me, I have not thought they had a case to make. It was clear from the judgment that a balance has to be struck—between the interest of the subject in keeping information private and the interest of internet users in having access to it. The effect will be removing information that may have been once completely justified in being there, but is now outdated or irrelevant."

We go on to discuss the changing face of privacy in the internet age. She firstly notes how relatively young privacy law is in

this country—only since 1998 have there been laws in place to protect privacy. Cases brought before this, such as that of *'Allo 'Allo* star Gordon Kaye, who in 1990 was photographed in his hospital bed badly battered following a car crash, had to prove that a breach of confidence had taken place. Collard points me to the recent Paul Weller case, in which the Modfather sued after being pictured in the *Daily Mail* out walking with his 16-year-old daughter and 10-month-old twins.

"A lot of these cases are *Mail* cases," she says with a twinkle. "It was the fact that the photos showed the children's faces that was found to be significant by the court. Weller brought the claim on behalf of all three children and it succeeded [although the *Mail* is appealing]." In his judgment, Justice Dingemans argued that the children's faces represented "one of the chief attributes of their respective personalities . . . These were photographs showing the expressions on faces of children, on a family afternoon out with their father. Publishing photographs of the children's faces, and the range of emotions that were displayed, and identifying them by surname, was an important engagement of their Article 8 rights."

Collard tells me: "The *Mail* argued very hard on a number of grounds, one of which was that the children didn't have a reasonable expectation of privacy, given that the teenager a couple of years earlier had done some modelling for *Teen Vogue* and the babies had had photos of them tweeted by their mother. However, she had been careful when tweeting not to show their faces. This thing about facial expressions is new and it will be interesting to see where it goes."

This year has not only seen a spate of news stories surrounding the issue of privacy but also a series of literary and artistic approaches to the subject. One of the most interesting was *Privacy*, a play at the Donmar Warehouse that came out of a close collaboration between director Josie Rourke and playwright James Graham. It was a groundbreaking production, from the moment the audience were urged to leave their telephones on as they entered the theatre. Over the course of the play, by turn intrusively intimate and angrily political, the audience (and their smartphones) found themselves at the centre of an attempt to chart the status of contemporary privacy—and the seemingly muted public reaction to its loss.

Within minutes of entering the theatre, I was squirming in my seat. An actor on stage was publicly analysing the results of a study designed by the psychometrics department of Cambridge University that used my Facebook profile to reveal my innermost secrets, questioning almost every aspect of my personality, from my political views to my sexuality. It was terrifying and compelling all at once. As the play ratcheted up to a coruscating finale, we, the audience, were made to see the enormous value of the rights we'd handed over as the mere cost of life in the 21st century (who, we were asked, had read the iTunes privacy policy? It's word for word as long as *The Tempest*).

I meet Rourke and Graham in Donmar's offices on Dryden Street in Covent Garden. We discuss the play, how charged tremors ran around the audience after each subsequent revelation and, above all, the sense of outrage that propels the narrative as it turns its fire on Facebook, Apple and finally on the American government. Are they worried, I ask, that there seems to be so little anger on behalf of the public? That it is beginning to feel (to me at least) as if we have given up our right to a private life with barely a whimper? Graham nods. "I think a lot of normal people, even if they did have the knowledge of how much they're publishing and how much they're giving away, and how much a corporate or government agency might know about them, would just go, 'That's fine, because I'm not interesting enough to be spied on.'"

There were moments in the play that were profoundly uncomfortable: for the audience and, I would imagine, for Rourke and Graham. Both director and playwright featured on stage and we delved deeply into their private lives, into their secret selves (and into our own). I ask about the dynamic between the two of them during the writing of the play and where they decided to draw the line between probing and invasive.

"We thought it through," Graham answers. "From the very beginning, we decided that we never wanted any of these interactions to be exposing or judgmental. We wanted them to be kind and benevolent and ask people to examine their data streams."

Rourke nods in agreement. "In order to research the show, we kept pushing at the boundaries of each other's privacy, really to see what that felt like. I don't want to make it sound like a piece of performance art, but we kept asking ourselves— oh look, we've found out that it's possible to do this. Are we prepared to do that to each other? The distinction between secret and private has been the guiding philosophical principle. We're not looking to get your secrets. We're asking you to test this thing which is less tangible and less transactable, which is your privacy."

A few days after our meeting, Rourke puts me in touch with Michal Kosinksi, the Cambridge academic who, with David Stillwell, has designed youarewhatyoulike.com, the psychometric algorithm that produces from your Facebook "likes" a map of your soul. I think of Ruskin, who in 1864 said: "Tell me what you like and I'll tell you what you are." I also think of Orwell's thought police and Philip K Dick's *The Minority Report*, where criminals are identified and arrested before they commit crimes. This is one of the problems about advances in technology: we are preconditioned to view them through a dystopian lens, with Orwell, Ballard, Burgess and others staring over our shoulders, marvelling, but fearful.

While I wait for my results, I ask Kosinski whether the potential for misuse worries him. "Most technologies have their bright and dark side," he replies, buoyantly. "My personal opinion is that a machine's ability to better understand us would lead to improved consumer experience, products, etc . . . But imagine that we published a clone of youarewhatyoulike.com that simply predicted which of your friends was gay (or Christian or liberal or HIV-positive, etc); lynches are not unlikely to follow . . ."

I'm left baffled by my results. According to the algorithm, I'm 26 (I'm actually 35). The program is unsure whether I'm male or female (I'm male). I'm borderline gay or, as Kosinski puts it in his analysis: "You are not yet gay, but very close." I'm most likely to be single, extremely unlikely to be married (I'm not sure what my wife will say to all this). The algorithm correctly predicts my professional life (art, journalism, psychology) and my politics (liberal) but claims that I exhibit low neuroticism. It should sit next to me on a turbulent flight. I realise that I'm viewing the results of a kind of double of myself, the public persona I present through social media (and over which I presume some sort of control), nothing like the real me. For that, I need a psychiatrist.

Alongside Rourke, Graham, William Hague and director of Liberty, Shami Chakrabarti, one of the real-world figures represented in the play *Privacy* is academic and psychoanalyst Josh Cohen. Cohen's book, *The Private Life* (2013), is an intelligent and highly literary exploration of the changing nature of privacy in the age of Facebook and *Celebrity Big Brother*. Skipping from Katie Price to Freud to Booker-winning author Lydia Davis, Cohen paints a convincing picture of a culture fighting a desperate psychological battle over the private self. He argues that both our ravenous hunger for celebrity gossip and the relentless attempts by the wealthy to protect their privacy have recast the private life as "a source of shame and disgust." The tabloid exposé and the superinjunction both "tacitly accede to the reduction of private life to the dirty secrets hidden behind the door."

And yet what neither the press nor the lawyers recognise when they treat privacy as they would secrecy—as something that can be revealed, possessed, passed on—is that the truly private has a habit of staying that way. Cohen argues that the private self is by definition unknowable, what George Eliot calls "the unmapped country within us." In an email conversation, Cohen gives me a condensation of this thesis: "When we seek to intrude on the other's privacy, whether with a telephoto lens, a hacking device or our own two eyes, we're gripped by the fantasy of seeing their most concealed, invisible self. But the frustration and disappointment is that we only ever get a photograph of the other, an image of their visible self—a mere shadow of the true substance we really wanted to see. The most private self is like the photographic negative that's erased when exposed to the light."

There is something strangely uplifting in this idea—that no matter how deep they delve, the organs of surveillance will never know my true self, for it is hidden even from me.

I ask Cohen about the differences between our "real" selves and those we project online. I think of the younger, gayer, less neurotic incarnation of myself that appears on Facebook. "I agree that the online persona has become a kind of double," he says. "But where in Dostoevsky or Poe the protagonist experiences his double as a terrifying embodiment of his own otherness (and especially his own voraciousness and destructiveness), we barely notice the difference between ourselves and our online double. I think most users of social media and YouTube would simply see themselves as creating a partial, perhaps preferred version of themselves."

I remember something James Graham had said to me: that early on in the writing of *Privacy*, he'd sat at Josie Rourke's kitchen table and read his tweets out loud to her. "I had to stop it was so awful . . . Just seeing the person there, listening as I said what I thought about my food, about politics, about what was on the television, it felt very exposing, like I'd sold myself badly."

This is the horror of social media—that it gives us the impression we are in control of our virtual identities, putting out messages that chime with our "real" selves (or some idealised version of them). In fact, there is always slippage and leakage, the subconscious asserting its obscure power. The internet can, as Cohen tells me, "provide a way of exploring and playing the multiplicity and complexity of the self." It can also prove to us just how little control we have over how we appear. As William Boyd put it in *Brazzaville Beach*: "The last thing we discover in life is our effect."

There is, of course, a flipside to the dystopian view of profit-hungry corporations and totalitarian governments relentlessly reaping our private selves. Josh Cohen describes the lifelogging movement as bearing "an overriding tone of utopian enthusiasm." Lifelogging involves the minute-by-minute transmission of data about one's life, whether by photographs, web journals or the sort of Quantified Self technologies—wearable watches, data-gathering smartphone apps–developed by German firm Datarella (and many others, Google Glass not least among them). An early proponent of lifelogging was conceptual artist Alberto Frigo, who in 2003 decided to record every object he would hold with his right hand for the next 36 years. He put the pictures on his website, 2004–2040.com.

Frigo's project started with photographs but has developed into a labyrinthine mapping of his thoughts and dreams, the music he is listening to and the world around him. The website is now a wormhole, a place in which it is possible to lose yourself in the beautiful but useless ephemera of a single existence.

Frigo tells me that his aim is to create for a future audience "some kind of a Rosetta Stone of this time, where different aspects of a person's life, recorded with different media, can be compared and interpreted."

2004–2040.com has come to dominate Frigo's life. He has insisted on radical honesty, writing down detailed dreams, a sophisticated map of his mental state. For his wife, this was problematic. "She did not accept that I dreamed of other girls," he tells me. "This slowly led to our separation." It also led to a hiatus in Frigo's lifelogging, when he carried on in private, recording but not publishing his material. "My ex-wife did not wish me to publish my dreams and I did not feel like presenting my project without one part. After the divorce, it took me sometime before I went online again."

Josh Cohen told me about the psychic risks of lifelogging. For some, he said, "shadowing your transient, irretrievable life is a permanent digital life, and the really frightening specter here is that the digital recording becomes more 'real', more authoritative than your memory." I asked Frigo about this. How would he look back on it once it had all finished? How will he feel to have this stunning, often baffling pictorial record of his life? "At the end of the project," he says, "I think I would feel that it is time to retire. I would love to go back to the Italian alps, when I am originally from, and have not so much to do with technology anymore, just have a little garden and look back, write a book perhaps, but mostly take care of a little land which I unfortunately never had the possibility to own as my father went off to Canada when I was little . . . I might well end up in a hospital connected to a machine for the rest of my life, who knows? Perhaps, in 2040 I might not reach my 60th birthday and the 1,000,000 photos of all the objects my right hand has used, the DNA code of my life, will remain incomplete, and no one will care about them or me."

Your privacy has a value. There are even companies such as RapLeaf.com that will tell you what your personal information is worth. The basic facts? Very little. More detailed information—for example, you own a smartphone, are trying to lose weight or planning a baby–are worth much more. Big life changes—marriage, moving home, divorce—bring with them fundamental changes in our buying patterns as we seek, through the brands with which we associate ourselves, to recast the narratives of our lives. Through analysis of buying patterns, US retailer Target predicted one of its customers was pregnant (and sent her coupons for maternity wear) before the teenager had broken the news to her disapproving parents.

Perhaps the reason people don't seem to mind that so much of their information is leaking from the private to the public sphere is not, as some would have it, that we are blind and docile, unable to see the complex web of commercial interests that surround us. Maybe it's that we understand very clearly the transaction. The internet is free and we wish to keep it that way, so corporations have worked out how to make money out of something we are willing to give them in return—our privacy. We have traded our privacy for the wealth of information the web delivers to us, the convenience of online shopping, the global village of social media.

Let me take you back to August 2006, the Chesterfield Hotel, Mayfair. My little brother (Preston from the Ordinary Boys) was marrying a girl he'd met on the telly (Chantelle Houghton). *Celebrity Big Brother* was still in its Channel 4 pomp, attracting 6 million viewers and upwards, the focus of water-cooler debate and gossip mag intrigue. The wedding was, briefly, an event. I remember a moment between the ceremony and the reception when we were queuing up in our gladrags to have our pictures taken for the *OK!* magazine spread. I felt a sudden, instinctive lurch—the thought of my phiz besmirching every hairdresser's salon and dentist's waiting room. I wasn't on Facebook, Twitter hadn't been invented, Friends Reunited? No thanks. I ran—to the bemusement of my family and the photographer.

Now, though, I post pictures of my breakfast on Instagram, unspool my soul in 140-character soundbites on Twitter, allow—even encourage—Facebook and Google and Apple to track my every move through the smartphone that has become less a piece of technology and more an extension of (and often a replacement for) my brain. I write articles on subjects I'd previously kept secret from my nearest and dearest. I let a Sunday newspaper take a (relatively tasteful) picture of me and my children when I was promoting my last novel. We have all—to a greater or lesser extent—made this same transaction and made it willingly (although my children didn't have much say in the matter).

We weren't private creatures in centuries past, either. In a 1968 talk on privacy in the electronic age, sociologist Marshall McLuhan argued that it was the coming of a new technology—books—and the "closed-off architecture" needed to read and study that had forged the sense of the private self. It may be that another new technology—the internet—is radically altering our sense of what (if anything) should remain private. We live in a liberal democracy, but, with recent lurches to the right, here and abroad, you don't need to be Philip K Dick to imagine the information you gave up so glibly being used against you by a Farage-led dictatorship.

More immediately, there is the normalising effect of surveillance. There is a barrier or check on our behaviour when we know we are being watched: deviancy needs privacy. This was the thinking behind Jeremy Bentham's Panopticon, a model for a jail where a single watching guard could survey a whole prison of inmates (the model, by the way, for Zamyatin's One

State). Soon, it didn't matter whether the guard was on duty or not, the mere possibility of surveillance was enough to ensure compliance. This is where we find ourselves now, under surveillance that may seem benign enough but which nonetheless asserts a dark, controlling power over us, the watched.

The message seems to be that if you really want to keep something private, treat it as a secret, and in the age of algorithmic analysis and big data, perhaps best to follow Winston Smith's bitter lesson from *Nineteen Eighty-Four*: "If you want to keep a secret, you must also hide it from yourself."

Here lies our greatest risk, one insufficiently appreciated by those who so blithely accept the tentacles of corporation, press and state insinuating their way into the private sphere. As Don DeLillo says in *Point Omega*: "You need to know things the others don't know. It's what no one knows about you that allows you to know yourself." By denying ourselves access to our own inner worlds, we are stopping up the well of our imagination, that which raises us above the drudge and grind of mere survival, that which makes us human.

I asked Josh Cohen why we needed private lives. His answer was a rallying cry and a warning. "Privacy," he said, "precisely because it ensures we're never fully known to others or to ourselves, provides a shelter for imaginative freedom, curiosity and self-reflection. So to defend the private self is to defend the very possibility of creative and meaningful life."

Critical Thinking

1. As of this writing, there is no Right to be Forgotten law in the U.S. Debate the pros and cons of this type of legislation.

2. To what extent should search engines be held responsible for search results?

3. What are the implications of your social media posts living on the Internet forever?

Internet References

Glenn Greenwald: Why Privacy Matters (TEDGlobal 2014)
https://goo.gl/dpWrPF

The Right to Be Forgotten from Google? Forget It, Says U.S. Crowd
https://goo.gl/WyZ7s6

The State of Privacy in America
https://goo.gl/q1MNNl

ALEX PRESTON'S most recent novel is *In Love and War*, published by Faber.

Article

Prepared by: Liz Friedman, *DePaul University* and
Daniel Mittleman, *DePaul University*

Privacy Is Dead, Long Live Privacy

Protecting social norms as confidentiality wanes.

JEAN-PIERRE HUBAUX AND ARI JUELS

Learning Outcomes

After reading this article, you will be able to:

- Identify privacy-enhancing technologies (PETs).

- Distinguish between four major trends that influence the assault on privacy.

- Differentiate between needs for privacy and confidentiality.

The past few years have been especially turbulent for privacy advocates. On the one hand, the global dragnet of surveillance agencies has demonstrated the sweeping surveillance achievable by massively resourced government organizations. On the other, the European Union has issued a mandate that Google definitively "forget" information in order to protect users.

Privacy has deep historical roots, as illustrated by the pledge in the Hippocratic oath (5th century B.C.), "Whatever I see or hear in the lives of my patients . . . which ought not to be spoken of outside, I will keep secret, as considering all such things to be private."[11] Privacy also has a number of definitions. A now common one among scholars views it as the flow of information in accordance with social norms, as governed by context.[10] An intricate set of such norms is enshrined in laws, policies, and ordinary conduct in almost every culture and social setting. Privacy in this sense includes two key notions: confidentiality and fair use. We argue that confidentiality, in the sense of individuals' ability to preserve secrets from governments, corporations, and one another, could well continue to erode. We call instead for more attention and research devoted to fair use.

To preserve existing forms of privacy against an onslaught of online threats, the technical community is working hard to develop *privacy-enhancing technologies* (PETs). PETs enable users to encrypt email, conceal their IP addresses, avoid tracking by Web servers, hide their geographic location when using mobile devices, use anonymous credentials, make untraceable database queries, and publish documents anonymously. Nearly all major PETs aim at protecting confidentiality; we call these *confidentiality-oriented* PETs (C-PETs). C-PETs can be good and helpful. But there is a significant chance that in many or most places, C-PETs will not save privacy. It is time to consider adding a new research objective to the community's portfolio: preparedness for a post-confidentiality world in which many of today's social norms regarding the flow of information are regularly and systematically violated.

Global warming offers a useful analogy, as another slow and seemingly unstoppable human-induced disaster and a worldwide tragedy of commons. Scientists and technologists are developing a portfolio of mitigating innovations in renewable energy, energy efficiency, and carbon sequestration. But they are also studying ways of coping with likely effects, including rising sea levels and displacement of populations. There is a scientific consensus that the threat justifies not just mitigation, but preparation (for example, elevating Holland's dikes).

The same, we believe, could be true of privacy. Confidentiality may be melting away, perhaps inexorably: soon, a few companies and surveillance agencies could have access to most of the personal data of the world's population. Data provides information, and information is power. An information asymmetry of this degree and global scale is an absolute historical novelty.

There is no reason, therefore, to think of privacy as we conceive of it today as an enduring feature of life.

Example: RFID

Radio-Frequency IDentification (RFID) location privacy concretely illustrates how technological evolution can undermine C-PETs. RFID tags are wireless microchips that often emit static identifiers to nearby readers. Numbering in the billions, they in principle permit secret local tracking of ordinary people. Hundreds of papers proposed C-PETs that rotate identifiers to prevent RFID-based tracking.[6]

Today, this threat seems quaint. Mobile phones with multiple RF interfaces (including Bluetooth, Wi-Fi, NFC), improvements in face recognition, and a raft of new wireless devices (fitness trackers, smartwatches, and other devices), offer far more effective ways to track people than RFID ever did. They render RFID C-PETs obsolete.

This story of multiplying threat vectors undermining C-PETs' power—and privacy more generally—is becoming common.

The Assault on Privacy

We posit four major trends providing the means, motive, and opportunity for the assault on privacy in its broadest sense. The adversaries include surveillance agencies and companies in markets such as targeted advertising, as well as smaller, nefarious players.

Pervasive data collection. As the number of online services and always-on devices grows, potential adversaries can access a universe of personal data quickly expanding beyond browsing history to location, financial transactions, video and audio feeds, genetic data[4], real-time physiological data—and perhaps eventually even brainwaves.[8] These adversaries are developing better and better ways to correlate and extract new value from these data sources, especially as advances in applied machine learning make it possible to fill in gaps in users' data via inference. Sensitive data might be collected by a benevolent party for a purpose that is acceptable to a user, but later fall into dangerous hands, due to political pressure, a breach, and other reasons. "Secondhand" data leakage is also growing in prevalence, meaning that one person's action impacts another's private data (for example, if a friend declares a co-location with us, or if a blood relative unveils her genome). The emerging Internet of Things will make things even trickier, soon surrounding us with objects that can report on what we touch, eat, and do.[16]

Monetization (greed). Political philosophers are observing a drift from what they term *having* a market economy to *being* a market society[13] in which market values eclipse non-market social norms. On the Internet, the ability to monetize nearly every piece of information is clearly fueling this process, which is itself facilitated by the existence of quasi-monopolies. A market place could someday arise that would seem both impossible and abhorrent today. (For example, for $10: "I know that Alice and Bob met several times. Give me the locations and transcripts of their conversations.") Paradoxically, tools such as anonymous routing and anonymous cash could facilitate such a service by allowing operation from loosely regulated territories or from no fixed jurisdiction at all.

Adaptation and apathy. Users' data curation habits are a complex research topic, but there is a clear generational shift toward more information sharing, particularly on social networks. (Facebook has more than one billion users regularly sharing information in ways that would have been infeasible or unthinkable a generation ago.). Rather than fighting information sharing, users and norms have rapidly changed, and convenience has trumped privacy to create large pockets of data-sharing apathy. Foursquare and various other microblogging services that encourage disclosure of physical location, for example, have led many users to cooperate in their own physical tracking. Information overload has in any event degraded the abilities of users to curate their data, due to the complex and growing challenges of "secondhand" data-protection weakening and inference, as noted previously.

Secret judgment. Traceability and accountability are essential to protecting privacy. Facebook privacy settings are a good example of visible privacy practice: stark deviation from expected norms often prompts consumer and/ or regulatory pushback.

Increasingly often, though, sensitive-data exploitation can happen away from vigilant eyes, as the recent surveillance scandals have revealed. (National security legitimately demands surveillance, but its scope and oversight are critical issues.) Decisions made by corporations—hiring, setting insurance premiums, computing credit ratings, and so forth—are becoming increasingly algorithmic, as we discuss later. Predictive consumer scores are one example; privacy scholars have argued they constitute a regime of secret, arbitrary, and potentially discriminatory and abusive judgment of consumers.[2]

A Post-Confidentiality Research Agenda

We should prepare for the possibility of a post-confidentiality world, one in which confidentiality has greatly eroded and in which data flows in such complicated ways that social norms are jeopardized. The main research challenge in such a world is to preserve social norms, as we now explain.

Privacy is important for many reasons. A key reason, however, often cited in discussions of medical privacy, is concern about abuse of leaked personal information. It is the potentially resulting unfairness of decision making, for example, hiring decisions made on the basis of medical history, that is particularly worrisome. A critical, defensible bastion of privacy we see in post-confidentiality world therefore is in the *fair use* of disclosed information.

Fair use is increasingly important as algorithms dictate the fates of workers and consumers. For example, for several years, some Silicon Valley companies have required job candidates to fill out questionnaires ("Have you ever set a regional-, state-, country-, or world-record?"). These companies apply classification algorithms to the answers to filter applications.[5] This trend will surely continue, given the many domains in which statistical predictions demonstrably outperform human experts.[7] Algorithms, though, enable deep, murky, and extensive use of information that can exacerbate the unfairness resulting from disclosure of private data.

On the other hand, there is hope that algorithmic decision making can lend itself nicely to protocols for enforcing accountability and fair use. If decision-making is algorithmic, it is possible to require decision-makers to prove that they are not making use of information in contravention of social norms expressed as laws, policies, or regulations. For example, an insurance company might prove it has set a premium without taking genetic data into account—even if this data is published online or otherwise widely available. If input data carries authenticated labels, then cryptographic techniques permit the construction of such proofs without revealing underlying algorithms, which may themselves be company secrets (for example, see Ben-Sasson et al.[1]). Use of information flow control[12] preferably enforced by software attested to by a hardware root of trust (for example, see McKeen et al.[9]) can accomplish much the same end. Statistical testing is an essential, complementary approach to verifying fair use, one that can help identify cases in which data labeling is inadequate, rendered ineffective by correlations among data, or disregarded in a system. (A variety of frameworks exist, for example, see Dwork et al.[3])

Conclusion

A complementary research goal is related to privacy quantification. To substantiate claims about the decline of confidentiality, we must measure it. Direct, global measurements are difficult, but research might look to indirect monetary ones: The profits of the online advertising industry per pair of eyeballs and the "precision" of advertising, perhaps as measured by click-through rates. At the local scale, research is already quantifying privacy (loss) in such settings as location based services.[14]

There remains a vital and enduring place for confidentiality. Particularly in certain niches—protecting political dissent, anti-censorship in repressive regimes—it can play a societally transformative role. It is the responsibility of policymakers and society as a whole to recognize and meet the threat of confidentiality's loss, even as market forces propel it and political leaders give it little attention. But it is also incumbent upon the research community to contemplate alternatives to C-PETs, as confidentiality is broadly menaced by technology and social evolution. If we cannot win the privacy game definitively, we need to defend paths to an equitable society. We believe the protection of social norms, especially through fair use of data, is the place to start. While C-PETs will keep being developed and will partially mitigate the erosion of confidentiality, we hope to see many "fair-use PETs" (F-PETs) proposed and deployed in the near future.[15]

References

1. Ben-Sasson, E. et al. SNARKs for C: Verifying program executions succinctly and in zero knowledge. In *Advances in Cryptology–CRYPTO,* (Springer, 2013), 90–108.

2. Dixon, P. and Gellman, R. The scoring of America: How secret consumer scores threaten your privacy and your future. Technical report, World Privacy Forum (Apr. 2, 2014).

3. Dwork, C. et al. Fairness through awareness. In *Proceedings of the 3rd Innovations in Theoretical Computer Science Conference.* (ACM, 2012), 214–226.

4. Erlich, Y. and Narayanan, A. Routes for breaching and protecting genetic privacy. *Nature Reviews Genetics 15,* 6 (2014), 409–421.

5. Hansell, S. Google answer to filling jobs is an algorithm. *New York Times* (Jan. 3, 2007).

6. Juels, A. RFID security and privacy: A research survey. *IEEE Journal on Selected Areas in Communication 24,* 2 (Feb. 2006).

7. Kahneman, D. *Thinking, Fast and Slow.* Farrar, Straus, and Giroux, 2012, 223–224.

8. Martinovic, I. et al. On the feasibility of side channel attacks with brain-computer interfaces. In *Proceedings of the USENIX Security Symposium,* (2012), 143–158.

9. McKeen, F. et al. Innovative instructions and software model for isolated execution. In *Proceedings of the 2nd International Workshop on Hardware and Architectural Support for Security and Privacy,* Article no. 10 (2013).

10. Nissenbaum, H. *Privacy in Context: Technology, Policy, and the Integrity of Social Life.* Stanford University Press, 2009.

11. North, M.J. Hippocratic oath translation. U.S. National Library of Medicine, 2002.

12. Sabelfeld, A. and Myers, C. Language-based information-flow security. *IEEE Journal on Selected Areas in Communications 21*, 1 (2003), 5–19.

13. Sandel, M.J. *What Money Can't Buy: The Moral Limits of Markets.* Macmillan, 2012.

14. Shokri, R. et al. Quantifying location privacy. In *Proceedings of the IEEE Symposium on Security and Privacy* (2011), 247–262.

15. Tramèr, F. et al. Discovering Unwarranted Associations in Data-Driven Applications with the FairTest Testing Toolkit, 2016; arXiv:1510.02377.

16. Weber, R.H. Internet of things—New security and privacy challenges. *Computer Law and Security Review 26*, 1 (2010), 23–30.

Critical Thinking

1. How can we prepare to protect privacy in a post-confidentiality world?

2. How has convenience influenced apathy toward the need for privacy?

3. How can fair use be regulated algorithmically?

Internet References

Glenn Greenwald: Why Privacy Matters (TEDGlobal 2014)
https://goo.gl/Eur8wW

Privacy Is Dead; Long Live Privacy
https://goo.gl/3qlG9Q

The Death of Privacy
https://goo.gl/ffQkjB

JEAN-PIERRE HUBAUX is a professor in the Computer Communications and Applications Laboratory at the Ecole Polytechnique Fédérale de Lausanne in Switzerland.

ARI JUELS is a professor at Cornell Tech (Jacobs Institute) in New York.

Prepared by: Liz Friedman, *DePaul University* and
Daniel Mittleman, *DePaul University*

Article

The Seven Veils of Privacy

Kieron O'Hara

Learning Outcomes

After reading this article, you will be able to:

- Summarize the seven levels of privacy.
- Discuss the impact of cultural norms on expectations of privacy.
- Define the "privacy paradox."

Privacy is very important. Whatever it is. The debate on privacy is notable for the lack of agreement—what is it for, is it a good or a bad thing, a right or a preference? As philosopher Judith Jarvis Thomson put it, "Perhaps the most striking thing about the right to privacy is that nobody seems to have any clear idea of what it is."[1] In a classic legal paper, William Prosser dismissed it as a set of interests "which are tied together by the common name, but otherwise have almost nothing in common except that each represents an interference with the right of the plaintiff . . . 'to be let alone'."[2] One of the most distinguished current commentators, Daniel Solove, pronounced that it was "a concept in disarray."[3]

Does this matter to anyone but a philosopher, a lawyer, or a nut who doesn't want his or her data to help humanity? It does: privacy has a role to play in our psychological well-being and the health of our democracies. Being undefined doesn't stop it playing that role, but the lack of definition opens up space for critics and skeptics with different priorities. Jeff Jarvis writes that instead of coherence he sees "a confused web of worries, changing norms, varying cultural mores, complicated relationships, conflicting motives, vague feelings of danger with sporadic specific evidence of harm, and unclear laws and regulations made all the more complex by context."[4] In short, he's saying it's a mélange that shouldn't stand in the way of social progress, and that we should ignore inchoate privacy concerns

and reap the benefits of sharing data with nary a backward glance. Maybe he has a point.

Do You Know What It Is Yet?

Jarvis' observation about the confusion is on the money, but we could get closer to some kind of consensus if we could leave the worries, norms, mores, and vague feelings behind, and then perhaps conduct a more sensible conversation. If you and I are addressing only a vague feeling of danger, then we shall not get far; we'll devise a set of vague solutions. If, on the other hand, you and I have a vague feeling of danger about something relatively concrete about whose limits we agree to some extent, then our discussion would be more productive, the solution set more coherent, and the costs and benefits clearer.

So there's mileage in thrashing this out. The first question is why it's so difficult. I think it's because we're having too many conversations simultaneously that ought to be separate—the result is cacophony, category error, and people talking past each other.

For example, one influential definition of privacy as "the freedom from unreasonable constraints on the construction of one's own identity,"[5] bundles up three separate ideas: a state in which a person is free of something (fine); freedom from unreasonable things, so necessarily a good thing for the individual, and plausibly something that should never be breached (since unreasonable things shouldn't happen if they can be prevented); and the construction of identity.

Yet privacy is sometimes breached for good reasons, and half the arguments about it are about how we identify those circumstances and legislate for them. Indeed, many cultures see privacy as a bad thing—privacy-related terms in ancient Greek (idiotes) and Latin (privare) had negative, not positive, connotations. And sometimes, privacy is a state in which someone has no interest in identity—that person just wants to get away from the madding crowd, or watch the ball game with a beer. The authors crammed contentious things about privacy into the above definition, and for good measure smuggled in their own opinions about what it is for. If someone denied, say, that privacy was required for identity, the debate would degenerate into the semantics of the definition, rather than remaining substantive and concerned with the application of an agreed (if contested) concept.

The Seven Veils

We can approach privacy at a number of levels and failure to recognize this ushers in the confusion and ambiguity that we find in writing on the topic. These levels conceal the roots of disputes and agreements and veil the nature of privacy itself. Had there been six or eight levels, I couldn't have used my catchy title, but there are seven, so here's to agreeable serendipity.

Level 1: conceptualization and realization. Underlying everything, there's a concept. This can't be simple; there are probably several of them in parallel. We know privacy varies across cultures, and that new technologies—writing, the portable camera, digital data storage, the Internet—create new problems. The first caveman to chisel a hole in his cave wall probably divided Neolithic opinion between those who welcomed the extra light and ventilation, and those who shook their heads and grunted about the shocking privacy implications.

For now, let's note that privacy takes many forms. It can be epistemological (Bob shouldn't acquire information about Alice), decisional (Bob shouldn't interfere with Alice's actions), spatial (Bob shouldn't intrude into Alice's space), ideological (Bob should tolerate Alice's beliefs), and economic (Bob shouldn't appropriate, use, or exchange Alice's property). All of these, particularly the first, have implications for online behavior. They are all states—Alice has her privacy when she is able to act freely, when her space is without a trespasser, when her data aren't being processed.

Do they have anything in common? Perhaps. Let's settle, for now, for the importance of a boundary. Bob crosses a line, metaphorically or otherwise, when he breaches Alice's privacy. And at any time a new type of behavior or technology can erect a new privacy boundary.

You can plug your own pet theory about privacy into level 1; I have my own views (detailed in the "Privacy at Level 1" sidebar), but they aren't essential to the six levels that follow. What I want to argue is that conceptual ambiguity resides here. The vague worries, changing norms, and complex relationships that concern Jarvis are distributed across the other six levels of discourse.

Level 2: empirical facts. Given a particular concept of privacy, then in principle, if not always easily, it's a simple matter to check whether someone actually has their privacy in this respect, or whether the line has been crossed. Either there's someone's eye at the spyhole into Alice's bathroom, or there isn't. Either someone is in possession of Alice's personal data, or no one is.

Privacy may occur because of someone trying to be private, but equally it might be unchosen, accidental, unnoticed, compulsory, or involuntary.[6] It may be given away freely or sold. Different concepts may come into play at the same time—an individual may be private in some respects but not others. A person may be private as part of a group but not be private within that group.

Level 3: phenomenology. This is a level often missing from discussion. A particular privacy situation will feel like something to Alice, and the way it feels will influence how tolerable she finds the state. Note that the empirical facts of Alice's privacy needn't be known to her.

Privacy isn't a matter of perception, but perception matters to the actions someone takes to preserve, or not preserve, his or her privacy. Alice showering unobserved, and Alice showering with Bob's eye at the spyhole feel identical to Alice; the phenomenology is unchanged, yet the privacy situation is radically different. Similarly, the phenomenology of privacy is culturally and contextually variable. Compare taking off clothes: with no observer; in front of your partner; in front of your mother; in the foyer of the Waldorf Astoria; on stage before a hundred people for a fee; on a nudist beach; in front of your doctor; in the dorm room for a bet; or at the behest of a zealous customs inspector. It's the same action in each case, but a very different feeling.

If we happen not to care about a privacy breach, then there's no reason even to notice it. Solove writes that "we are frequently seen and heard by others without perceiving this as even the slightest invasion of privacy."[3] True, but that just means that it's unimportant. We aren't private, in the relevant respect, when being seen and heard by others, whether we care, and whether we notice.

E-commerce and social networking sites work hard at this level in their service provision.[7] Social networkers feel private as they share information and chit-chat with their small group of friends. It feels warm and social, not like the chit-chat is owned by the network. Even if a social network is open about its use of information, via its privacy policy, and its users cognizant of the widespread exploitation of their personal data in the advertising business, that doesn't mean that social networking will feel as if it is exploited by advertisers and site owners.

Level 4: preferences. Given Alice's perceptions of privacy and her feelings about it, she will have certain preferences for or against it. She may prefer to be private in her dealings with the church, but online may prefer to be visible to her network. She will have preferences about other people's privacy—she may wish to keep her children's digital footprints as small as possible, for example. She may not want Bob to tell her all his troubles—she wishes he were more private. Preferences vary widely between individuals and across contexts for the same individual, and needn't be consistent. We need to be careful to separate the facts of privacy from our concern about it. Ruth Gavison argues that "our interest in privacy . . . is related to our concern over our accessibility to others."[8] That's true, but our interest being related to the concern doesn't make our concern part of the concept. Alice may be private or in a breach of privacy, while having no preference about it. She may make a fuss when her preferences aren't satisfied and may only take note of privacy when it's problematic, but that doesn't mean that its being problematic is part of the concept.

Privacy at Level I

The characteristics of privacy have only been sketched. Indeed, this may be all that can be done if the concept itself suggests no more than a family resemblance.[1] The framework of seven veils sketched here is a modular structure—if you have your own pet theory of privacy (and there are plenty of them), you can just plug it in at level 1. As long as your theory takes privacy as a state, and not a right, preference, norm, or legal concept, then the framework will separate the facts of privacy from our individual and social attitudes to it.

Is there more to say about what goes on at level I? How do we recognize a concept of privacy when, for example, new technology or new practices emerge?

I think much has to do with the psychology of ownership. By this, I absolutely do not mean property ownership in a legal sense, or even in John Locke's sense of "every man [having] a property in his own person."[2] I mean ownership as signaled by a compulsion to use possessive adjectives—my face, my body, my information, our beliefs, my space, our house, my name. "This is my business" means keep your nose out (your nose is your business, of course). This is a basic social instinct, and our legal ideas of property ownership are derivative from it. If I say "this is my business," I might be referring to my hairstyle, my beliefs about Donald Trump, the way I discipline my children, or the number of cigarettes I smoke on average per day; I own none of these, and can't sell them or leave them in my will.

Compare that to the notion of this is my house, but I don't own it (I rent it). This is my information, but I don't have any rights over it (Facebook has the rights, but it's still, in this non-legal sense, my data, because it's about me). Suppose Alice has a prosthetic leg; in that case, having bought it, she probably is the legal owner of the limb, yet she has a different, more profound sense of ownership of her real leg. I refer to ownership in the latter sense. Note that such adjectives may define an individual's private sphere, or that of a group. These are my friends (so that we have a collective privacy interest); I don't own them, and can't sell them to a passing slave trader.

The feeling of ownership is a deep component in the construction of one's identity, the self, although there are many competing ideas as to how that might function.[3,4] Ownership implies some kind of central and exclusive interest, or a privileged position. Alice gets to decide who enters her house (even if she doesn't legally own it). Alice decides who uses or disposes of her material possessions. Alice decides whether and when to reveal her body, or (in many cultures) her face,[5] or her name. The privilege may only be conceptual: Alice's information is about Alice, and if it's not about her it's not her information. As noted, she may not be able to defend these privileges without the cooperation of her fellows, but her privileged position is socially accepted.

Sometimes the privileged position is more nominal than effective. Private information about Alice may be unknown to her, and may be shared by others; but in most cultures, including Western liberal democracies, there are some taboos that protect privacy without her knowledge. Even the controversial US third-party doctrine,[6,7] under which information disclosed to third parties isn't defended by the US Constitution's Fourth Amendment against unreasonable searches, implies that the subject must take the first step in stripping away the legal protections. The doctrine is also founded on the individual's (and no one else's) "reasonable expectations of privacy."

Ownership, in this non-legal sense, subtends a boundary. There are my/our business, feelings, states, and decisions, and then there are bits of business, feelings, states and decisions that aren't mine/ours, over which society recognizes none of my/our privileges. The taxman may probe the financial affairs of many people, but only Alice's financial affairs affect her privacy.

A breach of privacy crosses a boundary, or challenges a privileged position. It implies attention toward some aspect of private behavior or position (Jed Rubenfeld writes of an "unarmed occupation of individuals' lives" a good phrase, although he focuses on privacy invasions by government).[8] Boundaries, (non-legal) ownership indicated by use of first-person possessive adjectives, and freedom from attention are all important indicators that privacy concepts are in place.

References

1. D.J. Solove, *Understanding Privacy,* Harvard Univ. Press, 2008.
2. J. Locke, "Second Treatise," *Two Treatises on Government,* Cambridge Univ. Press, 1988, pp. 265–428.
3. J. Dokic, "The Sense of Ownership: An Analogy between Sensation and Action," *Agency and Self-Awareness: Issues in Philosophy and Psychology,* J. Roessler and N. Eilan, eds., Oxford Univ. Press, 2003, pp. 321–344.
4. S. Gallagher, *How the Body Shapes the Mind,* Oxford Univ. Press, 2005.
5. F. El Guindi, *Veil: Modesty, Privacy and Resistance,* Berg, 1999.
6. O.S. Kerr, "The Case for the Third-Party Doctrine," *Michigan Law Rev.,* vol. 107, 2009, pp. 561–601.
7. E. Murphy, "The Case against the Case for Third-Party Doctrine: A Response to Epstein and Kerr," *Berkeley Technology Law J.,* vol. 24, no. 3, 2009, pp. 1239–1253.
8. J. Rubenfeld, "The Right of Privacy," *Harvard Law Rev.,* vol. 102, 1989, pp. 737–807.

Much of the discussion so far has been psychological, about the self. Yet now a social element emerges, because society has preferences about the privacy of individuals, too. Alice may wish to keep her financial details private, but the Internal Revenue Service, for perfectly good reasons, wants to see them (and were Alice Swedish, her society would wish her not only to give up the details to the taxman, but also to expect them to be published online). Alice doesn't want the police to have access to her heating bills, but—if she's growing marijuana in her attic—they may have grounds to seize them. Pace commentators such as Amitai Etzioni,[9] however, it's not always the case that individuals like Alice benefit from their privacy while society benefits from transparency and exposure.[10] Alice may prefer to sell her vote, but society wishes her to make her decision as to who to support privately. Alice may anticipate a life of partying, but society prefers her to care for children for whom she is responsible in her domestic sphere. Sociologist Irwin Altman described the endless process of negotiation of the boundaries between individuals, groups, and society, and this is no less apposite in the digitally networked age.[11]

Level 5: norms. Without assuming a naïve linear route through the levels, when sufficiently many people share similar preferences, we might expect these preferences to ossify into norms, expectations, conventions, and regularities of action and attitude. If Alice admonishes Bob to block up the spyhole because she doesn't like it, that's a level-4 claim. But if she admonishes Bob because spying on others is not the thing done around here, then she has moved to level 5. Helen Nissenbaum's theory of contextual integrity sits at this level.[12] She argues, for instance, that when considering putting some process online, someone should consider the norms that apply in the offline process (for instance, who gets to see customer information in a commercial transaction), and ensure that those norms are respected online, thereby preserving the situation's contextual integrity.

Level 5 normative aspects of privacy aren't part of the concept. Solove writes that "few would contend that when a crime victim tells the police about the perpetrator, it violates the criminal's privacy,"[3] but actually it does exactly that. And a good thing, too—the norm in that case works against privacy, for good social reasons. Privacy is about whether the details of someone's behavior are passed on; we need to separate the empirical question about what has happened from the normative one about what ought to have happened.

Social norms are vital for the protection of privacy, and explain much of its cultural diversity. They allow people to pursue their preferences (when preferences and norms are congruent) without needing to establish control. For instance, if Alice wants to mark out her personal space, all she needs is a little picket fence around her property; remarkably few people will be minded to cross it, although there's nothing physical to stop them.

Norms also influence the management of privacy with other concepts and mechanisms. Alice might give up privacy, for example, by discussing something personal with her doctor. In return, she expects confidentiality (that is, that her confidence won't leave the medical system).

Level 6: law. Norms can be formalized by turning them into laws or regulations, making the normalized behavior not only conventional but compulsory. This can have the effect of moving us from an adaptable, understandable, and context-sensitive norm to a more rigid, less-intuitive rule.[13] Equally, laws can be devised to extinguish or create norms.

A law requires more than mere social agreement, and so we move beyond civil society toward a notion of governance, and the application of sanctions by a state. Privacy law is important in understanding firms' and governments' practice with personal data, but the legal level has a hegemonic tendency—discussions about privacy tend to become discussions of law. We must remember that privacy isn't a legal concept, even though (in some countries) some types of privacy breach are illegal or actionable. One aim of a (level 6) law is to enable as many citizens as possible to satisfy their (level 4) preferences. At level 6, Alice can take legal action against Bob for his use of the spyhole, allowing her to satisfy her privacy preference for showering without an audience; at level 5, she can only appeal to social conventions.

Level 7: rights. Finally, privacy has moral and ethical connotations. It has political worth (for example, Beate Rössler argues that privacy supports individuals' autonomy, vital for the functioning of liberal democracy).[14] At level 7, Alice can argue that Bob is morally wrong to spy on her in her bathroom. We go beyond socially endorsed notions of what's right and wrong, to questions of value, logic, and conceptual analysis, separate from the other six levels, yet bringing us back to the conceptual evolution that characterizes level 1.

Views of rights vary. A legalist position, prominent in classic works by American scholars (such as Samuel Warren and Louis Brandeis[15] and Prosser[2]) is that we can "read off" our rights as a generalization, or a direction of travel, detectable in law (for example, in the US Constitution). The common law roots of US law locate much of this in financial or reputational harms that people have taken to court. In the EU, the position is somewhat different; universal rights are made explicit in treaties and documents, and laws enacted in Europe are expected to respect them. A court judges whether there's a conflict. The issue for lawyers and philosophers is whether, for example, a social network selling Alice's personal data to a third-party advertising broker intrudes so far into the private sphere that it threatens her private life.

Across the Levels

If we're discussing privacy, then it helps—actually, it's vital—not to jumble these levels. Suppose we're considering whether there's a right to privacy. Much will depend, for example, on whether the right protects the individual (like the right to life) or the collective (like the right to an open trial). Yet we can't have that discussion if we've written the presumed benefits into the definition of privacy in the first place. And if indeed we've done that, then we'll be shocked to discover that there are people in the world who don't care much about it. Our response may then be that such people are unaware of the issues, or have some kind of cognitive dissonance (the so-called privacy paradox). Yet it may actually be that such people just don't care

much to be in that kind of state, and would dispute the nature of the supposed benefits.

There are causal links between truths at the different levels, but we shouldn't generalize too much about their direction. One common sense type of reasoning will take us up through the levels—some particular type of privacy feels good or right to Alice (level 3), so she prefers it (level 4), as do many of her fellow citizens, leading to expectations or conventions emerging (level 5), which may at a later date be valorized in regulation (level 6), from which we abstract to create a right (level 7).

But the links may go in the opposite direction, or skip levels. Bob doesn't want to be spied upon (level 4) because it's just not done in his society (level 5), not the other way around. The sale of Alice's personal data annoys her (level 3), because she has a right to her privacy (level 7). There are norms in many cultures (level 5) which are designed to make individuals feel private (level 3); Mireille Hildebrandt writes of Japan, where, despite paper-thin walls in houses, people behave as if they're unaware of private conversations that they must have overheard,[13] while Robert Murphy writes that in communal living areas in some cultures, people simply avert their gaze from other people's space.[16]

Mention of norms reminds us that control—often assumed as a factor in defining privacy[17]—is secondary context, not a first-order facet of the concept. Alice may be able to protect her privacy herself (by destroying evidence of an event, perhaps), or she may use the law (by suing trespassers), or exploit social norms (by putting a small fence around her property), or she may be granted her privacy by the people around her. Only in the first case does she have total control, and she may feel less secure in her privacy as we go down the list. Self-determination often remains where control is ineffective, but beyond that, privacy may be conferred by a person's fellows.

If we can keep the question of whether someone actually has privacy free of value-related discourse, we might be able to unpick the different questions about the psychology, sociology, law, and morality of privacy. Tangling them up is a route to bafflement.

If, for example, you think that privacy is by definition a good thing or even a human right (a level 7 thing), then your definition will be complicated by an evaluation of the goodness or rightness of what you define. You may be thrown by the fact that, for example, in digital contexts, few people seem to be bothered by the loss of this good. On the other hand, if you decide that privacy is located in norms of concealment and exposure (a level 5 thing), you might agree with Mark Zuckerberg (who of course has no axe to grind in this area), that it's a thing of the past, as evidenced by the fact that a billion people are quite comfortable giving all their information to, er, Mark Zuckerberg.[18]

So how does this affect the digital citizen's experience of privacy and its lack? My aim is to separate the effects and affects of privacy from the facts. Privacy is too often defined as a good thing (and then it's a mystery why people give it away). It's often defined as law (so we have to go to court to find out how much of it we deserve). Sometimes it's defined as control (so we don't have very much of it). Removing these complicating factors from the simple state in which a boundary is crossed or not enables us to think about when that's problematic, and why this differs not only across cultures but also across generations and even for the same individuals.

This framework of the seven veils won't solve the myriad philosophical and political difficulties of privacy. It won't divulge whether the EU is right or wise to count privacy as a right, nor whether the United States is right to insist that privacy protections in law should be triggered by harms.[19] It does tell us that privacy goes wider than whatever we have a right to, and that privacy breaches needn't be (and usually aren't) accompanied by harm, whether financial or reputational.

Post-Snowden, security services have argued that bulk collection of data doesn't breach privacy—only analyzing it counts as surveillance. We can now see that collecting and analyzing are two different types of breach of privacy (level-1 concepts, the difference between them being the amount of attention paid to the data), and the first one may have few effects on the data subject (data collection will usually be completely invisible at the phenomenological level 3). The effects of data analysis and profiling may be evident to the data subject (she may be denied a seat on an airplane), but she may not associate those effects with a privacy breach. And if we ascend to level 6, we can ask the separate question about whether bulk collection is legal.

The framework tells of the importance of affective design in, say, social networks or e-commerce.[7] The way an experience of (breach of) privacy feels, or is concealed, will change the phenomenology and preferences of individuals, which may result in behavior that apparently shows a disregard on their part of assumed norms. For instance, after a profiling scandal in which the supermarket chain Target discovered that a teenager was pregnant before her parents did, "we started mixing in all these ads for things we knew pregnant women would never buy, so the baby ads looked random. . . . As long as we don't spook her, it works."[20] That's level-3 thinking, indeed. The seven-level framework encourages us to tease the different levels apart, and to consider that the individual's understanding of the situation may not include the recognition that a particular privacy norm is operative in the context in which he finds himself.

Indeed, we might even be able to unpick the so-called privacy paradox,[21] which suggests that individuals are irrational or lack self-knowledge when their behavior transgresses their stated privacy preferences. Perhaps people do adhere to particular norms at level 5, but their level-4 preferences are concerned with a whole Gestalt, crafted by system interface designers to affect them at level 3, involving much more than a simple experience of a privacy breach or otherwise. Any norm, including those of privacy, will be disregarded if the context makes it appropriate to do so. The privacy paradox isn't such a paradox when we see how easy it is to put people into situations where privacy doesn't seem like such a big deal.

References

1. J.J. Thomson, "The Right to Privacy," *Philosophy and Public Affairs,* vol. 4, 1975, pp. 295–314.

2. W.L. Prosser, "Privacy," *California Law Rev.,* no. 48, 1960, pp. 338–423.

3. D.J. Solove, *Understanding Privacy,* Harvard Univ. Press, 2008.

4. J. Jarvis, *Public Parts: How Sharing in the Digital Age Improves the Way We Work and Live,* Simon & Schuster, 2011.

5. P.E. Agre and M. Rotenberg, *Technology and Privacy: The New Landscape,* M.I.T. Press, 2001.

6. D.M. O'Brien, *Privacy, Law and Public Policy,* Praeger, 1979.

7. F.N. Egger, "Affective Design of E-Commerce User Interfaces: How to Maximise Perceived Trustworthiness," *Proc. Conf. Affective Human Factors Design,* 2001, pp. 317–324.

8. R. Gavison, "Privacy and the Limits of Law," *Yale Law J.,* vol. 89, 1980, pp. 421–471.

9. A. Etzioni, *The Limits of Privacy,* Basic Books, 1999.

10. K. O'Hara, "Are We Getting Privacy the Wrong Way Round?" *IEEE Internet Computing,* vol. 17, no. 4, 2013, pp. 88–92.

11. I. Altman, *The Environment and Social Behavior: Privacy, Personal Space, Territory, Crowding,* Brooks/Cole, 1975.

12. H. Nissenbaum, *Privacy in Context: Technology, Policy and the Integrity of Social Life*, Stanford Law Books, 2010.

13. M. Hildebrandt, *Smart Technologies and the End(s) of Law,* Edward Elgar, 2015.

14. B. Rössler, *The Value of Privacy*, Polity Press, 2005.

15. S.D. Warren and L.D. Brandeis, "The Right to Privacy," *Harvard Law Rev.*, vol. 4, 1890, pp. 193–220.

16. R.F. Murphy, "Social Distance and the Veil," *Am. Anthropologist,* vol. 66, 1964, pp. 1257–1274.

17. A.F. Westin, *Privacy and Freedom,* Athaneum, 1967.

18. I. Paul, "Facebook CEO Challenges the Social Norm of Privacy," *PCWorld,* Jan. 2010; www.pcworld.com /article/186584/facebook_ceo_challenges_the_social_ norm_of_privacy.html.

19. D. Solove, *Privacy and Data Security Violations: What's the Harm?* 25 June 2014; www.linkedin.com /pulse/20140625045136-2259773-privacy-and-data-security -violations-what-s-the-harm.

20. C. Duhigg, "How Companies Learn Your Secrets," *New York Times,* 16 Feb. 2012; www.nytimes.com/2012/02/19 /magazine/shopping-habits.html?_r=0.

21. S.B. Barnes, "A Privacy Paradox: Social Networking in the United States," *First Monday*, vol. 11, no. 9, 2006; http:// firstmonday.org/ojs/index.php/fm/article/viewArticle/1394.

Critical Thinking

1. Why is there no consensus around a defintion of privacy?

2. When might privacy be breached for good reasons?

3. How does context change an individual's privacy expectation?

Internet References

Americans' Attitudes About Privacy, Security and Surveillance
https://goo.gl/ZiI4Ou

There Is No Such Thing as Private Data
https://goo.gl/Vb5r0Y

UN Report Finds Mass Surveillance Violates International Treaties and Privacy Rights
https://goo.gl/j1U5VR

KIERON O'HARA is a senior lecturer and a principal research fellow in the Web and Internet Science Group in the Electronics and Computer Science Department at the University of Southampton. His research interests include trust, privacy, open data, and Web science. O'Hara has a DPhil in philosophy from the University of Oxford.

Article

Prepared by: Liz Friedman, *DePaul University* and
Daniel Mittleman, *DePaul University*

The Secret Things You Give Away Through Your Phone Metadata

NSIKAN AKPAN

Learning Outcomes

After reading this article, you will be able to:

- Explain how metadata can be used to identify sensitive information.
- Discuss the findings of the Stanford University experiment.
- Understand the differential privacy approach.

The word "metadata" achieved buzzword status in 2013. That's when whistleblower Edward Snowden leaked documents exposing a National Security Agency program that collected telephone metadata in bulk—along with other surveillance schemes deemed unsavory by electronic rights watchdogs. Since then, metadata collection has been invoked in court proceedings, innumerable opinion pieces and an Oscar-winning documentary as one of the most egregious violations of personal privacy. On Monday, former U.S. Attorney General Eric Holder said Snowden "performed a public service"—albeit an "inappropriate and illegal" one—by sharing the secrets.

Yet, most people couldn't describe, step-by-step, how metadata are used to piece together personal secrets.

This study shows that sensitive information, like health services or lifestyle choices, are easily discernible from metadata with little digging.

You're in luck. A new study from Stanford University charts exactly what can be learned from telephone metadata. The researchers used rudimentary techniques to show that your name or relationship status are immediately apparent from telephone metadata, but so are countless other personal details.

Don't want your parents to know that you're pregnant? Hope that they don't hack your smartphone's metadata.

The results clarify a longstanding debate. Metadata have historically received fewer legal protections than actual communications content, such as audio from a phone conversation or text message transcripts, to the disdain of privacy advocates. This study shows that sensitive information, like health services or lifestyle choices, are easily discernible from metadata with little digging.

"People have testified in Congress, saying that metadata definitely carries sensitive information, but there hadn't been a lot of science done," Patrick Mutchler, study co-author and member of Stanford's Computer Security Laboratory, told NewsHour. "What our study does is confirm a lot of the suspicions that people held about metadata."

Even though the NSA shuttered its bulk collection program six months ago, the researchers' findings remain pertinent. The NSA and Federal Bureau of Investigation can still obtain telephone metadata on individual suspects via the U.S. foreign intelligence surveillance court, which didn't deny any of the 1,457 requests made last year. (In fact, the FISA court hasn't refused an application since 2009). Plus, the NSA is holding on to boatloads of metadata collected over the last five years due to ongoing legal cases with privacy advocates.

The controversy also crosses borders. After last November's Paris attacks, France enhanced its surveillance powers to monitor phone calls without a warrant. Meanwhile, the U.K. government is debating similar legislation nicknamed the "snooper's charter." Regardless of what governments decide, companies continue to collect phone and internet metadata on customers, whether it's to sell ads or build better apps—and they've done so for decades.

"With these data, people are able to make more informed decisions about whether or not they approve or disapprove of these policies," Mutchler said. Tech innovators can also use the research to devise shields against the practice of metadata collection.

But let's start at the beginning with MetaPhone.

"Wait, you're pregnant!?"

MetaPhone is an Android app, designed by Mutchler and his labmates to collect telephone metadata. Over an eight-month window, the smartphones of 823 adult volunteers beamed call and text logs to the team's secure server. This data comprised when a call or text was made, whether it was an incoming or outgoing transmission, the duration of the call or the text message's length (in characters). The app also noted the phone numbers of the senders and recipients, but no identifiable information, audio recordings or textual content.

At least in one case, we were able to identify a person with a cardiac arrhythmia.

"The same stuff is available to the NSA, but they'd have more of it," Mutchler said of his May 17 report in the Proceedings of the National Academy of Sciences. "The volunteers hailed from 45 states, D.C. and Puerto Rico."

This small pool yielded 62,229 unique phone numbers, 251,788 calls and 1,234,231 texts. Basic machine-learning algorithms did the rest of the heavy lifting. The team relied on these quasi-intuitive programs to make inferences about people's identities or lifestyles.

The team started with child's play. They had the algorithms skim public information from Facebook, Yelp or Google Places in order to match 30,000 randomly selected phone numbers to individuals or businesses. Using these three sources, the researchers matched identities for 32 percent of the phone numbers. When the hunt expanded to include a public records service—a $19.95 investment—and 70 minutes of Google searches, the algorithms caught 82 percent of the identities.

The researchers could also pinpoint the identity of romantic partners—as verified by Facebook relationship statuses—with 80 percent accuracy using call volume and 76 percent accuracy using how often the couple texted each day.

The shocks came when the researchers looked for sensitive connections. In the report, they presented five typical examples.

"I would have guessed general inferences—like religious affiliation. But at least in one case we were able to identify a person with a cardiac arrhythmia," Mutchler said.

This participant received a long phone call from a cardiology group at a regional medical center, according to the paper, talked briefly with a medical laboratory and answered several short calls from a local drugstore. But the key giveaway may have been brief calls to a self-reporting hotline for a cardiac arrhythmia monitoring device. The team followed up and confirmed the cardiac arrhythmia, as well as a case where the analysis accurately concluded a person had purchased an automatic rifle.

Metadata from an NSA request involving a single suspect could uncover information on approximately 25,000 individuals.

Another volunteer called a pharmaceutical hotline for a drug prescribed only for multiple sclerosis, while a third vignette involved a person who spoke her sister early one morning for an extended period of time. Two days later, she made multiples calls to a nearby Planned Parenthood clinic. She repeated the pattern two weeks later . . . and then again, a month after the first call.

Communications with health services were the most common form of sensitive information caught by MetaPhone's surveillance, accounting for 57 percent of calls among participants. Financial services accounted for 40 percent.

Another case involved a person who "placed calls to a hardware outlet, locksmiths, a hydroponics store, and a head shop in under three weeks," the report stated.

"The call patterns are indicative of starting to grow marijuana," Mutchler said.

Overall, the analysis found metadata from an NSA request involving a single suspect could uncover information on approximately 25,000 individuals. Extend the search by one degree of separation—you, your friend and their contacts—and an agent could recover personal information on 20 million people. Kevin Bacon, eat your heart out. This latter scenario, known as three-hop surveillance, was the NSA's legal standard until recently.

"Maybe these [metadata] separately are innocuous, but there is a more meaningful picture that doesn't appear until you look at the data."

Metadata collection for the masses

Not long after Snowden outed the NSA, President Obama asked the National Academy of Sciences to convene a panel of 13 computer security experts. Over the course of five months in late 2014, they tackled whether there were currently technological alternatives to bulk collection of metadata that could still let intelligence agencies to do their work.

"In a sense, the short answer was not really," said Michael Kearns, a computer scientist at the University of Pennsylvania who served on the committee.

The reason is a sensible one, he said. The whole premise of intelligence work is maybe some individuals don't have the right to privacy. It's difficult to know in advance who you should and shouldn't be collecting data on, for the very reason that if you knew already, then you wouldn't need any data in the first place.

Kearns believes that future technology can strike a balance for surveillance agencies. In January, his team published a set of algorithms that can take a social network—like Facebook or a database of phone contacts—and filter perps from the innocent. Here's how it works.

Suppose I tell you the average salary of the PBS NewsHour editorial staff immediately before and after a reporter resigns. If you know those two values, you can easily figure out how much the reporter was making. Kearns' algorithm rely on differential privacy—a statistical masking that adds a bit of noise or randomness to the data. You can still make the salary calculation, but you can't identify the reporter.

Certain types of info, they'd rather not collect. They don't want to be on the hook for a subpoena "You want to limit the amount of information that's passing through the barrier between the place where all the data is held and the people who can act on the data," said Adam Smith, a security and privacy data scientist at Pennsylvania State University who wasn't involved with the research. "Differential privacy gives you a way to publish approximate stats to guarantee that there isn't too much information about one person."

Smith said companies like Google employ similar techniques to gather stats on how people people use apps on their phones but maintain privacy.

"Certain types of info, they'd rather not collect," Smith said. "They don't want to be on the hook for subpoena."

This info could be as simple as a person's homepage on their browser. The companies monitor these browser settings because some types of viruses and malware create false default homepages that take a user to another webpage. By using differential privacy, the company can track webpage traffic that raises a red flag and see if a piece of malware is responsible.

"Differential privacy allows them to collect approximate statistics about how people are setting their homepage without knowing the precise details of how you and I set our homepage," Smith said.

As an individual, you don't have a lot of control over how your data is used or manipulated once it's left you and gone to the telecommunication companies.

One team at MIT wants to apply the differential privacy approach, which primarily suits centralized databases, and apply it to individual smartphones. They've developed an app called SafeAnswers that allows a downloader to share parts of their metadata without forking over personal identifying content. The idea isn't completely novel. A handful of startups have created personal data storage platforms, so people can charge third-parties for access to metadata.

Yet, both Kearns and Smith said differential privacy works as a solution only if surveillance agencies or communications companies buy into it.

Individuals can end-to-end encrypt their phone calls, texts and WhatsApp messages with a service like OpenWhisperSystems. However, it requires an internet connection to create a secure channel. Mutchler couldn't think of an app that automatically anonymizes or creates false metadata to throw off possible snoops.

"As an individual, you don't have a lot of control over how your data is used or manipulated once it's left you and gone to the telecommunication companies. As it stands now, we would need to make a bunch of changes," Mutchler said. "From a public policy perspective, the next step is a continued discussion about metadata privacy and whether metadata should be considered separate or not" from content communications.

Critical Thinking

1. How accurate do you think alogrithms are at identifying your identity or lifestyle based on the metadata they collect on you?

2. What is the trade-off between personal privacy and national security? And who should decide which is more important in any given scenario?

3. To what extent should you be able to control what data others can retrieve?

Internet References

Metadata: Your City's Secret Weapon (Industry Perspective)
https://goo.gl/Z6r5dN

No, NSA Phone Spying Has Not Ended
https://goo.gl/4JR9yf

The Feds Are Prepping Strict Rules to Protect Your Online Privacy
https://goo.gl/Y6CxNq

NSIKAN AKPAN is the digital science producer for PBS NewsHour.

Prepared by: Liz Friedman, *DePaul University* and
Daniel Mittleman, *DePaul University*

Article

Privacy Not Included: Federal Law Lags Behind New Tech

The federal privacy law known as HIPAA doesn't cover home paternity tests, fitness trackers or health apps. When a Florida woman complained after seeing the paternity test results of thousands of people online, federal regulators told her they didn't have jurisdiction.

CHARLES ORNSTEIN

Learning Outcomes

After reading this article, you will be able to:

- Identify weaknesses in HIPPA protections as it relates to technology.

- Discuss the trade-off between privacy and convenience as it relates to health tracking apps.

This story was co-published with the Washington Post.

Jacqueline Stokes spotted the home paternity test at her local drugstore in Florida and knew she had to try it. She had no doubts for her own family, but as a cybersecurity consultant with an interest in genetics, she couldn't resist the latest advance.

At home, she carefully followed the instructions, swabbing inside the mouths of her husband and her daughter, placing the samples in the pouch provided and mailing them to a lab.

Days later, Stokes went online to get the results. Part of the lab's website address caught her attention, and her professional instincts kicked in. By tweaking the URL slightly, a sprawling directory appeared that gave her access to the test results of some 6,000 other people.

The site was taken down after Stokes complained on Twitter. But when she contacted the Department of Health and Human Services about the seemingly obvious violation of patient privacy, she got a surprising response: Officials couldn't do anything about the breach.

The Health Insurance Portability and Accountability Act, a landmark 1996 patient-privacy law, only covers patient information kept by health providers, insurers and data clearinghouses, as well as their business partners. At-home paternity tests fall outside the law's purview. For that matter, so do wearables like Fitbit that measure steps and sleep, testing companies like 23andMe, and online repositories where individuals can store their health records.

In several instances, the privacy of people using these newer services has been compromised, causing embarrassment or legal repercussions.

In 2011, for instance, an Australian company failed to properly secure details of hundreds of paternity and drug tests, making them accessible through a Google search. The company said that it quickly fixed the problem.

That same year, some users of the Fitbit tracker found that data they entered in their online profiles about their sexual activity and its intensity—to help calculate calories burned—was accessible to anyone. Fitbit quickly hid the information.

And last year, a publicly accessible genealogy database was used by police to look for possible suspects in a 1996 Idaho murder. After finding a "very good match" with the DNA of semen found at the crime scene, police obtained a search warrant to get the person's name. After investigating further, authorities got another warrant ordering the man's son to provide a DNA sample, which cleared him of involvement.

The incident spooked genealogy aficionados; AncestryDNA, which ran the online database, pulled it this spring.

"When you publicly make available your genetic information, you essentially are signing a waiver to your past and future medical records," said Erin Murphy, a professor at New York University School of Law.

The true extent of the problem is unclear because many companies don't know when the health information they store has been accessed inappropriately, experts say. A range of potentially sensitive data is at risk, including medical diagnoses, disease markers in a person's genes and children's paternity.

What is known is that the Office for Civil Rights, the HHS agency that enforces HIPAA, hasn't taken action on 60 percent of the complaints it has received because they were filed too late or withdrawn or because the agency lacked authority over the entity that's accused. The latter accounts for a growing proportion of complaints, an OCR spokeswoman said.

A 2009 law called on HHS to work with the Federal Trade Commission—which targets unfair business practices and identity theft—and to submit recommendations to Congress within a year on how to deal with entities handling health information that falls outside of HIPAA. Six years later, however, no recommendations have been issued.

The report is in "the final legs of being completed," said Lucia Savage, chief privacy officer of the HHS Office of the National Coordinator for Health Information Technology.

None of this was useful to the 30-year-old Stokes, a principal consultant at the cybersecurity firm Mandiant. Four months after she filed her complaint with OCR, it suggested she contact the FTC. At that point, she gave up.

"It just kind of seems like a Wild West right now," she said.

Protection of Consumer-app Data Varies

Advances in technology offer patients ways to monitor their own health that were impossible until recently: Internet-connected scales to track their weight; electrodes attached to their iPhones to monitor heart rhythms; virtual file cabinets to store their medical records.

"Consumer-generated health information is proliferating," FTC Commissioner Julie Brill said at a forum last year. But many users don't realize that much of it is stored "outside of the HIPAA silo."

HIPAA seeks to facilitate the flow of electronic health information, while ensuring that privacy and security are protected along the way. It only applies to health providers that transmit information electronically; a 2009 law added business partners that handle health information on behalf of these entities. Violators can face fines and even prison time.

"If you were trying to draft a privacy law from scratch, this is not the way you would do it," said Adam Greene, a former OCR official who's now a private-sector lawyer in Washington.

In 2013, the Privacy Rights Clearinghouse studied 43 free and paid health and fitness apps. The group found that some did not provide a link to a privacy policy and that many with a policy did not accurately describe how the apps transmitted information. For instance, many apps connected to third-party websites without users' knowledge and sent data in unencrypted ways that potentially exposed personal information.

"Consumers should not assume any of their data is private in the mobile app environment—even health data that they consider sensitive," the group said.

Consider a woman who is wearing a fetal monitor under her clothes that sends alerts to her phone. The device "talks" to her smartphone via wireless Bluetooth technology, and its presence on a network could be detected by others, alerting them to the fact that she's pregnant or that she may have concerns about her baby's health.

"That is a fact that you may not want to share with others around you—co-workers or family members or strangers in a café," said David Kotz, a computer science professor at Dartmouth College who is principal investigator of a federally funded project that is developing secure technology for health and wellness.

"We've seen this in the tech market over and over again," he added. "What sells devices or applications are the features for the most part, and unless there's a really strong business reason or consumer push or federal regulation, security and privacy are generally a secondary thought."

'Walking Through an Open Door'

In Florida, Stokes is one of those people enamored with emerging health technologies. Several years ago, she rushed to sign up for 23andMe to analyze her genetic profile. And when she was pregnant with her daughter, she purchased a test that said it could predict the sex of the fetus. (It was wrong.)

The paternity test kit that piqued her interest earlier this year advertised "accuracy guaranteed" for "1 alleged father and 1 child." She remembers the kit costing about $80 at a nearby Walgreens. Such tests sell for about $100 online.

"It was kind of a nerdy thing that I was interested in doing," Stokes said.

The test was processed in New Mexico by GTLDNA Genetic Testing Laboratories, then a division of General Genetics Corp. Stokes was directed to log into a website and enter a unique code for her results. When they appeared, she noticed an unusual Web address on her screen, and she wondered what would happen if she modified it to remove the ID assigned to her.

She tried that and saw a folder containing the results of thousands of other people. She was able to click through and read them. "You wouldn't call that hacking," she said. "You would call that walking through an open door."

Stokes downloaded those publicly accessible records so that she would have proof of the lax security. "There were no safeguards," she said. She complained to the HHS Office for Civil Rights in early February. It answered in June, writing that the office "does not have authority to investigate your complaint, and therefore, is closing this matter."

Bud Thompson, who until last month was the chief executive of General Genetics, initially said he had not heard about Stokes' discovery. A subsequent email provided an explanation.

"There was a coding error in the software that resulted in the person being able to view results of other customers. The person notified the lab, and the website was immediately taken down to solve this problem," he wrote. "Since this incident, we have sold this line of business and have effectively ceased all operations of the lab."

The DNA testing company 23andMe, which helps people learn about their genetic backgrounds and find relatives based on those profiles, had a highly publicized lab mix-up in which as many as 96 customers were given the wrong DNA test results, sometimes for people of a different gender. A spokeswoman for the California-based company said she was unaware of any privacy or security breaches since that 2010 incident.

Kate Black, its privacy officer and corporate counsel, said that 23andMe tries to provide more protection than HIPAA would require.

"No matter what, no law is ever going to be narrow enough or specific enough to appropriately protect each and every business model and consumer health company," she said.

California lawmakers have twice considered a measure to prohibit anyone from collecting, analyzing or sharing the genetic information of another person without written permission, with some exceptions.

Then-Sen. Alex Padilla, who sponsored the bill, cited a California company that marketed DNA testing, including on samples collected from people without their knowledge. In a recent interview, he said that he was amazed state law did not protect "what's arguably the most personal of our information and that's our genetic makeup, our genetic profile."

The legislation failed. And Padilla, now California's secretary of state, remains concerned: "I don't think this issue is going away any time soon."

Too Many Complaints To Pursue

While Stokes was troubled by her experience, she was particularly disheartened by the OCR's response. "It was shocking to me to get that message back from the government saying this isn't covered by the current legislation and, as a result, we don't care about it," she said.

The agency's deputy director for health information privacy says there is no lack of interest. While it refers certain cases to law enforcement, OCR can barely keep up with those complaints that fall within its jurisdiction.

"I wish we had the bandwidth to do so," Deven McGraw said. "We would love to be able to be a place where people can get personalized assistance on every complaint that comes in the door, but the resources just don't allow us to do that."

For its part, the FTC has taken action against a few companies for failing to secure patients' information, including a 2013 settlement with Cbr Systems Inc., a blood bank where parents store the umbilical cord blood of newborns in case it is ever needed to treat subsequent diseases in the children or relatives. That settlement requires Cbr to implement comprehensive security and submit to independent audits every other year for 20 years. It also bars the company from misrepresenting its privacy and security practices.

But FTC officials say the number of complaints pursued hardly reflects the scope of the problem. Most consumers are never told when a company sells or otherwise shares their health information without their permission, said Maneesha Mithal, associate director of the FTC's division of privacy and identity protection.

"It may be done behind the scenes, without consumers' knowledge," she noted. "Those are the cases where consumers may not even know to complain."

Has your medical privacy been compromised? Help ProPublica investigate by filling out a short questionnaire. You can also read other stories in our Policing Patient Privacy series.

Critical Thinking

1. What are the ethical implications of companies selling your health or fitness app data?

2. What steps can you take to protect the privacy of your data?

Internet References

Are Fitness Apps Fit for Privacy Protection?
https://goo.gl/N5bcVe

Employer-Sponsored Wellness Programs Put Your Health Privacy on Life Support
https://goo.gl/WqN17Z

Stanford Computer Scientists Show Telephone Metadata Can Reveal Surprisingly Sensitive Personal Information
https://goo.gl/4K1Ivh

CHARLES ORNSTEIN is a senior reporter for ProPublica covering health care and the pharmaceutical industry.

Article

Prepared by: Liz Friedman, *DePaul University* and
Daniel Mittleman, *DePaul University*

Google's European Conundrum: When Does Privacy Mean Censorship?

Though Google is a U.S. company, its American rights don't transpose across the pond. A court case will determine whether Google has to comply with EU law, which could have far-reaching consequences for European users.

Zack Whittaker

Learning Outcomes

After reading this article, you will be able to:

- Understand how data placed on the Internet is virally replicated in a manner that no one entity can control it, let alone erase it.

- Articulate how information available on the Internet impacts the trade-off of concerns between free speech rights and privacy rights.

- Know the risks of maintaining an online presence.

How Google and other American Internet companies operate in Europe could come down to a link that, depending on what side of the Atlantic Ocean you're on, should or should not be deleted.

A case heard Tuesday before the European Court of Justice (ECJ) hinges on a complaint submitted by a Spanish citizen who searched Google for his name and found a news article from several years earlier, saying his property would be auctioned because of failed payments to his social security contributions.

Spanish authorities argued that Google, other search engines, and other Web companies operating in Spain should remove information such as that if it is believed to be a breach of an individual's privacy. Google, however, believes that it should not have to delete search results from its index [http://www.reuters.com/article/2013/02/26/us-eu-googledataprotection-idUSBRE91P0A320130226] because the company didn't create it in the first place. Google argued that it is the publisher's responsibility and that its search engine is merely a channel for others' content.

The ECJ's advocate-general will publish its opinion on the case on June 25, with a judgment expected by the end of the year. The outcome of the hearing will affect not only Spain but also all of the 27 member states of the European Union.

In principle, this fight is about freedom of speech versus privacy, with a hearty dash of allegations of censorship mixed in. In reality, this could be one of the greatest changes to EU privacy rules in decades—by either strengthening the rules or negating them altogether.

The European view is simple: If you're at our party, you have to play by our rules. And in Europe, the "right to be forgotten" is an important one.

"Facebook and Google argue they are not subject to EU law as they are physically established outside the EU," a European Commission spokesperson told CNET. In new draft privacy law proposals, the message is, "as long as a company offers its goods or services to consumers on the EU territory, EU law must apply."

While Europe has some of the strongest data protection and privacy laws in the world, the U.S. doesn't. And while the U.S. has some of the strongest free speech and expression laws in the world, enshrined by a codified constitution, most European countries do not, instead favoring "fair speech" principles.

Google is also facing another legal twist: Spanish authorities are treating it like a media organization without offering it the full legal protection of one.

The European view is simple: If you're at our party, you have to play by our rules. And in Europe, the "right to be forgotten" is an important one.

Newspapers should be exempt from individual takedown requests to preserve freedom of speech, according to Spanish authorities, but Google should not enjoy the same liberties, despite having no editorial control and despite search results being determined by algorithms. Though Google is branded a "publisher" like newspapers, the search giant does not hold media-like protection from takedowns under the country's libel laws. This does not translate across all of Europe, however. Some European member states target newspapers directly and are held accountable through press regulatory authorities in a bid to balance freedom of speech and libel laws.

One of Spain's highest courts, the Agencia Espanola de Proteccion de Datos (AEPD), found in favor of the complainant in early 2011 and ruled that Google should delete the search result [http://online.wsj.com/article/SB10001424052748703396604576087573944344348.html]. This case is one of around 180 other ongoing cases in the country.

Google appealed the decision and the case was referred to the highest court in Europe, the ECJ, which will eventually determine if the search giant is the "controller" of the data or whether it is merely a host of the data.

The case will also decide on whether U.S.-based companies are subject to EU privacy law, which may mean EU citizens have to take their privacy cases to U.S. courts to determine whether Google is responsible for the damage caused by the "diffusion of personal information."

In a blog post on Tuesday [http://googlepolicyeurope.blogspot.com/2013/02/judging-freedom-of-expression-at.html], Bill Echikson, Google's "head of free expression," said the search giant "declined to comply" with a request by Spanish data protection authorities, as the search listing "includes factually correct information that is still publicly available on the newspaper's Web site."

"There are clear societal reasons why this kind of information should be publicly available. People shouldn't be prevented from learning that a politician was convicted of taking a bribe, or that a doctor was convicted of malpractice," Echikson noted.

"We believe the answer to that question is 'no'. Search engines point to information that is published online—and in this case to information that had to be made public, by law. In our view, only the original publisher can take the decision to remove such content. Once removed from the source webpage, content will disappear from a search engine's index."

EU's Latest Privacy Proposal: The "Right To Be Forgotten"

Should the ECJ find in favor of the Spanish complainant, it will see the biggest shakeup to EU privacy rules in close to two decades and would enable European citizens a "right to be forgotten."

In January 2011, the European Commission lifted the lid on draft proposals for a single one-size-fits-all privacy regulation for its 27 member states. One of the proposals was the "right to be forgotten," empowering every European resident the right to force Web companies as well as offline firms to delete or remove their data [http://www.cnet.com/8301-1009_3-57363585-83/new-eu-dataprotection-rules-due-this-week/] to preserve their privacy.

For Europeans, privacy is a fundamental right to all residents, according to Article 8 of the European Convention of Human Rights, in which it states [http://www.hri.org/docs/ECHR50.html#C.Art8]: "Everyone has the right to respect for his private and family life, his home and his correspondence." It does however add a crucial exception. "There shall be no interference by a public authority with the exercise of this right except . . . for the protection of the rights and freedoms of others."

Because U.S.-based technology giants like Google, Facebook, and Twitter have users and in many cases a physical presence in Europe, they must comply with local laws. The "right to be forgotten" would force Facebook and Twitter to remove any data it had on you, as well as Google removing results from its search engine. It would also extraterritorially affect users worldwide outside the European Union who would also be unable to search for those removed search terms.

Such Web companies have said (and lobbied to that effect) [http://www.telegraph.co.uk/technology/news/9070019/EU -Privacy-regulations-subject-to-unprecedented-lobbying.html] that the "right to be forgotten" should not allow data to be removed or manipulated at the expense of freedom of speech. This, however, does not stop with republished material and other indexed content, and most certainly does not apply to European law enforcement and intelligence agencies.

Two Continents, Separated by "Free" and "Fair Speech"

The U.S. and the EU have never seen eye-to-eye on data protection and privacy. For Americans and U.S.-based companies, the belief is that crossover between freedom of speech and privacy overlaps in "a form of censorship," according to Google's lawyers [http://www.bbc.co.uk/news/technology-12239674] speaking during the Spanish court case.

In the U.S., you can freely say the most appalling words, so long as they don't lead to a crime or violence against a person or a group of people. In European countries such as the U.K. words can lead to instant arrest. Europe's laws allow for "fair speech" in order to prevent harassment, fear of violence, or even alarm and distress. It's a dance between the American tradition of protecting the individual and the European tradition of protecting society.

Google is fundamentally so very American in this regard. That said, Google already filters and censors its own search results at the behest of governments and private industry, albeit openly and transparently [http://www.google.com /transparencyreport/]. Google will agree to delete links that violate copyrights under the Digital Millennium Copyright Act, which seeks to remove content from Google's search results that may facilitate copyright infringement.

Google also complies, when forced by a court, with numerous types of government requests, not limited to subpoenas, search warrants, and National Security Letters [http://www .zdnet.com/what-google-does-when-a-government-requests-your -data-7000010418/], or so-called "gagging orders." It also discloses those requests and when it complies with them. And it's a system not that dissimilar to what it's being asked to do in Europe.

Whose Jurisdiction Is Google Under: U.S., EU, or Both?

While Europe's privacy principles apply to the Web, it's unclear whether they apply to data "controllers" established outside of the European Union. But several European court cases have sided with local law. A German court found that Facebook fell under Irish law [http://www.bloomberg.com/news/2013-02-15 /facebook-scores-win-in-legal-regime-dispute-with-germany .html] because the social networking company had a physical presence in Ireland, another EU member state. In Google's case, Spanish authorities are making a similar argument, claiming that Google is processing data in a European state and therefore EU law should apply.

Many American companies have voiced their objections to the proposed EU privacy law [http://www.zdnet.com/blog /london/european-draft-data-law-announced-what-you-need-to -know/2609], including Amazon, eBay, and Yahoo, according to a lobbying watchdog [http://www.lobbyplag.eu/#/compare /overview]. It could still take a year or two for the law to be ratified.

"Exempting non-EU companies from our data protection regulation is not on the table. It would mean applying double standards," said Europe's Justice Commissioner Viviane Reding, the top politician in Europe on data protection and privacy rules in the region, in an interview with the *Financial Times of London* [http://www.ft.com/intl/cms/s/0/903b3302 -7398-11e2-bcbd-00144feabdc0.html#axzz2MCRmwDfo].

The new EU Data Protection Regulation, proposed by the European Commission and currently being debated in the European Parliament, will likely be voted on by June.

But this fight isn't as much about censorship as one might think. It's about a cultural difference between two continents and perspectives on what freedom of speech can and should be. It's also about privacy, and whether privacy or free speech is more important.

Critical Thinking

1. Explain why it is so difficult to completely remove information placed on the Internet.

2. Assuming it were technologically feasible to completely remove information from the Internet, should a public figure be permitted to selectively remove information from the Internet about himself or herself? Should a private person be permitted to do so? Should someone under 18 be permitted to do so? What about someone who had embarrassing information posted with their consent?

3. Should a potential employer be permitted to sift through old Internet information when making an employment decision? Should an existing employer be permitted to look and potentially terminate an employee? Should a potential spouse be able to look? Should a potential first date? If your answers are split between yes and no, what general policy should guide when a historical search is appropriate and when it is not?

Internet References

California "Eraser Law" Lets Minors Remove Embarrassing Online Content
www.pbs.org/newshour/rundown/2013/09/california-eraser-law-lets
-minors-remove-embarrassing-online-content.html

EU Report: The "Right To Be Forgotten" Is Technically Impossible . . . So Let's Do It Anyway
www.techdirt.com/articles/20121205/08425221239/eu-report-right-to-be
-forgotten-is-technically-impossible-so-lets-do-it-anyway.shtml

Juan Enriquez: Your Online Life, Permanent as a Tattoo [TED Talk]
www.ted.com/talks/juan_enriquez_how_to_think_about_digital_tattoos.html

Reputation 3.0: The Internet Is Your Resume
www.forbes.com/sites/dorieclark/2013/07/19/reputation-3-0-the
-internet-is-your-resume

Survey: One-Third of Youths Engage in Sexting
www.wired.com/threatlevel/2009/12/sexting-survey

Temporary Social Media
www.technologyreview.com/featuredstory/513731/temporary-social-media

---

ZACK WHITTAKER writes for ZDNet, CNET, and CBS News. He is based in New York City.

Unit 5

UNIT

Prepared by: Liz Friedman, *DePaul University* and
Daniel Mittleman, *DePaul University*

Personal Security

Security is the yang to privacy's yin. And our online security today is under siege. Global cybercrime is likely costing victims something over $400 billion a year, with estimates the cost will reach $2.1 trillion by 2019.[1] And cybercrime is evolving as well. Not only are exploits to acquire personal identity information becoming more sophisticated, but whole new forms of cyber-crime are emerging and growing. For example, the crime of ransomware—encrypting an innocent user's data as hostage and selling the decryption key for large amounts of untraceable money, usually Bitcoin—has grown from about $200 million of ransom payments in 2015 to over $1 billion in ransom payments in 2016 according to the FBI.[2] Of course, ransom payments account for only a fraction of the real loss to a business that may suffer from days to weeks of downtime and hundreds of man-hours rebuilding systems. Some security firms believe that the actual loss to ransomware is four times the FBI's estimate as they find ransomware cases are reported to authorities only about 25% of the time.

Our security is at risk from cybercrime because the economic, social, and civic fabric of our lives has moved to the virtual and become more tightly coupled with these networks and data repositories. Our modern Internet-based society is dominated by several types of complementary networks and data repositories, many of them coexisting on the Internet. Among those data repositories are the vast collections of information held by Google, Apple, Facebook, LinkedIn, Amazon, eBay, and others about our personal surfing, posting, and shopping habits. Also potentially accessible out there in more secured spaces are our credit card and banking information, our credit histories, our medical histories, and government data such as property holdings, license and registration data, criminal and traffic history, and voter registration records. The rare exception among us who has largely stayed offline is impacted nevertheless by institutional data placed online outside of that person's control. Therefore, it is reasonable to conclude that all of us run the risk of getting hurt.

Beyond our personal data that is stored on the Internet cloud are institutional and public data. The aforementioned medical, insurance, and credit information is held for the most part by private companies doing the best job they can (we hope) to successfully steward our data. Further, many banks, retail stores, and other institutions employ networked security cameras to track the comings and goings of their patrons. Beyond that are the police and criminal databases often referred to during cop shows on TV. And there exist databases and active networks used to manage civic security cameras, and public works such as water and power distribution. And our national security infrastructure makes use of networks (sometimes, but not always, separate and more secure than the Internet) to undertake their mission. This includes, but is not limited to, work by Homeland Security departments, the military, and the various government spy agencies.

None of these networks is 100% secure. Many, likely most, of these networks are under regular attack—though security protocols automatically block the common and more amateur attacks. There have been multiple reports of late, however, of more skilled and determined attacks on our public networks from groups within China and, perhaps, Iran.[3,4,5]

With the realization in 2013 from documents leaked by Edward Snowden that the U.S. government has been collecting domestic telephone and Internet data, concern has focused on the potential vulnerability to everyday Americans from the government holding this information. But large Internet and communication companies possess as much—perhaps more—information about our online activities. And many of these companies, due to license agreements we agree to, maintain rights to make use of this data in a variety of ways. Google's vast database of our web browsing and related history contains far more detailed personal interests and behaviors than any government could know.[6] And Facebook is aiming to capture every one of everyone's relationships with objects, organizations, and each other.[7] What are the implications of having such personal and complete information about almost all of us sitting in corporate databases?

[1]See: http://www.forbes.com/sites/stevemorgan/2016/01/17/cyber-crime-costs-projected-to-reach-2-trillion-by-2019/
[2]See: https://pdf.ic3.gov/2015_IC3Report.pdf
[3]S. Gorman, J. Barnes, "Iran Blamed for Cyberattacks," *Wall Street Journal*, October 13, 2012.
[4]E. Nakashima, "China Testing Cyber-attack Capabilities, Report Says," *Washington Post*, March 7, 2012.
[5]J. Winter, J. Kaplan, "Washington Confirms Chinese Hack Attack on White House Computer," FoxNews.com (accessed 10/13/12 at http://www.foxnews.com/tech/2012/10/01/washington-confi rmschinese-hack-attack-on-white-house-computer/#ixzz29D5gQjKp)
[6]James Gleick, "How Google Dominates Us," *The New York Review of Books*, August 13, 2011.
[7]Tom Simonite, "What Facebook Knows," *Technology Review*, July/August 2012.

What is a reasonable person to make of all of this? We can communicate with almost anyone almost anywhere on the planet at almost no cost. The wealth of the world is available on Amazon or eBay for those with credit cards. Google, Wikipedia, and an ocean of other sites provide information in abundance and at a speed that would have seemed like science fiction a generation ago. Yet thieves get hold of digitally stored personal information. Our digital records are disintegrating even as we digitize more and more of them. The government compiles massive databases about terrorism and catches the innocent in its nets. Disruption of the global communications network could be catastrophic, as financial markets and global supply chains collapse. One strives for the equanimity of Neil Postman: "Technology giveth and technology taketh away."

Prepared by: Liz Friedman, *DePaul University* and
Daniel Mittleman, *DePaul University*

Article

Cybersecurity: The Age of the Megabreach

We haven't stopped huge breaches. The focus now is on resilience, with smarter ways to detect attacks and faster ways to respond to them.

DAVID TALBOT

Learning Outcomes

After reading this article, you will be able to:

- Understand the breadth of the threat of theft due to lack of encryption.

- Understand the kinds of crimes that can occur when thieves are able to access unencrypted data.

- Articulate a role for government, if any, for ensuring corporate data is encrypted.

In November 2014, an especially chilling cyberattack shook the corporate world—something that went far beyond garden-variety theft of credit card numbers from a big-box store. Hackers, having explored the internal servers of Sony Pictures Entertainment, captured internal financial reports, top executives' embarrassing e-mails, private employee health data, and even unreleased movies and scripts and dumped them on the open Web. The offenders were said by U.S. law enforcement to be working at the behest of the North Korean regime, offended by a farcical movie the company had made in which a TV producer is caught up in a scheme to kill the country's dictator.

The results showed how profoundly flat-footed this major corporation was. The hack had been going on for months without being detected. Data vital to the company's business was not encrypted. The standard defensive technologies had not worked against what was presumed to have been a "phishing" attack in which an employee clicked a link that downloaded powerful malware. Taken together, all this showed that many of today's technologies are not adequate, that attacks can now be more aggressive than ever, and that once breaches occur, they are made worse by slow responses.

The Sony hack was one in a series of recent data breaches—including many "megabreaches," in which at least 10 million records are lost—that together reveal the weakness of today's cybersecurity approaches and the widening implications for the global economy. In 2015, the U.S. Office of Personnel Management was hacked, exposing 21.5 million records, including background checks on millions of people—among them copies of 5.6 million sets of fingerprints. Later in the year, 37 million visitors to Ashley Madison, a dating site for people seeking extramarital affairs, learned that their real e-mail addresses and other data had been released. The theft of data from 83 million customers of Wall Street giant J.P. Morgan, allegedly by an Israel-based team trying to manipulate the stock market, revealed chilling possibilities from how cyberattacks could undermine the financial sector.

Since companies and other organizations can't stop attacks and are often reliant on fundamentally insure networks and technologies, the big question for this report is how they can effectively respond to attacks and limit the damage—and adopt smarter defensive strategies in the future. New approaches and new ways of thinking about cybersecurity are beginning to take hold. Organizations are getting better at detecting fraud and other attacks by using algorithms to mine historical information in real time. They are responding far more quickly, using platforms that alert security staff to what is happening and quickly help them take action. And new tools are emerging from a blossoming ecosystem of cybersecurity startups, financed by surging venture capital investment in the area.

Cyber Breaches Hit Staggering Levels

Exceptionally harmful hacks have recently struck organizations in the global insurance, finance, telecom, and entertainment industries and at the heart of a U.S. federal agency—inflicting hundreds of millions of dollars in damage and added costs.

		How They Were Exploited	Data Stolen and Scale	Costs	Suspected Culprit
7/2014	**JPMorgan Chase** New York City	Two-factor authentication upgrade not fully implemented.	Names, addresses, and phone numbers of 76 million household and seven million small-business accounts.	The company says it plans to spend $250 million annually on security.	Three people have been charged with the attack as part of a stock manipulation scheme.
11/2014	**Sony Pictures Entertainment** Culver City, California	Malware and lack of intrusion detection.	E-mails, salary information, and terabytes of other data, including movie scripts and contracts.	$41 million, according to public filings.	North Korean regime.
2/2015	**Anthem Health** Indianapolis	Malware specifically designed to attack the company.	Names, birth dates, addresses, employment information, and Social Security numbers for 78 million people.	Much or all of the $100 million value of its cyberinsurance policy.	China-based hackers, suspected to be affiliated with the government.
6/2015	**U.S. Office of Personnel Management** Washington, D.C.	Likely social-engineering attacks and lack of modern intrusion detection services.	A mix of names, birth dates, addresses, fingerprints, and background information on as many as 21.5 million people.	More than $133 million just for credit monitoring for victims.	China-based hackers, suspected to be affiliated with the government.
7/2015	**Ashley Madison** Toronto	Unknown, but attackers cited weak passwords and almost nonexistent internal security.	Names, addresses, birth dates, phone numbers, and credit card history of 37 million users, plus the CEO's e-mails.	Unknown. The company faces numerous lawsuits.	A previously unknown group that calls itself Impact Team.
9/2015	**T-Mobile US** Bellevue, Washington	Security weaknesses at a partner (Experian) that was managing credit check data.	Names, birth dates, addresses, and Social Security and driver's license numbers of 15 million people.	Experian has spent at least $20 million on credit monitoring and other corrective actions.	Unknown.
10/2015	**TalkTalk Telecom** London	Distributed-denial-of-service attack and malicious code.	Names, birth dates, addresses, and phone numbers of more than 150,000 customers.	About $50 million in lost sales and incident response costs.	A teenager in Northern Ireland.

But hindering progress everywhere is the general lack of encryption on the devices and messaging systems that hundreds of millions of people now use. Nearly three years ago, when National Security Agency contractor Edward Snowden revealed that intelligence agencies were freely availing themselves of data stored by the major Internet companies, many of those companies promised to do more to encrypt data. They started using encryption on their own corporate servers, but most users remain exposed unless they know to install and use third-party apps that encrypt their data.

All these measures will help protect data in today's relatively insecure networks. But it's clear that the very basics of how networked technologies are built need to be rethought and security given a central role. A new national cybersecurity strategy is expected to chart an R&D plan to make sure software is verifiably secure and that users know when it's not working.

There's a big opportunity: the number of Internet-connected devices—not including smartphones, PCs, and tablets—could reach two billion in just five years. A **2015 McKinsey report** predicts that this will become a multitrillion-dollar industry by 2025. All these new devices will present an opportunity to build things robustly from the start—and avoid having them play a role in Sony-like hacks in the future.

Critical Thinking

1. What is encryption and how does it protect data on corporate servers? How does it protect data being sent by e-mail or texting?

2. Why isn't more being done to protect data?

3. How much responsibility does an industry have to protect your data and how much of that responsibility lies with you?

Internet References

Cluster of "Megabreaches" Compromises a Whopping 642 Million Passwords
   https://goo.gl/Ytm21U

Security News This Week: A Deluge of Mega-Breaches Dumps on the Dark Web
   https://goo.gl/hf8Uh5

Yahoo! and the Mega Breaches That Keep Happening
   https://goo.gl/jk0E51

Prepared by: Liz Friedman, *DePaul University* and
Daniel Mittleman, *DePaul University*

Article

Machine Bias

JULIA ANGWIN et al.

Learning Outcomes

After reading this article, you will be able to:

- Understand the role of mathematical algorithms in affecting American life.

- Articulate the pros and cons of using an algorithmic assessment to inform sentencing in of a conflicted criminal.

- Articulate a position as to whether or not the use of algorithms can have a racial bias built in.

On a spring afternoon in 2014, Brisha Borden was running late to pick up her god-sister from school when she spotted an unlocked kid's blue huffy bicycle and a silver Razor scooter. Borden and a friend grabbed the bike and scooter and tried to ride them down the street in the Fort Lauderdale suburb of Coral Springs.

Just as the 18-year-old girls were realizing they were too big for the tiny conveyances—which belonged to a 6-year-old boy—a woman came running after them saying, "That's my kid's stuff." Borden and her friend immediately dropped the bike and scooter and walked away.

But it was too late—a neighbor who witnessed the heist had already called the police. Borden and her friend were arrested and charged with burglary and petty theft for the items, which were valued at a total of $80.

Compare their crime with a similar one: The previous summer 41-year-old Vernon Prater was picked up for shoplifting $86.35 worth of tools from a nearby Home Depot store.

Prater was the more seasoned criminal. He had already been convicted of armed robbery and attempted armed robbery, for which he served 5 years in prison, in addition to another armed robbery charged. Borden had a record, too, but it was for misdemeanors committed when she was a juvenile.

Yet something odd happened when Borden and Prater were booked into jail: A computer program spat out a score predicting the likelihood of each committing a future crime. Borden—who is black—was rated a high risk. Prater—who is white—was rated a low risk.

Two years later, we know the compute algorithm got it exactly backward. Borden has not been charged with any new crimes. Prater is serving an 8-year prison term for subsequently breaking into a warehouse and stealing thousands of dollars' worth of electronics.

Scores like this—known as risk assessments—are increasingly common in courtrooms across the nation. They are used to inform decisions about who can be set free at every stage of the criminal justice system, from assigning bond amounts—as is the case in Fort Lauderdale—to even more fundamental decisions about defendants' freedom. In Arizona, Colorado, Delaware, Kentucky, Louisiana, Oklahoma, Virginia, Washington, and Wisconsin, the results of such assessments are given to judges during criminal sentencing.

Rating a defendant's risk of future crime is often done in conjunction with an evaluation of a defendant's rehabilitation needs. The Justice Department's National Institute of Corrections now encourages the use of such combined assessments at every stage of the criminal justice process. And a landmark sentencing reform bill currently pending in Congress would mandate the use of such assessments in federal prisons.

Two Petty Theft Arrests

Vernon Prater

Low Risk	3

Brisha Borden

High Risk	8

Borden was rated high risk for future crime after she and a friend took a kid's bike and scooter that were sitting outside. She did not reoffend.

In 2014, then U.S. Attorney General Eric Holder warned that the risk scores might be injecting bias into the courts. He called for the U.S. Sentencing Commission to study their use. "Although these measures were crafted with the best of intentions, I am concerned that they inadvertently undermine our efforts to ensure individualized and equal justice," he said, adding, "they may exacerbate unwarranted and unjust disparities that are already far too common in our criminal justice system and in our society."

The sentencing commission did not, however, launch a study of risk scores. So ProPublica did, as part of a larger examination of the powerful, largely hidden effect of algorithms in American life.

We obtained the risk scores assigned to more than 7,000 people arrested in Broward County, Florida, in 2013 and 2014 and checked to see how many were charged with new crimes over the next 2 years, the same benchmark used by the creators of the algorithm.

The score proved remarkably unreliable in forecasting violent crime: Only 20 percent of the people predicted to commit violent crimes actually went on to do so.

When a full range of crimes were taken into account—including misdemeanors such as driving with an expired license—the algorithm was somewhat more accurate than a coin flip. Of those deemed likely to reoffend , 61 percent were arrested for any subsequent crimes within 2 years.

We also turned up significant racial disparities, just as Holder feared. In forecasting who would reoffend, the algorithm made mistakes with black and white defendants at roughly the same rate but in very different ways.

- The formula was particularly likely to falsely flag black defendants as future criminals, wrongly labeling them this way at almost twice the rate as white defendants.
- White defendants were mislabeled as low risk more often than black defendants.

Could this disparity be explained by defendants' prior crimes or the type of crimes they were arrested for? No. We ran a statistical test that isolated the effect of race from criminal history and recidivism, as well as from defendants' age and gender. Black defendants were still 77 percent more likely to be pegged as at higher risk of committing a future violent crime and 45 percent more likely to be predicted to commit a future crime of any kind.

The algorithm used to create the Florida risk scores is a product of a for-profit company, Northpointe. The company disputes our analysis.

In a letter, it criticized ProPublica's methodology and defended the accuracy of its test: "Northpointe does not agree that the results of your analysis, or the claims being made based upon that analysis, are correct or that they accurately reflect the outcomes from the application of the model."

Northpointe's software is among the most widely used assessment tools in the country. The company does not publicly disclose the calculations used to arrive at defendants' risk scores, so it is not possible for either defendants or the public to see what might be driving the disparity. (On Sunday, Northpointe gave ProPublica the basics of its future crime formula—which includes factors such as education levels, and whether a defendant has a job. It did not share the specific calculations, which it said are proprietary.)

Northpointe's core product is a set of scores derived from 137 questions that are either answered by defendants or pulled from criminal records. Race is not one of the questions. The survey asks defendants such things as: "Was one of your parents ever sent to jail or prison?" "How many of your friends/acquaintances are taking drugs illegally?" and "How often did you get in fights while at school?" The questionnaire also asks people to agree or disagree with statements such as "A hungry person has a right to steal" and "If people make me angry or lose my temper, I can be dangerous."

The appeal of risk scores is obvious: The United States locks up far more people than any other country, a disproportionate number of them black. For more than two centuries, the key decisions in the legal process, from pretrial release to sentencing to parole, have been in the hands of human beings guided by their instincts and personal biases.

If computers could accurately predict which defendants were likely to commit new crimes, the criminal justice system could be fairer and more selective about who is incarcerated and for how long. The trick, of course, is to make sure the computer gets it right. If it's wrong in one direction, a dangerous criminal could go free. If it's wrong in another direction, it could result in someone unfairly receiving a harsher sentence or waiting longer for parole than is appropriate.

The first time Paul Zilly heard of his score—and realized how much was riding on it—was during his sentencing hearing on Feb. 15, 2013, in court in Barron County, Wisconsin. Zilly had been convicted of stealing a push lawnmower and some tools. The prosecutor recommended a year in county jail and follow-up supervision that could help Zilly with "staying on the right path." His lawyer agreed to a plea deal.

But Judge James Babler had seen Zilly's scores. Northpointe's software had rated Zilly as a high risk for future violent crime and a medium risk for general recidivism. "When I look at the risk assessment," Babler said in court, "it is about as bad as it could be."

Then Babler overturned the plea deal that had been agreed on by the prosecution and defense and imposed 2 years in state prison and 3 years of supervision.

Criminologists have long tried to predict which criminals are more dangerous before deciding whether they should be released. Race, nationality and skin color were often used in making such predictions until about the 1970s, when it became politically unacceptable, according to a survey of risk assessment tools by Columbia University law professor Bernard Harcourt.

In the 1980s, as a crime wave engulfed the nation, lawmakers made it much harder for judges and parole boards to exercise discretion in making such decisions. States and the federal government began instituting mandatory sentences and, in some cases, abolished parole, making it less important to evaluate individual offenders.

But as states struggle to pay for swelling prison and jail populations, forecasting criminal risk has made a comeback.

Two Drug Possession Arrests

Dylan Fugett

Low Risk	3

Bernard Parker

High Risk	10

Fugett was rated low risk after being arrested with cocaine and marijuana. He was arrested three times on drug charges after that.

Dozens of risk assessments are being used across the nation—some created by for-profit companies such as Northpointe and others by nonprofit organizations. (One tool being used in states including Kentucky and Arizona, called the Public Safety Assessment, was developed by the Laura and John Arnold Foundation, which also is a funder of ProPublica.)

There have been few independent studies of these criminal risk assessments. In 2013, researchers Sarah Desmarais and Jay Singh examined 19 different risk methodologies used in the United States and found that "in most cases, validity had only been examined in one or two studies" and that "frequently, those investigations were completed by the same people who developed the instrument."

Their analysis of the research through 2012 found that the tools "were moderate at best in terms of predictive validity,"

Desmarais said in an interview. And she could not find any substantial set of studies conducted in the United States that examined whether risk scores were racially biased. "The data do not exist," she said.

Since then, there have been some attempts to explore racial disparities in risk scores. One 2016 study examined the validity of a risk assessment tool, not Northpointe's, used to make probation decisions for about 35,000 federal convicts. The researchers, Jennifer Skeem at University of California, Berkeley, and Christopher T. Lowenkamp from the Administrative Office of the U.S. Courts, found that blacks did get a higher average score but concluded that the differences were not attributable to bias.

The increasing use of risk scores is controversial and has garnered media coverage, including articles by the Associated Press, and the Marshall Project and Five Thirty Eight last year.

Most modern risk tools were originally designed to provide judges with insight into the types of treatment that an individual might need—from drug treatment to mental health counseling.

"What it tells the judge is that if I put you on probation, I'm going to need to give you a lot of services or you're probably going to fail," said Edward Latessa, a University of Cincinnati professor who is the author of a risk assessment tool that is used in Ohio and several other states.

But being judged ineligible for alternative treatment—particularly during a sentencing hearing—can translate into incarceration. Defendants rarely have an opportunity to challenge their assessments. The results are usually shared with the defendant's attorney, but the calculations that transformed the underlying data into a score are rarely revealed.

"Risk assessments should be impermissible unless both parties get to see all the data that go into them," said Christopher Slobogin, director of the criminal justice program at Vanderbilt Law School. "It should be an open, full-court adversarial proceeding."

Black Defendants' Risk Scores

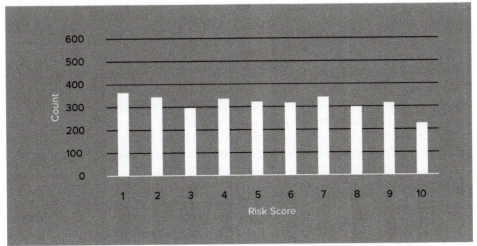

White Defendants' Risk Scores

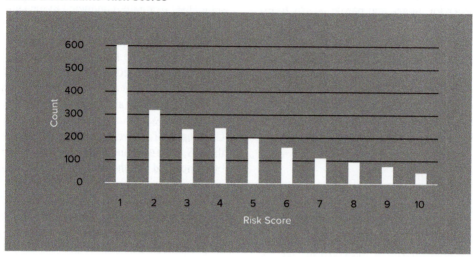

These charts show that scores for white defendants were skewed toward lower-risk categories. Scores for black defendants were not. (Source: ProPublica analysis of data from Broward County, Fla.)

Proponents of risk scores argue they can be used to reduce the rate of incarceration. In 2002, Virginia became one of the first states to begin using a risk assessment tool in the sentencing of nonviolent felony offenders statewide. In 2014, Virginia judges using the tool sent nearly half of those defendants to alternatives to prison, according to a state sentencing commission report. Since 2005, the state's prison population growth has slowed to 5 percent from a rate of 31 percent the previous decade.

In some jurisdictions, such as Napa County, California, the probation department uses risk assessments to suggest to the judge an appropriate probation or treatment plan for individuals being sentenced. Napa County Superior Court Judge Mark Boessenecker said he finds the recommendations helpful. "We have a dearth of good treatment programs, so filling a slot in a program with someone who doesn't need it is foolish," he said.

However, Boessenecker, who trains other judges around the state in evidence-based sentencing, cautions his colleagues that the score doesn't necessarily reveal whether a person is dangerous or if they should go to prison.

"A guy who has molested a small child every day for a year could still come out as a low risk because he probably has a job," Boessenecker said. "Meanwhile, a drunk guy will look high risk because he's homeless. These risk factors don't tell you whether the guy ought to go to prison or not; the risk factors tell you more about what the probation conditions ought to be."

"I'm surprised [my risk score] is so low. I spent five years in state prison in Massachusetts." (Josh Ritchie for ProPublica)

Sometimes, the scores make little sense even to defendants.

James Rivelli, a 54-year old Hollywood, Florida, man, was arrested 2 years ago for shoplifting seven boxes of Crest Whitestrips from a CVS drugstore. Despite a criminal record that included aggravated assault, multiple thefts and felony drug trafficking, the Northpointe algorithm classified him as being at a low risk of reoffending.

"I am surprised it is so low," Rivelli said when told by a reporter he had been rated a 3 out of a possible 10. "I spent 5 years in state prison in Massachusetts. But I guess they don't count that here in Broward County." In fact, criminal records from across the nation are supposed to be included in risk assessments.

Less than a year later, he was charged with two felony counts for shoplifting about $1,000 worth of tools from Home Depot. He said his crimes were fueled by drug addiction and that he is now sober.

Northpointe was founded in 1989 by Tim Brennan, then a professor of statistics at the University of Colorado, and Dave Wells, who was running a corrections program in Traverse City, Michigan.

Wells had built a prisoner classification system for his jail. "It was a beautiful piece of work," Brennan said in an interview conducted before ProPublica had completed its analysis. Brennan and Wells shared a love for what Brennan called "quantitative taxonomy"—the measurement of personality traits such as intelligence, extroversion and introversion. The two decided to build a risk assessment score for the corrections industry.

Brennan wanted to improve on a leading risk assessment score, the LSI, or Level of Service Inventory, which had been developed in Canada. "I found a fair amount of weakness in the LSI," Brennan said. He wanted a tool that addressed the major theories about the causes of crime.

Brennan and Wells named their product the Correctional Offender Management Profiling for Alternative Sanctions, or COMPAS. It assesses not just risk but also nearly two dozen so-called "criminogenic needs" that relate to the major theories of criminality, including "criminal personality," "social isolation," "substance abuse" and "residence/stability." Defendants are ranked low, medium or high risk in each category.

Two DUI Arrests

Gregory Lugo

Low Risk	1

Mallory Williams

Medium Risk	6

Lugo crashed his Lincoln Navigator into a Toyota Camry while drunk. He was rated as a low risk of reoffending despite the fact that it was at least his fourth DUI.

As often happens with risk assessment tools, many jurisdictions have adopted Northpointe's software before rigorously testing whether it works. New York State, for instance, started using the tool to assess people on probation in a pilot project in 2001 and rolled it out to the rest of the state's probation departments—except New York City—by 2010. The state didn't publish a comprehensive statistical evaluation of the tool until 2012. The study of more than 16,000 probationers found the tool was 71 percent accurate, but it did not evaluate racial differences.

A spokeswoman for the New York state division of criminal justice services said the study did not examine race because it only sought to test whether the tool had been properly calibrated to fit New York's probation population. She also said judges in nearly all New York counties are given defendants' Northpointe assessments during sentencing.

In 2009, Brennan and two colleagues published a validation study that found that Northpointe's risk of recidivism score had an accuracy rate of 68 percent in a sample of 2,328 people. Their study also found that the score was slightly less predictive for black men than white men—67 percent versus 69 percent. It did not examine racial disparities beyond that, including whether some groups were more likely to be wrongly labeled higher risk.

Brennan said it is difficult to construct a score that doesn't include items that can be correlated with race—such as poverty, joblessness and social marginalization. "If those are omitted from your risk assessment, accuracy goes down," he said.

In 2011, Brennan and Wells sold Northpointe to Toronto-based conglomerate Constellation Software for an undisclosed sum.

Wisconsin has been among the most eager and expansive users of Northpointe's risk assessment tool in sentencing decisions. In 2012, the Wisconsin Department of Corrections launched the use of the software throughout the state. It is used at each step in the prison system, from sentencing to parole.

In a 2012 presentation, corrections official Jared Hoy described the system as a "giant correctional pinball machine" in which correctional officers could use the scores at every "decision point."

Wisconsin has not yet completed a statistical validation study of the tool and has not said when one might be released. State corrections officials declined repeated requests to comment for this article.

Some Wisconsin counties use other risk assessment tools at arrest to determine if a defendant is too risky for pretrial release. Once a defendant is convicted of a felony anywhere in the state, the Department of Corrections attaches Northpointe's assessment to the confidential presentence report given to judges, according to Hoy's presentation.

In theory, judges are not supposed to give longer sentences to defendants with higher risk scores. Rather, they are supposed to use the tests primarily to determine which defendants are eligible for probation or treatment programs.

Prediction Fails Differently for Black Defendants

	White	African American
Labeled Higher Risk, But Didn't Reoffend	23.5%	44.9%
Labeled Lower Risk, Yet Did Reoffend	47.7%	28.0%

Overall, Northpointe's assessment tool correctly predicts recidivism 61 percent of the time. But blacks are almost twice as likely as whites to be labeled a higher risk but not actually reoffend. It makes the opposite mistake among whites: They are much more likely than blacks to be labeled lower risk but go on to commit other crimes. (Source: ProPublica analysis of data from Broward County, Fla.)

But judges have cited scores in their sentencing decisions. In August 2013, Judge Scott Horne in La Crosse County, Wisconsin, declared that defendant Eric Loomis had been "identified, through the COMPAS assessment, as an individual who is at high risk to the community." The judge then imposed a sentence of 8 years and 6 months in prison.

Loomis, who was charged with driving a stolen vehicle and fleeing from police, is challenging the use of the score at sentencing as a violation of his due process rights. The state has defended Horne's use of the score with the argument that judges can consider the score in addition to other factors. It has also stopped including scores in presentencing reports until the state Supreme Court decides the case.

"The risk score alone should not determine the sentence of an offender," Wisconsin Assistant Attorney General Christine Remington said last month during state Supreme Court arguments in the Loomis case. "We don't want courts to say, this person in front of me is a 10 on COMPAS as far as risk, and therefore I'm going to give him the maximum sentence."

That is almost exactly what happened to Zilly, the 48-year-old construction worker sent to prison for stealing a push lawnmower and some tools he intended to sell for parts. Zilly has long struggled with a meth habit. In 2012, he had been working toward recovery with the help of a Christian pastor when he relapsed and committed the thefts.

After Zilly was scored as a high risk for violent recidivism and sent to prison, a public defender appealed the sentence and called the score's creator, Brennan, as a witness.

Brennan testified that he didn't design his software to be used in sentencing. "I wanted to stay away from the courts," Brennan said, explaining that his focus was on reducing crime rather than punishment. "But as time went on I started realizing that so many decisions are made, you know, in the courts. So I gradually softened on whether this could be used in the courts or not."

Still, Brennan testified, "I don't like the idea myself of COMPAS being the sole evidence that a decision would be based upon."

After Brennan's testimony, Judge Babler reduced Zilly's sentence, from 2 years in prison to 18 months. "Had I not had the COMPAS, I believe it would likely be that I would have given 1 year, 6 months," the judge said at an appeals hearing on November 14, 2013.

Zilly said the score didn't take into account all the changes he was making in his life—his conversion to Christianity, his struggle to quit using drugs and his efforts to be more available for his son. "Not that I'm innocent, but I just believe people do change."

Florida's Broward county, where Brisha Borden stole the Huffy bike and was scored as high risk, does not use risk assessments in sentencing. "We don't think the [risk assessment] factors have any bearing on a sentence," said David Scharf, executive director of community programs for the Broward County Sheriff's Office in Fort Lauderdale.

Broward County has, however, adopted the score in pretrial hearings, in the hope of addressing jail overcrowding. A court-appointed monitor has overseen Broward County's jails since 1994 as a result of the settlement of a lawsuit brought by inmates in the 1970s. Even now, years later, the Broward County jail system is often more than 85 percent full, Scharf said.

In 2008, the sheriff's office decided that instead of building another jail, it would begin using Northpointe's risk scores to help identify which defendants were low risk enough to be released on bail pending trial. Since then, nearly everyone arrested in Broward has been scored soon after being booked. (People charged with murder and other capital crimes are not scored because they are not eligible for pretrial release.)

The scores are provided to the judges who decide which defendants can be released from jail. "My feeling is that if they don't need them to be in jail, let's get them out of there," Scharf said.

Two Shoplifting Arrests

James Rivelli

Low Risk	**3**

Robert Cannon

Medium Risk	**6**

After Rivelli stole from a CVS and was caught with heroin in his car, he was rated a low risk. He later shoplifted $1,000 worth of tools from a Home Depot.

Scharf said the county chose Northpointe's software over other tools because it was easy to use and produced "simple yet effective charts and graphs for judicial review." He said the system costs about $22,000 a year.

In 2010, researchers at Florida State University examined the use of Northpointe's system in Broward County over a 12-month period and concluded that its predictive accuracy was "equivalent" in assessing defendants of different races. Like others, they did not examine whether different races were classified differently as low or high risk.

Scharf said the county would review ProPublica's findings. "We'll really look at them up close," he said.

Broward County Judge John Hurley, who oversees most of the pretrial release hearings, said the scores were helpful when he was a new judge, but now that he has experience he prefers to rely on his own judgment. "I haven't relied on COMPAS in a couple years," he said.

Hurley said he relies on factors including a person's prior criminal record, the type of crime committed, ties to the community, and their history of failing to appear at court proceedings.

ProPublica's analysis reveals that higher Northpointe scores are slightly correlated with longer pretrial incarceration in Broward County. But there are many reasons that could be true other than judges being swayed by the scores—people with higher risk scores may also be poorer and have difficulty paying bond, for example.

Most crimes are presented to the judge with a recommended bond amount, but he or she can adjust the amount. Hurley said he often releases first-time or low-level offenders without any bond at all.

However, in the case of Borden and her friend Sade Jones, the teenage girls who stole a kid's bike and scooter, Hurley raised the bond amount for each girl from the recommended $0 to $1,000 each.

Hurley said he has no recollection of the case and cannot recall if the scores influenced his decision.

The girls spent two nights in jail before being released on bond.

"We literally sat there and cried" the whole time they were in jail, Jones recalled. The girls were kept in the same cell. Otherwise, Jones said, "I would have gone crazy." Borden declined repeated requests to comment for this article.

Jones, who had never been arrested before, was rated a medium risk. She completed probation and got the felony burglary charge reduced to misdemeanor trespassing, but she has still struggled to find work.

"I went to McDonald's and a dollar store, and they all said no because of my background," she said. "It's all kind of difficult and unnecessary."

Critical Thinking

1. In a review of risk assessment software, the authors found that the algorithm predicted who would commit a violent crime wrong 80 percent of the time over a 2-year period. What responsibility should the makers of tools such as this have to test, retest, analyze?

2. In what ways where the assessments racially biased? What are solutions to this outcome?

3. In what instances do you think it makes sense to use assessments such as those described in the article? Pre-trial incarceration? Probation? Sentencing?

Internet References

Are Machines Biased, or Are We Biased Against Machines?
https://goo.gl/M6wfUQ

PropPublica Responds to Company's Critique of Machine Bias Story
https://goo.gl/2M2d1r

Why We Should Expect Algorithms to Be Biased
https://goo.gl/FtsHGh

JULIA ANGWIN is a senior reporter at ProPublica. From 2000 to 2013, she was a reporter at The Wall Street Journal, where she led a privacy investigative team that was a finalist for a Pulitzer Prize in Explanatory Reporting in 2011 and won a Gerald Loeb Award in 2010.

JEFF LARSON is the Data Editor at ProPublica. He is a winner of the Livingston Award for the 2011 series Redistricting: How Powerful Interests are Drawing You Out of a Vote.

LAUREN KIRCHNER is a senior reporting fellow at ProPublica.

SURYA MATTU is a contributing researcher. Design and production by Rob Weychert and David Sleight.

Article

Prepared by: Liz Friedman, *DePaul University* and
Daniel Mittleman, *DePaul University*

Own a Vizio Smart TV? It's Watching You

Vizio, one of the most popular brands on the market, is offering advertisers "highly specific viewing behavior data on a massive scale."

JULIA ANGWIN

Learning Outcomes

After reading this article, you will be able to:

- Understand the kinds of data that technology in our homes can capture about us including behavioral data, use data, metadata, and anonymized data.
- Understand how data from multiple sources can be combined to create a comprehensive picture of an individual.
- Articulate the pros and cons of direct data collection by home appliances.

TV makers are constantly crowing about the tricks their smart TVs can do. But one of the most popular brands has a feature that it's not advertising: Vizio's Smart TVs track your viewing habits and share it with advertisers, who can then find you on your phone and other devices.

The tracking—which Vizio calls "Smart Interactivity"—is turned on by default for the more than 10 million Smart TVs that the company has sold. Customers who want to escape it have to opt-out.

In a statement, Vizio said customers' "non-personal identifiable information may be shared with select partners . . . to permit these companies to make, for example, better-informed decisions regarding content production, programming and advertising."

Vizio's actions appear to go beyond what others are doing in the emerging interactive television industry. Vizio rivals Samsung and LG Electronics only track users' viewing habits if customers choose to turn the feature on. And unlike Vizio, they don't appear to provide the information in a form that allows advertisers to reach users on other devices.

Vizio's technology works by analyzing snippets of the shows you're watching, whether on traditional television or streaming Internet services such as Netflix. Vizio determines the date, time, channel of programs—as well as whether you watched them live or recorded. The viewing patterns are then connected your IP address—the Internet address that can be used to identify every device in a home, from your TV to a phone.

IP addresses can increasingly be linked to individuals. Data broker Experian, for instance, offers a "data enrichment" service that provide "hundreds of attributes" such as age, profession and "wealth indicators" tied to a particular IP address.

Vizio recently updated its privacy policy to say it has begun providing data about customers' viewing habits to companies that "may combine this information with other information about devices associated with that IP address." The company does not promise to encrypt IP addresses before sharing them.

Cable TV companies and video rental companies are prohibited by law from selling information about the viewing habits of their customers. However, Vizio says that those laws—the Video Privacy Protection Act and cable subscriber protections—don't apply to its business.

Vizio hopes its new tracking forays will provide a boost to the thin profit margins it earns in the competitive television manufacturing business. In an October filing for an initial public offering, Vizio touted its ability to provide "highly specific viewing behavior data on a massive scale with great accuracy."

The company said in its filing that revenues from its viewing data business are not yet significant. But people familiar with the company said that Vizio has begun working to combine its viewing data with information about users that it gets from data broker Neustar.

Neustar declined to comment about the relationship but said the company does not handle or distribute viewing information about Vizio users.

A spokeswoman for Tapad, a company that helps identify users across their many devices, said that its contracts prevent it from sharing the name of the companies it works with.

An Experian spokeswoman said, "We currently do not have a relationship with Vizio."

Critical Thinking

1. How do you feel about your television sending information about your viewing habits out to advertisers who can then track you across multiple devices?

2. Is an opt-out process such as the one used by Vizio enough to qualify as consent or should they (and others) be required to get your consent (opt-in) on the front end? What are the advantages and disadvantages of each model?

3. Should companies that collect information such as this be required to encrypt the data?

Internet References

Now Advertisers Can Watch You Watch TV
https://goo.gl/BWyhDy

The Internet of Things: How Your TV, Car and Toys Could Spy on You
https://goo.gl/LblyKH

Your TV May Be Watching You
https://goo.gl/KPN06I

Article

Prepared by: Liz Friedman, *DePaul University* and
Daniel Mittleman, *DePaul University*

Ransomware in Real Time: How Hackers Infiltrate Secured Systems

Shane Dingman

Learning Outcomes

After reading this article, you will be able to:

- Describe the cybercrime of ransomware and how it threatens current business practices.
- Articulate common best practice strategies for combating ransomware.

Security-software providers are in a constant cat-and-mouse game with ransomware makers who can find ways to penetrate even well-guarded systems. The following is an account of a real attack that happened in February of this year, as described by Chris Whidden, a security engineer based out of New York who works for Canadian security consultancy eSentire Inc.

Thursday, February 25, 7:43 A.M.:

Employees at an unnamed registered investment adviser begin receiving invoices in their e-mail inboxes that suggest they have racked up huge fees on a well-known car service. Within seconds, dozens of employees get these messages, which are very convincing fakes of a real invoice e-mail, at the New York and London offices. One employee in New York opens the e-mail and clicks the link that says "download this invoice."

This is a security-conscious company that has had employee training to avoid doing this very thing and also employs the real-time monitoring of eSentire—not to mention that the company has next-generation anti-virus firewalls. Still, the so-called "phishing" e-mail attack works because humans are naturally curious; clicking bad links and opening Microsoft Office docs remains the top vector for phishing ransomware attacks.

Clicking the link in this case downloads Javascript software that tries to download a file called 87.exe, which is actually a version of ransomware called TeslaCrypt first discovered in February, 2015, from several different IP addresses that are blacklisted by eSentire's Asset Manager Protect software as known hacker nodes, and so the download is blocked. A second later, 87.exe is successfully downloaded from an IP address that is not yet on the hacker blacklist.

7:44 A.M.:

The ransomware begins to install on the user's PC. Because it is a new variant of TeslaCrypt, the firewalls do not recognize it as malware as it installs itself; it bears no signatures of previous hacker products. What it is doing, Mr. Whidden says, is "introducing anomalous signals on the network." Twenty seconds after installation, it "beacons" or sends a message back to the IP address it came from, blasting a message that says in essence: "Hey, I got into the victim, give me a key so I can start encrypting files." This communication triggers an alert in eSentire's operations centre where, for the first time, a human will look at what's going on.

As this is happening, TeslaCrypt is looking for files to encrypt, avoiding recently used files so as not to tip off the user. It rewrites data it finds with the Advanced Encryption Standard (AES) developed in 2001 by the U.S. National Institute of Standards and Technology (NIST), which features a 128-bit block (which means it takes any 128-bit block of data and replaces it with a same-sized block of garbled text). This version has a 256-bit key, which means it cycles that same 128-bit block 14 times, so the encrypted data is many generations removed from the original. Given time, a supercomputer might be able to untangle that garbling in what's called a "brute force" attack: In the case of AES-256 standard crypto, it would take a supercomputer roughly 13 billion years. Effectively, that encryption is unbreakable unless you buy the decryption key from the hacker who possesses it.

Where once TeslaCrypt would ask for the equivalent of a few hundred dollars in mostly anonymous bitcoin, nowadays hackers will means-test extortion demands based on a victim's ability to pay. Ransomware will sometimes pretend to be a police agency demanding that a user pay fines for cybercrimes. TeslaCrypt is more direct, giving the users a countdown before the key to unlock their files is deleted and a Web address they can send payment to. There are only two options: Pay or lose your files. Turning off your computer, unplugging it from the Internet, praying over it—none of that will work.

7:54 A.M.:

An analyst has evaluated the attack in eSentire's Security Operations Centre in Cambridge, Ont., and calls the client directly with the warning: You've got ransomware in your building. The company remotely deactivates the phishing victim's connection to the internal network and to the Internet before staff set off to find the physical machine. The files on the PC are continuing to be encrypted.

The company catches a lucky break, because TeslaCrypt is designed to immediately look for shared folders, connected servers and any data-backup systems that the PC might connect to. In this case, the infection stayed on a single PC.

Mr. Whidden relates a similar incident, weeks earlier, at a similar-sized financial company where the infection was not detected. In the just more than five hours between infection and discovery, more than 700 gigabytes of data were encrypted, locking away an active project for 15 billable workers. The company restored the data from backups and believed it had removed the malicious software across its 20 office locations. The company was wrong. A week later, a dormant version of the same ransomware kicked into life in another office. A week after that, it happened again.

Some individuals and companies will pay to get files back. Data on how many is hard to collect, though the U.S. Federal Bureau of Investigation believes one variant called CryptoWall cost U.S. businesses $18 million between 2014 and 2015. But paying does not guarantee file recovery: Ransomware is not developed by the world's great software designers—sometimes there are bugs in the code that can destroy files forever. In 2015, some 1,641 ransomware attacks a day were reported in Canada, compared with almost 25,000 a day in the United States, according to security-software firm Symantec's Internet Security Threat report.

8:30 A.M.:

Client notifies eSentire that the machine has been located, physically separated from the network (or air-gapped) and that they are wiping the device and restoring it from a fresh "master" rather than a backup. Any files that local user had stored on the PC are now gone.

In some cases, that is not the end of the story. Some variants of ransomware encrypt and then send the files to a remote server controlled by the hackers, to be used for potential blackmail. The data can be decrypted by hackers and the plain text read for possible intelligence on future attacks. Increasingly, Mr. Whidden says, hackers are targeting companies that hold onto sensitive documents: Law firms, insurance companies and hospitals are increasingly targeted by actors who once focused mainly on quick, low-dollar blackmail from individuals or large-dollar extortion of financial institutions.

In a bizarre post-script, On May 18, security researchers released a new tool that can decrypt machines infected by the TeslaCrypt ransomware, with some unexpected help from the creators of the malevolent software. As the company wrote in a blog post: "One of ESET's analysts contacted the group anonymously, using the official support channel offered to the ransomware victims by the TeslaCrypt's operators, and requested the universal master decryption key. Surprisingly, they made it public."

Critical Thinking

1. Why to cyber criminals target businesses rather than individuals for ransomware attacks?

2. If you found most all your personal data encrypted and received a message demanding ransom to unencrypt it, how badly would this impact you? How much, if anything, would you pay in ransom to get your data back?

3. Why do most cyber criminals demand Bitcoin for ransom payments rather than cash or credit card? Does this impact your opinion about the value of Bitcoin as an online currency?

Internet References

FBI: Incidents of Ransomware on the Rise
   https://goo.gl/GLQvXe
How Bitcoin Helped Fuel an Explosion in Ransomware Attacks
   https://goo.gl/fynCZe
Ransomware Dominates the Threat Landscape
   https://goo.gl/O5BHJY

Article

Prepared by: Liz Friedman, *DePaul University* and
Daniel Mittleman, *DePaul University*

10 Ways to Make the Internet Safe from Cyber Attacks

Patrick Tucker

Learning Outcomes

After reading this article, you will be able to:

- Understand why a policy-driven response to cyber attacks is vital to security.
- Describe the European Union's Right to Be Forgotten initiative.
- Discuss the critical importance of being able to function when forced to operate offline.

A single well-designed cyber weapon could "take down the entire Internet," according to Dan Geer, chief information security officer for In-Q-Tel, the CIA's venture capital company.

Here are his 10 policy proposals for protecting the Internet from cyber attacks:

1. Companies Should Be Mandated To Report Big Hacks

We report big disease outbreaks the moment that they happen and the Centers for Disease Control sends out an advance team to deal with them. Why not mandate that companies must do the same thing when they experience a big hack or breach on the federal level? It's a proposal that goes well beyond the largely toothless White House Cybersecurity Framework released earlier this year. It's a move that companies would likely fight, arguing that most of the hacks they face don't constitute the sort of threat that they need to inform the public about. Geer says large companies or the government should have no expectation of privacy in the wake of major cyber attacks, just as individuals

with a highly communicable disease lose any expectation of privacy in the event of an Ebola or other major disease outbreak.

"Wouldn't it make sense to have a regime of mandatory reporting for cyber-security failures?" Geer said. "Should you face criminal charges if you fail to make such a report?" He points out that 46 states require mandatory reporting of some cyber attacks in the form of their cyber-breach laws, but 70 to 80 percent of data breaches are discovered by unrelated third parties. Geer says every security failure "above some threshold we have yet to negotiate" should be reported to the federal government. In broaching this, he drew from a recent paper by former Navy Secretary Richard Danzig titled *Surviving On a Diet of Poisoned Fruit,* in which Danzig argues that software hacks should be treated with the same urgency as airplane near-misses.

2. Net-Neutrality Shouldn't Be Left to the FCC

He recommends not one single proposal, but stresses that what's most important to understand is that the Federal Communications Commission is not the sort of agency that can effectively manage something as important to the future as Internet traffic.

"What I can say is that the varied tastes need to be reflected in constrained choice rather than the idea that . . . some . . . agency can assure happiness if and only if it—rather than corporations or individuals—does the choosing."

3. Companies Should Be Held Liable for Making Hackable Software

It's a measure that, had it been in place 20 years ago, Microsoft would be on the hook for every time some piece of malware crashed a computer and Bill Gates would be nowhere near the richest man in the world list.

"The software houses will yell bloody murder the minute legislation like this is introduced, and any pundit and lobbyist they can afford will spew their dire predictions that 'this law will mean the end of computing as we know it!' To which our considered answer will be: 'Yes, please! That was exactly the idea.'"

4. Striking Back Should Be Legal But There Should Perhaps Be Oversight

Strike back is the ability to attack those that attack you. "I suspect that a fair number of you have, in fact, struck back at some attacker somewhere or, at least, done targeting research even if you didn't pull the trigger," Geer said. "I'd trust many of you to identify targets carefully enough to minimize collateral damage, but what we are talking about here is the cyber equivalent of the smart bomb. As I implied earlier, cyber smart bombs are what the national laboratories of several countries are furiously working on. In that sense, you do know what is happening behind the curtain, and you know how hard that targeting really is because you know how hard attribution—real attribution—really is." He called it "expensive therapy" not open to most small players.

5. Software Needs Resilient Fallbacks

Software makers should be legally obliged to have fallbacks in place in the event of a major attack of service disruption and those fallbacks should be in place prior to deployment of the software. Geer calls this resiliency. The best way to assure resiliency is to build systems that can be managed from afar, so-called remote managed systems. If you can't build remote management into your system, you should design in an expiration date.

"Resiliency is an area where no one policy can be sufficient, so I've suggested a trio of baby steps: Embedded systems cannot be immortal if they have no remote management interface, embedded systems must have a remote management interface if they are to be immortal, and swap-over is preferable to swap-out when it comes to data protection."

6. The Government Should Pay Top Dollar to Hackers To Find Vulnerabilities

This is called vulnerability finding and Geer says the U.S. should corner the market on it and pay people who find vulnerabilities 10 times what anyone else could pay them for keeping the vulnerability secret. Once the government learns of a new vulnerability, the next step is to make it public.

"If a couple of Texas brothers could corner the world silver market, there is no doubt that the U.S. government could openly corner the world vulnerability market. That is, we buy them all and we make them all public. Simply announce: 'Show us a competing bid, and we'll give you 10 times.'" In a subsequent Q&A session, Geer elaborated further. "Vulnerabilities that you keep to yourself for use as a future weapon is a hostile act. So let's corner the market. . . . If there are a limited number of

them . . . by making them no longer weaponizable, have we not contributed to world peace?"

7. The Right To Be Forgotten Should Be Put in Place in the United States

The European Union's Right to Be Forgotten initiative, which mandates that European citizens have a right to have some information kept off the web (or at least out of Google search results), is "appropriate, advantageous [but] doesn't go far enough," Geer said. The definition of privacy that he lives by is this: "You have privacy if you have the effective capacity to misrepresent yourself."

It's becoming a hugely important issue for individuals, but it's not a small issue for the military either. Intelligence agents, Geer says, are having an ever more difficult time keeping their identities a secret. "Crafting good cover is getting harder and for the same reasons. Misrepresentations are getting harder."

In a sense, we are moving toward a post-spy world, according to the guy that runs the CIA's venture capital arm. And protecting the right to be forgotten is one way around that. But more importantly, "a right to be forgotten is the only check on the tidal wave of observability that a ubiquitous sensor fabric is birthing now—observability that changes the very quality of what 'in public' means."

The Obama administration's issuance of a National Strategy for Trusted Identities in Cyberspace is a "case-in-point; it 'calls for the development of interoperable technology standards and policies—an Identity Ecosystem'—where individuals, organizations, and underlying infrastructure—such as routers and servers—can be authoritatively authenticated."

Anonymity is something we give government witnesses and whistleblowers. He says it should be a right for everyone. Moreover, if the U.S. were to follow the European lead on right to be forgotten, it would help curb the balkanization of the Internet, and decrease foreign suspicion of U.S. tech companies.

8. Internet Voting? No

Geer said very little on the question of whether or not the United States or other countries should allow for voting over the Internet or become more reliant on Internet-connected voting machines. But as soon as he said the words, "Internet voting," the crowd in the ballroom of the Mandalay Hotel erupted in laughter and he quickly moved on to the next subject.

9. Abandoned Software Should Be Treated Like Abandoned Stuff

If any company abandons a software codebase then the same rules that apply to discarded furniture should apply to the software—it becomes public and open-source. That means that there would in effect never be any devices out there using software that was proprietary but that wasn't supported. "Apple computers running 10.5 or less get no updates (comprising a significant fraction of the installed base). Any Microsoft computer running XP gets no updates (likewise comprising a significant fraction of the installed base). The end of security updates follows abandonment. It is certainly ironic that freshly pirated copies of Windows get security updates when older versions bought legitimately do not. . . . Either you support it or you give it to the public."

10. Make Sure There's an Offline Backup

"The more we put on the Internet, the broader and more unmitigable Internet surprises become," Geer said. He called this "dependence," and it's a growing problem.

He cited a recent Bloomberg story pointing out that some of the nation's largest banks were calling on the government to protect them from the threat of cyber attack. The article was titled *"Banks Dreading Computer Hacks Call for Cyber War Council."*

"The biggest financial firms [are] saying that their dependencies are no longer manageable, and that the state's monopoly on the use of force must be brought to bear. What they are talking about is that they have no way to mitigate the risk of common mode failure."

Bottom line: Everything that is a critical infrastructure component *must* show that it can run without the Internet and the makers have to be able to prove it. Geer is proposing a massive stress test for every bank, utility, or any other company that fulfills a critical public role to see how well they operate when they are thrown offline. We stress tested the banks after the 2008 market crash, he points out. "We need stress tests in our field even more."

In his remarks, Geer acknowledged that cyber attacks would get worse before they get better, that maintaining online anonymity would become ever more difficult and inconvenient,

and that in the present political environment, many of the proposals would face enormous, if not insurmountable, resistance. Only the second policy proposal has any real chance of passing. But that could change—if things get worse. "There's the political will to do a stress test but only after a bad event. Let's hope it's not catastrophic," he said.

Critical Thinking

1. Of the 10 policy proposals suggested here, which one may be the most difficult to implement? Why?
2. Does the maintenance of online anonymity justify the multitude of inconveniences that are inevitably required? Why or why not?
3. Will anything short of a catastrophe break through the barriers of political resistance when it comes to legislating serious cyber security?

Internet References

Daily Mail: "Think you're safe on the internet? Think again: Map reveals millions of cyber attacks happening around the world in real time"
www.dailymail.co.uk/sciencetech/article-2670710/Think-youre-safe-internet-Think-Map-reveals-millions-cyber-attacks-happening-world-real-time.html#ixzz3JAA9dHls

Entrepreneur: "How to Protect Your Small Business Against a Cyber Attack"
www.entrepreneur.com/article/225468

UTG Solutions: "Network Security—Is Your Company Safe from Cyber Attacks?"
www.utgsolutions.com/network-security-is-your-company-safe-from-cyber-attacks

Unit 6

UNIT

Prepared by: Liz Friedman, *DePaul University* and
Daniel Mittleman, *DePaul University*

IT, Business, and Economy

Innovation may be defined as radical or breakthrough change that improves products, services, or business processes. It is innovation that drives growth in an economy by sparking new investment, creating new markets, and pruning deadwood companies who failed to innovate from the marketplace. When we think of innovation, we think of breakthrough new product design or establishment of new product categories.

Apple computer has seen both. The iPhone, in 2007, quickly dominated its market by completely re-envisioning mobile phone user experience. And the iPad created a whole new market category essentially zooming an iPhone interface to tablet size, which permitted effective movie or business document viewing.

Information technology has been a major driver of innovation the past half century not only by creating new products and product categories (who would have imagined an iTunes store in 1965?) but also by vastly improving productivity through more effective workflow processes. For example, Amazon has 24/7 distribution centers with highly automated "pick, pack, and ship" processes. Amazon's supply-chain automation is responsible, at least in part, for the company's growth and success.

Innovation, however, has a dark side; more than one, actually. First, there is the issue of patents. Patents are intended to encourage innovation by protecting the inventor and giving him or her an ample head start to earn back development costs, while at the same time promoting more innovation by requiring the details of each invention be revealed, and limiting the amount of time a patent monopoly right can be maintained. While patents, perhaps, work well in other industries to promote innovation, in computer and communication technologies they have become a morass, slowing innovation and adding significant costs to new startups.

A typical new computing device (such as a tablet or cell phone) may contain hundreds of patents, and a networking technology can contain many more. For example, as of 2008, a 4G wireless network would utilize over 18,300 patents, with over 16,000 new patent applications under review. And this is beyond the 80,000 patents used in its underlying backbone.[1] How can a new network vendor innovate in this environment without violating a patent (or worse, have a threatened competitor perceive their patent was violated and sue to delay development of the product)? How can a network innovator even know whether their product violates one of 114,000 potential patents?

It is not surprising, then, that patent lawsuits have become the norm for almost all large-scale IT development efforts. And paying patent licensing fees, rather than fighting patent claims, has become the norm as well. Many large firms, Google, Apple, and Microsoft among them, have purchased companies simply to acquire their patent holdings and protect their own development efforts. Further exacerbating the situation is the presence of patent trolls: Small companies who have acquired patents from others and exist solely to sue others for patent violation, which given the number of outstanding patents, the complexity of development efforts, and the cost of fighting a patent lawsuit, are easy pickings.

Second to the issue of patents is the issue of innovation and jobs. Economists have long debated whether innovation creates jobs or costs jobs. Today, most economists would agree that in the long term innovation builds a larger economy and with that growth comes more jobs. However, the new jobs may not be direct replacement for the old jobs. The new jobs may require different education or training. The new jobs may be at a different location. And the new jobs, if at the same skill level, may not pay nearly as well. So, the people who lose jobs because of innovation are not necessarily the same people who get jobs. And that leaves specific individuals out of work and unhappy about the change.

---

[1] L. Gilroy, T. D'Amato, How many patents does it take to build an iPhone? *Intellectual Property Today*, November 2009 (accessed on October 13, 2012 at http://www.iptoday.com/issues/2009/11/articles/how-many-patents-take-build-iPhone.asp)

Article

Prepared by: Liz Friedman, *DePaul University* and
Daniel Mittleman, *DePaul University*

Social Capital: The Secret behind Airbnb and Uber

The true promise of a connected society is helping one another.

—Biz Stone, cofounder of Twitter, in *Things a Little Bird Told Me*

BARBARA GRAY

Learning Outcomes

After reading this article, you will be able to:

- Articulate the concepts of "social capital" and "social economy."

- Articulate the layers of the Social Economy Pyramid.

- Understand how the emergence of Web 2.0 technologies enables growth of the Social Economy.

Ironically, although I had been on an intellectual journey for the previous four years, it was only when I undertook a physical journey to New York City (I had traveled east to speak at the CFA Society Toronto event Social Media's Impact to the Investment Process) and used Airbnb and Uber for the first time that the dots finally connected. This inspired me to write the article "Social Capital: The Secret behind Airbnb and Uber," which I published on Linked In in June 2014. It ended up going viral, and as of August 2016 it has been viewed by over 396,000 professionals. The article serves as a good summary of what I've discussed thus far and shows how my thinking evolved to what I go on to discuss in the rest of the book.

When I was 30 years old and single and living in New York City, I had a dream: to return one day with my husband and push our baby in a stroller through Central Park. In May 2014, my dream came true, albeit more than a decade later. But we did not stay in a hotel and travel by yellow taxicab; instead we used Airbnb to book a guy's condo on the Upper East Side and we traveled by Uber to the airport.

How is it that Airbnb and Uber have been able to build thriving ecosystems in just over five years, with such significant scale and influence that they were then valued at US$10 billion and US$12 billion? And how have these companies become such a disruptive force that they are the target of deafening protests from the highly ensconced hotel and taxi industries in cities around the world? Two words: *social capital.*

In this new social era of transparency, connectedness, and stakeholder empowerment, social media exchanges are acting as catalysts to accelerate the formation of bonding, bridging, and linking capital among its stakeholders (i.e., employees, customers, and business partners).

There are three levels of companies that operate in the social economy. And the higher a company moves up what I term the Social Economy Pyramid, the faster the rate of value acceleration, as they are able to achieve a higher level of disruption and access multiple social value drivers. The first social value driver is advocacy, which creates abundance of demand through the democratization of influence. The second social value driver is connection, which creates abundance of supply through the democratization of data. And the third social value driver is collaboration, which creates abundance of both supply and demand through the democratization of physical and human capital.

Starbucks, Whole Foods Market, Chipotle Mexican Grill, and Lululemon create abundance of demand through advocacy of a social mission. By creating positive social capital (shared values and positive externalities) for stakeholders, these companies are able to attract people looking to align their values with the companies they buy from, work for, and work with. This leads to the creation of a thriving stakeholder ecosystem. Because social mission companies are founded on movements and follow a blue ocean strategy, they are on the low-end of the disruption scale, as they created new uncontested marketplaces. And their ability to grow revenue and free cash flow is limited by time and capital constraints on the supply side.

LinkedIn creates abundance of supply through connection by building a unique structural asset base that empowers people to connect with one another and build bridging and linking capital through their platforms. By revolutionizing the way professionals manage their reputation and contacts, LinkedIn has been able to create a unique and invaluable structural asset base from the profiles and highly interconnected networks of its now 450 million members. This provides LinkedIn with a low-cost supply of constantly updated data (i.e., raw material) from which to extract value. Although LinkedIn may appear unthreatening, with nascent business lines, it has been able to establish a long tail and is beginning to gain footholds in the low-end markets. The revolutionary power of its consumer-centric marketplace platforms makes it, as Clayton Christensen and Michael E. Raynor deem in *The Innovator's Solution,* a "ubiquitous disruptive force" to be reckoned with. However, LinkedIn is challenged on the demand side: I estimate that its paid customer penetration is less than 2%

Airbnb and Uber create abundance of demand and supply through collaboration by creating social platforms that facilitate trust and enable individuals to form weak ties (bridging capital) with one another, leading to the personal sharing of assets, goods, and services (linking capital). By accessing an untapped market of nonsuppliers of latent and underutilized personal assets, goods, and services, these companies are not only creating blue oceans of demand but discovering a new frontier below the corporate ocean with no capital or time constraints: the social ecosystem reef. And by creating a long tail in rival assets, goods, and services, these companies are able to directly match supply and demand, and collect a cut of each transaction.

When I stayed at my first Airbnb in May 2014, the company had already processed a total of 11 million reservations and created a compelling accommodation alternative for its guests by offering them a fun way to discover and book unique accommodations with its then base of over 350,000 hosts offering 600,000 home listings. And at that time, Uber operated in over 70 cities in 36 countries around the world. As of August 2016, Airbnb has more than tripled its inventory of home listings to over 2 million, and Uber has more than quintupled its operational base to over 400 cities. These rapidly expanding social-sharing companies are directly attacking the incumbent hotel and taxi industries on both the supply and demand side and are threatening to erode their traditional economic moats in terms of low-cost production, high switching costs, intangible assets, and the network effect.

In terms of being a low-cost producer, the incumbents' high fixed-cost structure (which provides them with process and scale cost advantages) is becoming a competitive disadvantage, as many travelers have grown tired of the impersonal experience of staying in cookie-cutter hotels and of the inefficient and impersonal experience of traveling in taxis. In comparison, companies such as Airbnb and Uber are the ultimate low-cost producers, as they have a close-to-zero marginal cost model, since they have the potential to create infinite supply by empowering individuals to generate income from underutilized personal assets (i.e., property, plant, and equipment such as a house or car, and human capital such as property management or chauffeuring services). In terms of high switching costs, customers are no longer held captive to the incumbents as Airbnb and Uber now present more attractive and personal alternatives.

In terms of intangible assets, the value of a brand name is depreciating as Airbnb and Uber create long tails in travel by replacing artificial institutional trust with social capital. They achieve this by democratizing the tools of production and distribution, and by connecting supply and demand by capitalizing on the filtering efficiency of social network reviews and facilitating trust through dual accountability systems (i.e., both the hosts and the guests rate each other). And in terms of the network effect, unlike hotel and taxi companies that seek to constrain supply to keep prices high, Airbnb and Uber are creating structural assets that appreciate in value as they attract more and more new hosts and drivers (i.e., supply) and travelers (i.e., demand) to their platforms, leading to the ultimate network effect.

I have no doubt that the social economy will transform how we travel, live, work, play, and consume. And the secret to understanding this accelerating tectonic shift starts with social capital.

Critical Thinking

1. What is social capital? And how have Uber and Airbnb been able to use it to great advantage?

2. What is it about Uber and Airbnb that makes consumers so readily trust them?

3. In what industry do you see transformation happening next?

Internet References

How Cryptocurrency Could Change the Sharing Economy
https://goo.gl/JhDPJl

Rethinking the Value of Customers in a Digital Economy
https://goo.gl/yKrP6o

Welcome to the 'Sharing Economy'
https://goo.gl/c8mwXF

Why Social Media Is Necessary for the Sharing Economy
https://goo.gl/N3pF18

Article

Prepared by: Liz Friedman, *DePaul University* and
Daniel Mittleman, *DePaul University*

Technology Is Changing How We Live, but It Needs to Change How We Work

Ezra Klein

Learning Outcomes

After reading this article, you will be able to:

- Articulate a definition of technology, and contrast it to several incorrect definitions in common use.

- Articulate what "total factor productivity" is and explain why it is an important economic concept.

- Articulate how productivity is measured and whether or not its measurement accurately reflects meaning changes to people and the economy.

What do you think of when you hear the word "technology"? Do you think of jet planes and laboratory equipment and underwater farming? Or do you think of smartphones and machine-learning algorithms?

Venture capitalist Peter Thiel guesses it's the latter. When a grave-faced announcer on CNBC says "technology stocks are down today," we all know he means Facebook and Apple, not Boeing and Pfizer. To Thiel, this signals a deeper problem in the American economy, a shrinkage in our belief of what's possible, a pessimism about what is really likely to get better. Our definition of what technology is has narrowed, and he thinks that narrowing is no accident. It's a coping mechanism in an age of technological disappointment.

"Technology gets defined as 'that which is changing fast,'" he says. "If the other things are not defined as 'technology,' we filter them out and we don't even look at them."

Thiel isn't dismissing the importance of iPhones and laptops and social networks. He founded PayPal and Palantir, was one of the earliest investors in Facebook, and now sits atop a fortune estimated in the billions. We spoke in his sleek, floor-to-ceiling-windowed apartment overlooking Manhattan— a palace built atop the riches of the IT revolution. But it's obvious to him that we're living through an extended technological stagnation. "We were promised flying cars; we got 140 characters," he likes to say.

The numbers back him up. The closest the economics profession has to a measure of technological progress is an indicator called total factor productivity, or TFP. It's a bit of an odd concept: It measures the productivity gains left over after accounting for the growth of the workforce and capital investments.

When TFP is rising, it means the same number of people, working with the same amount of land and machinery, are able to make more than they were before. It's our best attempt to measure the hard-to-define bundle of innovations and improvements that keep living standards rising. It means we're figuring out how to, in Steve Jobs's famous formulation, work smarter. If TFP goes flat, then so do living standards.

And TFP has gone flat—or at least flatter—in recent decades. Since 1970, TFP has grown at only about a third the rate it grew from 1920 to 1970. If that sounds arid and technical, then my mistake: It means we're poorer, working longer hours, and leaving a worse world for our grandchildren than we otherwise would be. The **2015 Economic Report of the President** (https://www.whitehouse.gov/sites/default/files/docs/cea_2015_erp.pdf) noted that if productivity growth had continued to roar along at its 1948–1973 pace, the average household's income would be $30,000 higher today.

What Thiel can't quite understand is why his fellow founders and venture capitalists can't see what he sees, why they're so damn optimistic and self-satisfied amidst an obvious, rolling disaster for human betterment.

Maybe, he muses, it's simple self-interest at work; the disappointments elsewhere in the economy have made Silicon Valley richer, more important, and more valued. With so few other advances competing for press coverage and investment dollars, the money and the prestige flow into the one sector of the economy that is pushing mightily forward. "If you're involved in the IT sector, you're like a farmer in the midst of a famine," Thiel says. "And being a farmer in a famine may actually be a very lucrative thing to be."

Or maybe it's mere myopia. Maybe the progress in our phones has distracted us from the stagnation in our communities. "You can look around you in San Francisco, and the housing looks 50, 60 years old," Thiel continues. "You can look around you in New York City and the subways are 100-plus years old. You can look around you on an airplane, and it's little different from 40 years ago—maybe it's a bit slower because the airport security is low-tech and not working terribly well. The screens are everywhere, though. Maybe they're distracting us from our surroundings rather than making us look at our surroundings."

But Thiel's peers in Silicon Valley have a different, simpler explanation. To many of them, the numbers are simply wrong.

What Larry Summers doesn't understand

If there was any single inspiration for this article, it was **a speech** (http://www.cspan.org/video/?324436-1/discussion-future-work) Larry Summers gave at the Hamilton Project in February 2015. Summers is known for his confident explanations of economic phenomena, not his befuddlement. But that day, he was befuddled.

"On the one hand," he began, "we have enormous anecdotal evidence and visual evidence that points to technology having huge and pervasive effects."

Call this the *but everybody know it* argument. *Everybody knows* technological innovation is reshaping the world faster than ever before. The proof is in our pockets, which now contain a tiny device that holds something close to the sum of humanity's knowledge, and it's in our children, who spend all day staring at screens, and it's in our stock market, where Apple and Google compete for the highest valuation of any company on Earth. How can anyone look at all this and doubt that we live in an age dominated by technological wonders?

"On the other hand," Summers continued, "the productivity statistics on the last dozen years are dismal. Any fully satisfactory view has to reconcile those two observations, and I have not heard it satisfactorily reconciled."

Many in Silicon Valley have a simple way of reconciling those views. The productivity statistics, they say, are simply broken.

"While I am a bull on technological progress," **tweeted** (https://twitter.com/pmarca/status/549524898410803200) venture capitalist Marc Andreessen, "it also seems that much that progress is deflationary in nature, so even rapid tech may not show up in GDP or productivity stats."

Hal Varian, the chief economist at Google, is also a skeptic. "The question is whether [productivity] is measuring the wrong things," he told me.

Bill Gates agrees. During our conversation, he rattled off a few of the ways our lives have been improved in recent years—digital photos, easier hotel booking, cheap GPS, nearly costless communication with friends. "The way the productivity figures are done isn't very good at capturing those quality of service–type improvements," he said.

There's much to be said for this argument. Measures of productivity are based on the sum total of goods and services the economy produces for sale. But many digital-era products are given away for free, and so never have an opportunity to show themselves in GDP statistics.

Take Google Maps. I have a crap sense of direction, so it's no exaggeration to say Google Maps has changed my life. I would pay hundreds of dollars a year for the product. In practice, I pay nothing. In terms of its direct contribution to GDP, Google Maps boosts Google's advertising business by feeding my data back to the company so they can target ads more effectively, and it probably boosts the amount of money I fork over to Verizon for my data plan. But that's not worth hundreds of dollars to Google, or to the economy as a whole. The result is that GDP data might undercount the value of Google Maps in a way it didn't undercount the value of, say, Garmin GPS devices.

This, Varian argues, is a systemic problem with the way we measure GDP: It's good at catching value to businesses but bad at catching value to individuals. "When GPS technology was adopted by trucking and logistics companies, productivity in that sector basically doubled," he says. "[Then] the price goes down to basically zero with Google Maps. It's adopted by households. So it's reasonable to believe household productivity has gone up. But that's not really measured in our productivity statistics."

The gap between what I pay for Google Maps and the value I get from it is called "consumer surplus," and it's Silicon Valley's best defense against the grim story told by the productivity statistics. The argument is that we've broken our country's productivity statistics because so many of our great new technologies are free or nearly free to the consumer. When Henry Ford began pumping out cars, people bought his cars, and so their value showed up in GDP. Depending on the day you check, the stock market routinely certifies Google—excuse me, Alphabet—as the world's most valuable company, but few of us ever cut Larry Page or Sergei Brin a check.

This is what Andreessen means when he says Silicon Valley's innovations are "deflationary in nature": Things like Google Maps are pushing prices down rather than pushing them up, and that's confounding our measurements.

The other problem the productivity skeptics bring up are so-called "step changes"—new goods that represent such a massive change in human welfare that trying to account for them by measuring prices and inflation seems borderline ridiculous. The economist Diane Coyle **puts this well** (https://www.uschamberfoundation.org/article/why-gdp-statisticsare-failing-us). In 1836, she notes, Nathan Mayer Rothschild died from an abscessed tooth. "What might the richest man in the world at the time have paid for an antibiotic, if only they had been invented?" Surely more than the actual cost of an antibiotic.

Perhaps, she suggests, we live in an age of step changes—the products we use are getting so much better, so much faster, that the normal ways we try to account for technological improvement are breaking down. "It is not plausible that the statistics capture the step changes in quality of life brought about by all of the new technologies," she writes, "any more than the price of an antibiotic captures the value of life."

One problem with the mismeasurement hypothesis: There's always been mismeasurement

"Yes, productivity numbers do miss innovation gains and quality improvements," sighs John Fernald, an economist at the San Francisco Federal Reserve Bank who has studied productivity statistics extensively. "But they've always been missing that."

This is a challenge to the mismeasurement hypothesis: We've *never* measured productivity perfectly. We've always been confounded by consumer surplus and step changes. To explain the missing productivity of recent decades, you have to show that the problem is getting worse—to show the consumer surplus is getting bigger and the step changes more profound. You have to prove that Facebook offers more consumer surplus than cars once did; that measures of inflation tracked the change from outhouses to toilets better than the change from telephones to smartphones. That turns out to be a very hard case to make.

Consider Google Maps again. It's true that using the app is free. But the productivity gains it enables should show in other parts of the economy. If we are getting places faster and more reliably, that should allow us to make more things, have more meetings, make more connections, create more value. That's how it was for cars and trains—their real value to the economy wasn't simply sales of automobiles or tickets or gasoline, but the way they revolutionized our work and lives.

Or take Coyle's point about the step change offered by antibiotics. Is there anything in our recent history that even remotely compares to the medical advances of the 20th century? Or the sanitation advances of the late 19th century? If so, it's certainly not evident in our longevity data: Life expectancy gains have slowed sharply in the IT era. A serious appreciation of step changes suggests that our measures of productivity might have missed more in the 20th century than they have in the 21st.

Another problem with the mismeasurement hypothesis: It doesn't fit the facts

The mismeasurement hypothesis fails more specific tests, too. In January, Chad Syverson, an economist at the University of Chicago's Booth School of Business, published **a paper** (http://faculty.chicagobooth.edu/chad.syverson/research/productivityslowdown.pdf) that is, in the understated language of economics research, a devastating rebuttal to the thesis.

Syverson reasoned that if productivity gains were being systematically distorted in economies dependent on informational technologies, then productivity would look better in countries whose economies were driven by other sectors. Instead, he found that the productivity slowdown—which is evident in every advanced economy—is "unrelated to the relative size of information and communication technologies in the country's economy."

Then he moved on to the consumer surplus argument. Perhaps the best way to value the digital age's advances is by trying to put a price on the time we spend using things like Facebook. Syverson used extremely generous assumptions about the value of our time, and took as a given that we would use online services even if we had to pay for them. Even then, he found the consumer surplus only fills a third of the productivity gap. (And that's before you go back and offer the same generous assumptions to fully capture the value of past innovations, which would widen the gap today's technologies need to close!)

A March **paper** (http://www.brookings.edu//media/projects/bpea/spring-2016/byrneetal_productivitymeasurement_conferencedraft.pdf) from David Byrne, John Fernald, and Marshall Reinsdorf took a different approach but comes to similar conclusions. "The major 'cost' to consumers of Facebook, Google, and the like is not the broadband access, the cell phone service, or the phone or computer; rather, it is the opportunity cost of time," they concluded. "But that time cost . . . is akin to the consumer surplus obtained from television (an old economy invention) or from playing soccer with one's children."

There is real value in playing soccer with one's children, of course—it's just not the kind of value economists are looking to measure with productivity statistics.

This is a key point, and one worth dwelling on: When economists measure productivity gains, they are measuring the kind of technological advances that power economic gains. What that suggests is that even if we were mismeasuring productivity, we would see the effects of productivity-enhancing technological change in other measures of economic well-being.

You can imagine a world in which wages look flat but workers feel richer because their paychecks are securing them wonders beyond their previous imagination. In that world, people's perceptions of their economic situation, the state of the broader economy, and the prospects for their children would be rosier than the economic data seemed to justify. That is not the world we live in.

According to **the Pew Research Center** (http://www .pewresearch.org/datatrend/national-conditions/personal -finances/), the last time a majority of Americans rated their own financial condition as "good or excellent" was 2005. Gallup **finds** (http://www.gallup.com/poll/1669/general-mood-country. aspx) that the last time most Americans were satisfied with the way things were going in the country was 2004. The last time Americans **were confident** (http://www.pollingreport.com/life. htm) that their children's lives would be better than their own was 2001. Hell, Donald Trump is successfully running atop the slogan "Make America Great Again"—the "again" suggests people many don't feel their lives are getting better and better.

Why isn't all this technology improving the economy? Because it's not changing how we work.

There's a simple explanation for the disconnect between how much it feels like technology has changed our lives and how absent it is from our economic data: It's changing how we play and relax more than it's changing how we work and produce.

As my colleague Matthew Yglesias has **written** (http:// www.vox.com/2015/7/27/9038829/automation-myth), "Digital technology has transformed a handful of industries in the media/entertainment space that occupy a mindshare that's out of proportion to their overall economic importance. The robots aren't taking our jobs; they're taking our leisure."

"Data from the **American Time Use Survey** (http://www. bls.gov/tus/charts/sleep.htm)," he continues, "suggests that on average Americans spend about 23 percent of their waking hours watching television, reading, or gaming. With Netflix, HDTV, Kindles, iPads, and all the rest, these are certainly activities that look *drastically* different in 2015 than they did in 1995 and can easily create the impression that life has been revolutionized by digital technology."

But as Yglesias notes, the entertainment and publishing industries account for far less than 23 percent of the workforce.

Retail sales workers and cashiers make up the single biggest tranche of American workers, and you only have to enter your nearest Gap to see how little those jobs have changed in recent decades. Nearly a tenth of all workers are in food preparation, and even the most cursory visit to the kitchen of your local restaurant reveals that technology hasn't done much to transform that industry, either.

This is part of the narrowing of what counts as the technology sector. "If you were an airplane pilot or a stewardess in the 1950s," Thiel says, "you felt like you were part of a futuristic industry. Most people felt like they were in futuristic industries. Most people had jobs that had not existed 40 or 50 years ago."

Today, most of us have jobs that did exist 40 or 50 years ago. We use computers in them, to be sure, and that's a real change. But it's a change that mostly happened in the 1990s and early 2000s, which is why there was a temporary increase in productivity (and wages, and GDP) during that period.

The question going forward is whether we're in a temporary technological slowdown or a permanent one.

The case for pessimism: The past 200 years were unique in human history

The scariest argument economist Robert Gordon makes is also the most indisputable argument he makes: There is no guarantee of continual economic growth. It's the progress of the 20th century, not the relative sluggishness of the past few decades, that should surprise us.

The economic historian Angus Maddison, who died in 2010, estimated that the annual economic growth rate in the Western world from AD 1 to AD 1820 was 0.06 percent per year—a far cry from the 2 to 3 percent we've grown accustomed to in recent decades.

The superpowered growth of recent centuries is the result of extraordinary technological progress—progress of a type and pace unknown in any other era in human history. The lesson of that progress, Gordon writes in *The Rise and Fall of American Growth* (https://www.amazon.com/Rise-Fall-American-Growth -Princetonebook/dp/B0131KW67U?ie=UTF8&btkr=1&ref _=dp-kindle-redirect), is simple: "Some inventions are more important than others," and the 20th century happened to collect some really, really important inventions.

It was in the 19th and particularly 20th centuries that we really figured out how to use fossil fuels to power, well, pretty much everything. "A newborn child in 1820 entered a world that was almost medieval," writes Gordon, "a dim world lit by candlelight, in which folk remedies treated health problems and in which travel was no faster than that possible by hoof or sail."

That newborn's great-grandchildren knew a world transformed:

> When electricity made it possible to create light with the flick of a switch instead of the strike of a match, the process of creating light was changed forever. When the electric elevator allowed buildings to extend vertically instead of horizontally, the very nature of land use was changed, and urban density was created. When small electric machines attached to the floor or held in the hand replaced huge and heavy steam boilers that transmitted power by leather or rubber belts, the scope for replacing human labor with machines broadened beyond recognition. And so it was with motor vehicles replacing horses as the primary form of intra-urban transportation; no longer did society have to allocate a quarter of its agricultural land to support the feeding of the horses or maintain a sizable labor force for removing their waste.

Then, of course, there were the medical advances of the age: sanitation, anesthetic, antibiotics, surgery, chemotherapy, and antidepressants. Many of the deadliest scourges of the 18th century were mere annoyances by the 20th century. Some, like smallpox, were eliminated altogether. Nothing improves a person's economic productivity quite like remaining alive.

More remarkable was how fast all this happened. "Though not a single household was wired for electricity in 1880, nearly 100 percent of U.S. urban homes were wired by 1940, and in the same time interval the percentage of urban homes with clean running piped water and sewer pipes for waste disposal had reached 94 percent," Gordon writes. "More than 80 percent of urban homes in 1940 had interior flush toilets, 73 percent had gas for heating and cooking, 58 percent had central heating, and 56 percent had mechanical refrigerators."

Gordon pushes back on the idea that he is a pessimist. He does not dismiss the value of laptop computers and GPS and Facebook and Google and iPhones and Teslas. He's just saying that the stack of them doesn't amount to electricity plus automobiles plus airplanes plus antibiotics plus indoor plumbing plus skyscrapers plus the Interstate Highway System.

But it is hard not to feel pessimistic when reading him. Gordon does not just argue that today's innovations fall short of yesterday's. He also argues, persuasively, that the economy is facing major headwinds in the coming years that range from an aging workforce to excessive regulations to high inequality. Our innovations will have to overcome all that, too.

The case for optimism

Gordon's views aren't universally held, to say the least. When I asked Bill Gates about *The Rise and Fall of American Growth,* he was unsparing. "That book will be viewed as quite ironic," he replied. "It's like the 'peace breaks out' book that was written in 1940. It will turn out to be that prophetic."

Gates's view is that the past 20 years have been an explosion of scientific advances. Over the course of our conversation, he marveled over advances in gene editing, machine learning, antibody design, driverless cars, material sciences, robotic surgery, artificial intelligence, and more.

Those discoveries are real, but they take time to turn up in new products, in usable medical treatments, in innovative startups. "We will see the dramatic effects of those things over the next 20 years, and I say that with incredible confidence," Gates says.

And while Gordon is right about the headwinds we face, there are tailwinds, too. We don't appear to be facing the world wars that overwhelmed the 20th century, and we have billions more people who are educated, connected, and working to invent the future than we did 100 years ago. The ease with which a researcher at Stanford and a researcher in Shanghai can collaborate must be worth something.

In truth, I don't have any way to adjudicate an argument over the technologies that will reshape the world 20 or 40 years from now. But if you're focused on gains over the next 5, 10, or even 20 years—and for people who need help soon, those are the gains that matter—then we've probably got all the technology we need. What we're missing is everything else.

Will there be a second IT boom?

By 1989, computers were fast becoming ubiquitous in businesses and homes. They were dramatically changing how any number of industries—from journalism to banking to retail—operated. But it was hard to see the IT revolution when looking at the economic numbers. The legendary growth economist Robert Solow quipped, "You can see the computer age everywhere but in the productivity statistics."

It didn't stay that way for long: The IT revolution powered a productivity boom from 1995 to 2004.

The lesson here is simple and profound: Productivity booms often lag behind technology. As Chad Syverson has **documented** (http://faculty.chicagobooth.edu/chad.syverson /research/ITrevolution.pdf), the same thing happened with electricity. Around the turn of the 20th century, electricity changed lives without really changing the economy much. Then, starting in 1915, there was a decade-long acceleration in productivity as economic actors began grafting electricity onto their operations. That boom, however, quickly tapered off.

But in the case of electrification, there was a *second* productivity boom that arrived sometime later. This was the boom that emerged as factories, companies and entire industries were rebuilt around the possibilities of electricity—the boom that only came as complex organizations figured out how electricity could transform their operations. "History shows that productivity growth driven by general purpose technologies can arrive in multiple waves," writes Syverson.

Could the same be true for IT?

Tyler Cowen, an economist at George Mason University and author of *The Great Stagnation,* believes so. "I think the internet is just beginning, even though that sounds crazy."

Phase one, he argues, was the internet as "an add-on." This is Best Buy letting you order stereos from a website, or businesses using Facebook ads to target customers. This is big companies eking out some productivity gains by adding some IT on to their existing businesses.

Phase two, he says, will be new companies built top to bottom around IT—and these companies will use their superior productivity to destroy their competitors, revolutionize industries, and push the economy forward. Examples abound: Think Amazon hollowing out the retail sector, Uber disrupting the taxi cab industry, or Airbnb taking on hotels. Now imagine that in *every* sector of the economy—what happens if Alphabet rolls out driverless cars powered by the reams of data organized in Google Maps, or if telemedicine revolutionizes rural health care, or if MOOCs (massive open online courses) can truly drive down the cost of higher education?

These are the big leaps forward—and in most cases, we have, or will soon have, the technology to make them. But that doesn't mean they'll get made.

We have the technology. What we need is everything else.

Chris Dixon, a venture capitalist at Andreessen Horowitz, has a useful framework for thinking about this argument. "In 2005, a bunch of companies pitched me the idea for Uber," he says. "But because they followed orthodox thinking, they figured they would build the software but let other people manage the cars."

This was the dominant idea of the add-on phase of the internet: Silicon Valley should make the software and then it should sell it to companies with expertise in all the other parts of the business. And that worked, for a while. But it could only take IT so far.

"The problem was the following," Dixon continues. "You build the software layer of Uber. Then you knock on the door of the taxi company. They're a family business. They don't know how to evaluate, purchase, or implement software. They don't have the budget for it. And even if you can make them a customer, the experience was not very good. Eventually Uber and Lyft and companies like this realized that by controlling the full experience and full product you can create a much better end-user experience." (Dixon's firm, I should note, is an investor in Lyft, though to their everlasting regret, they passed on Uber.)

The point here is that really taking advantage of IT in a company turns out to be really, really hard. The problems aren't merely technical; they're personnel problems, workflow problems, organizational problems, and regulatory problems.

The only way to solve those problems (and thus to get the productivity gains from solving them) is to build companies designed to solve those problems. That is, however, a harder, slower process than getting consumers to switch from looking at one screen to looking at another, or to move from renting DVDs to using Netflix.

In this telling, what's holding back our economy isn't so much a dearth of technological advances but a difficulty in turning the advances we already have into companies that can actually use them.

In health care, for instance, there's more than enough technology to upend our relationships with doctors—but a mixture of status quo bias on the part of patients, confusion on the part of medical providers, regulatory barriers that scare off or impede new entrants, and anti-competitive behavior on the part of incumbents means most of us don't even have a doctor who stores our medical records in an electronic form that other health providers can easily access and read. And if we can't even get that done, how are we going to move to telemedicine?

Uber's great innovation wasn't its software so much as its brazenness at exploiting loopholes in taxi regulations and then mobilizing satisfied customers to scare off powerful interest groups and angry local politicians. In the near term, productivity increases will come from companies like Uber—companies whose competency isn't so much technology as it is figuring out how to apply existing technologies to resistant industries.

"It turns out the hardest things at companies isn't building the technology but getting people to use it properly," Dixon says.

My best guess is that's the answer to the mystery laid out by Summers. Yes, there's new technology all around us, and some of it is pretty important. But developing the technology turns out to be a lot easier than getting people—and particularly companies—to use it properly.

Critical Thinking

1. How do you reconcile declining productivity statistics with the "huge and pervasive" effects of technology?

2. Compare and contrast the changes technology has made to time at leisure versus time at work. Where has technology made the greatest impact? And how does this influence Americans' level of satisfaction.

3. How does the fact that so many technologies are free to the end user (e.g., Google Maps) influence productivity statistics?

Internet References

This Is When the Jobs "Recovery" Goes KABOOM
https://goo.gl/ep1veN

Web 2.0 Is Everywhere, Except in the Productivity Statistics
https://goo.gl/Jouiw8

What Happened to the Internet Productivity Miracle?
https://goo.gl/xbJDOH

Why This Golden Era of Innovation Isn't Improving Productivity
https://goo.gl/2oKZk5

EZRA KLEIN is founder and editor-in-chief of Vox.com—a site dedicated to explaining the news.

Prepared by: Liz Friedman, *DePaul University* and
Daniel Mittleman, *DePaul University*

Article

The Mirage of the Marketplace

The disingenuous ways Uber hides behind its algorithm.

TIM HWANG AND MADELEINE CLARE ELISH

Learning Outcomes

After reading this article, you will be able to:

- Articulate how an algorithm can capture—and perhaps misrepresent—supply and demand for a product.

- Articulate positives and negatives of the use of real-time algorithms to manage price and availability of product or service.

- Articulate the pros and cons of differential product and service pricing.

In June, the California Labor Commission ruled in favor of classifying Uber driver **Barbara Ann Berwick as an employee** and not as an independent contractor. But the battle over ride-hailing apps continues to rage as companies, governments, activists, and incumbent businesses all seek to shape how a new generation of companies will be regulated. A class-action suit with potentially even bigger implications continues to wind its way through the federal courts, with **Uber resisting every step of the way.** All this has continued to take place on a backdrop of violent **protests, accusations of gender bias,** and revelations about less-than-savory **techniques of message control.**

But the battle isn't about Uber, Lyft, or any of the other hot ride-hailing startups leveraging similar technology. Increasingly, what underlies the debate over the so-called sharing economy is a nascent, bigger battle about how society wants machines coordinating and governing human activity. These apps don't match and route people by hand. Instead, **software and underlying algorithms** make these technologies work. Companies throughout the "sharing economy"—like Postmates, Handy, and TaskRabbit—all depend on the use of machines to match, sort, and assign tasks effectively at massive scale.

To date, the industry has used language that portrays itself as a mere facilitator. As Uber **CEO Travis Kalanick told** Wired **in 2013,** "[Uber is] not setting the price. The market is setting the price. . . . We have algorithms to determine what that market is."

So: Is the Uber algorithm really a reflection of the marketplace? The stakes here are high. If Uber is merely a system humbly facilitating a relationship between supply and demand, then it supports the argument that Uber does not exert the kind of control over drivers that would deem them employees in the eyes of the law.

However, if Uber is **more than simply a platform** for allowing buyers and sellers of transportation to connect, then it may exert a kind of control that renders its drivers effectively employees. At its core, the debate over Uber drivers as employees is about the relative power of the algorithm.

Part of what is so difficult about Uber and many "sharing economy" platforms is that the lived experience of these applications so closely reflects a marketplace. The app connects drivers with riders, with a fluctuating price that seems to correlate with demand. You rate the performance of the driver as you would an independent seller on Amazon or eBay. The app, in short, looks like a market and quacks like a market. But companies like Uber and Lyft merely adopt tropes of a marketplace. The apps' user interface suggests a reality that doesn't exist in practice.

In a real marketplace, supply responds directly to the pressures of demand. This isn't the case with Uber: According to a forthcoming paper by researchers **Alex Rosenblat** and **Luke Stark** at **Data & Society** (where we work), the supply of drivers is instead mobilized to meet *predicted* passenger demand, as through surge pricing.

Drivers are shown a map of "surge zones," which ostensibly reflect the demand for rides in different parts of the city at a given time. While this is **how the company frames it,** it actually isn't the case in practice. According to its patents, **Uber generates surge based on the projected demand of riders at some point in the future.** When it works, this system produces low latency—a rider requesting a car can get one quickly. When it doesn't, drivers can spend precious time and gas in a neighborhood with no or slow demand. The suppliers get to see only what a system expects the state of the market to be, and not the market itself. (**Update, July 28, 2015:** For more on Uber's "phantom cabs," read Rosenblat's piece on Motherboard.)

Demand is also walled off from supply. When you open the Uber app as a rider, you see a map of your local pickup area, with little sedans around that appear to be drivers available for a request. While you might assume that these reflect an accurate picture of market supply, the way drivers are configured in Uber's marketplace can be misleading. According to Rosenblat and Stark, the presence of those virtual cars on the passenger's screen does not necessarily reflect an accurate number of drivers who are physically present or their precise locations. Instead, these phantom cars are part of a "visual effect" that Uber uses to emphasize the proximity of drivers to passengers. Not surprisingly, the visual effect shows cars nearby, even when they might not actually exist. Demand, in this case, sees a simulated picture of supply. Whether you are a driver or a rider, the algorithm operating behind the curtain at Uber shows a through-the-looking-glass version of supply and demand.

What the company has produced is a *mirage* of a marketplace—an app experience that produces the sensation of independent riders and drivers responding to the natural fluctuations of supply and demand. But a look underneath the hood reveals a system that intermediates and influences more than it facilitates free exchange.

This mirage has effectively confused the debate by allowing the companies to adopt the mantle of a passive marketplace. Uber has persistently characterized itself in its suits as simply **"a software application . . . that permits riders to arrange trips with nearby transportation providers,"** implying that it is the users who "arrange" the rides. But in reality, it is Uber that does much more than "arrange": It sets the price, coordinates the trip, and has the power to exclude both **riders** and **drivers.**

Hiding behind the algorithm has also created negotiating leverage for the companies. Perhaps hedging the risk from the wave of legal challenges that would render their workers employees, **some representatives of the industry** support the creation of a third category—something between employee and contractor. (Sen. **Mark Warner** and **Hillary Clinton** have both voiced interest in this proposal.)

Creating a middle ground *does* make a good deal of sense. To use the language of **legal scholar Adam Kolber,** the employer–employee distinction is a good example of a "bumpy" law since it only permits two extreme states, one with low costs to the platforms and another one with considerable costs. This structure creates all sorts of distortions, not least of which is that small variations in the specific behavior of platforms might result in radically different legal outcomes. That might raise risks and hinder experimentation with new forms of work and employment.

Machines' ability to coordinate the work of many people at low cost could reorganize the workplace in novel and better ways. To that end, the technology that we see at play in ride-hailing apps might indeed hold the promise of flexible work, financial independence, and much of the other technological advantages trumpeted by boosters of the "sharing economy." But the question is not whether a middle ground makes sense in some abstract sense. The key issue is whether these technologies, as currently constituted, necessitate a middle ground.

That's a much less clear proposition. **As many have depicted more evocatively,** companies like Uber and Lyft continue to exert a great deal of control over drivers, though they may use novel systems of employee discipline and monitoring. While the specifics have shuffled around, the balance of power between company and worker has in large part remained the same.

If the "sharing economy" were to take advantage of a third category, it should have to make significant changes. Categorizing workers in the middle zone between employee and contractor ought to require ride-hailing technologies to create work conditions that match the truly novel kind of employment they **aggressively market to drivers.** The reality of command and control, in short, would have to change to meet the promises of a flexible and free market mirage.

What the ride-hailing experience shows is the extent to which the behavior of these artificial intelligence systems can diverge significantly from the trappings they adopt. Similar mirages are cast elsewhere throughout the "sharing economy" and even in **the design of our social platforms.** They downplay the responsibility of the platform designer, masking the more active role these technologies play in the sectors they exist in.

As the uses of artificial intelligence continue to broaden, society will increasingly confront questions around the power these technologies can and should have. As we move toward regulation, we need to question the narratives offered by companies and make sure that policy reflects reality.

Critical Thinking

1. The article states the underlyng controversies at Uber and Lyft boil down to "how society wants machines [and algorithms] coordinating and governing human activity." What do the authors mean by this statement, and what are the two basic positions in conflict?

2. What are Uber's ethical obligations to its drivers: honesty, full information, or maximizing revenue opportunities? What are Uber's ethical obligations to its rider customers?

3. Other companies use algorithms to set market pricing. Amazon, for example, may show different shoppers a different price for the exact same item based on what it knows about the shopper's demographics, shopping history, and browsing patterns. In what situations do you think differential pricing is or isn't ethical?

Internet References

Big Data and Differential Pricing
https://goo.gl/N3bth0

Different Customers, Different Prices, Thanks to Big Data
https://goo.gl/QttRRY

Judge Calls Uber Algorithm "Genius," Green-Lights Surge-Pricing Lawsuit
https://goo.gl/TNa1zc

The Secrets of Uber's Mysterious Surge Pricing Algorithm, Revealed
https://goo.gl/1A464M

When Your Boss Is an Uber Algorithm
https://goo.gl/AUEWI6

Prepared by: Liz Friedman, *DePaul University* and
Daniel Mittleman, *DePaul University*

Article

How Technology Is Destroying Jobs

DAVID ROTMAN

Learning Outcomes

After reading this article, you will be able to:

- Articulate the arguments both for why technology innovation causes unemployment and why it does not.

- Understand what workplace robots are and how the growth in their use may affect employment today.

Given his calm and reasoned academic demeanor, it is easy to miss just how provocative Erik Brynjolfsson's contention really is. Brynjolfsson, a professor at the MIT Sloan School of Management, and his collaborator and coauthor Andrew McAfee have been arguing for the last year and a half that impressive advances in computer technology—from improved industrial robotics to automated translation services—are largely behind the sluggish employment growth of the last 10 to 15 years. Even more ominous for workers, the MIT academics foresee dismal prospects for many types of jobs as these powerful new technologies are increasingly adopted not only in manufacturing, clerical, and retail work but in professions such as law, financial services, education, and medicine.

That robots, automation, and software can replace people might seem obvious to anyone who's worked in automotive manufacturing or as a travel agent. But Brynjolfsson and McAfee's claim is more troubling and controversial. They believe that rapid technological change has been destroying jobs faster than it is creating them, contributing to the stagnation of median income and the growth of inequality in the United States. And, they suspect, something similar is happening in other technologically advanced countries.

Perhaps the most damning piece of evidence, according to Brynjolfsson, is a chart that only an economist could love. In economics, productivity—the amount of economic value created for a given unit of input, such as an hour of labor—is a

crucial indicator of growth and wealth creation. It is a measure of progress. On the chart Brynjolfsson likes to show, separate lines represent productivity and total employment in the United States. For years after World War II, the two lines closely tracked each other, with increases in jobs corresponding to increases in productivity. The pattern is clear: as businesses generated more value from their workers, the country as a whole became richer, which fueled more economic activity and created even more jobs. Then, beginning in 2000, the lines diverge; productivity continues to rise robustly, but employment suddenly wilts. By 2011, a significant gap appears between the two lines, showing economic growth with no parallel increase in job creation. Brynjolfsson and McAfee call it the "great decoupling." And Brynjolfsson says he is confident that technology is behind both the healthy growth in productivity and the weak growth in jobs.

It's a startling assertion because it threatens the faith that many economists place in technological progress. Brynjolfsson and McAfee still believe that technology boosts productivity and makes societies wealthier, but they think that it can also have a dark side: technological progress is eliminating the need for many types of jobs and leaving the typical worker worse off than before. Brynjolfsson can point to a second chart indicating that median income is failing to rise even as the gross domestic product soars. "It's the great paradox of our era," he says. "Productivity is at record levels, innovation has never been faster, and yet at the same time, we have a falling median income and we have fewer jobs. People are falling behind because technology is advancing so fast and our skills and organizations aren't keeping up."

Brynjolfsson and McAfee are not Luddites. Indeed, they are sometimes accused of being too optimistic about the extent and speed of recent digital advances. Brynjolfsson says they began writing *Race Against the Machine,* the 2011 book in which they laid out much of their argument, because they wanted to explain the economic benefits of these new technologies (Brynjolfsson spent much of the 1990s sniffing out evidence that information technology was boosting rates of productivity). But it became clear to them that the same technologies making many jobs safer, easier, and more productive were also reducing the demand for many types of human workers.

Anecdotal evidence that digital technologies threaten jobs is, of course, everywhere. Robots and advanced automation have been common in many types of manufacturing for decades. In the United States and China, the world's manufacturing powerhouses, fewer people work in manufacturing today than in 1997, thanks at least in part to automation. Modern automotive plants, many of which were transformed by industrial robotics in the 1980s, routinely use machines that autonomously weld and paint body parts—tasks that were once handled by humans. Most recently, industrial robots like Rethink Robotics' Baxter more flexible and far cheaper than their predecessors, have been introduced to perform simple jobs for small manufacturers in a variety of sectors. The website of a Silicon Valley startup called Industrial Perception features a video of the robot it has designed for use in warehouses picking up and throwing boxes like a bored elephant. And such sensations as Google's driverless car suggest what automation might be able to accomplish someday soon.

A less dramatic change, but one with a potentially far larger impact on employment, is taking place in clerical work and professional services. Technologies like the Web, artificial intelligence, big data, and improved analytics—all made possible by the ever increasing availability of cheap computing power and storage capacity—are automating many routine tasks. Countless traditional white-collar jobs, such as many in the post office and in customer service, have disappeared. W. Brian Arthur, a visiting researcher at the Xerox Palo Alto Research Center's intelligence systems lab and a former economics professor at Stanford University, calls it the "autonomous economy." It's far more subtle than the idea of robots and automation doing human jobs, he says: it involves "digital processes talking to other digital processes and creating new processes," enabling us to do many things with fewer people and making yet other human jobs obsolete.

It is this onslaught of digital processes, says Arthur, that primarily explains how productivity has grown without a significant increase in human labor. And, he says, "digital versions of human intelligence" are increasingly replacing even those jobs once thought to require people. "It will change every profession in ways we have barely seen yet," he warns.

McAfee, associate director of the MIT Center for Digital Business at the Sloan School of Management, speaks rapidly and with a certain awe as he describes advances such as Google's driverless car. Still, despite his obvious enthusiasm for the technologies, he doesn't see the recently vanished jobs coming back. The pressure on employment and the resulting inequality will only get worse, he suggests, as digital technologies—fueled with "enough computing power, data, and geeks"—continue their exponential advances over the next several decades. "I would like to be wrong," he says, "but when all these science-fiction technologies are deployed, what will we need all the people for?"

New Economy?

But are these new technologies really responsible for a decade of lackluster job growth? Many labor economists say the data are, at best, far from conclusive. Several other plausible explanations, including events related to global trade and the financial crises of the early and late 2000s, could account for the relative slowness of job creation since the turn of the century. "No one really knows," says Richard Freeman, a labor economist at Harvard University. That's because it's very difficult to "extricate" the effects of technology from other macroeconomic effects, he says. But he's skeptical that technology would change a wide range of business sectors fast enough to explain recent job numbers.

Employment trends have polarized the workforce and hollowed out the middle class.

David Autor, an economist at MIT who has extensively studied the connections between jobs and technology, also doubts that technology could account for such an abrupt change in total employment. "There was a great sag in employment beginning in 2000. Something did change," he says. "But no one knows the cause." Moreover, he doubts that productivity has, in fact, risen robustly in the United States in the past decade (economists can disagree about that statistic because there are different ways of measuring and weighing economic inputs and outputs). If he's right, it raises the possibility that poor job growth could be simply a result of a sluggish economy. The sudden slowdown in job creation "is a big puzzle," he says, "but there's not a lot of evidence it's linked to computers."

To be sure, Autor says, computer technologies are changing the types of jobs available, and those changes "are not always for the good." At least since the 1980s, he says, computers have increasingly taken over such tasks as bookkeeping, clerical work, and repetitive production jobs in manufacturing—all of which typically provided middle-class pay. At the same time, higher-paying jobs requiring creativity and problem-solving skills, often aided by computers, have proliferated. So have low-skill jobs: demand has increased for restaurant workers, janitors, home health aides, and others doing service work that is nearly impossible to automate. The result, says Autor, has been a "polarization" of the workforce and a "hollowing out" of the middle class—something that has been happening in numerous industrialized countries for the last several decades. But "that is very different from saying technology is affecting the total number of jobs," he adds. "Jobs can change a lot without there being huge changes in employment rates."

What's more, even if today's digital technologies are holding down job creation, history suggests that it is most likely a temporary, albeit painful, shock; as workers adjust their skills and entrepreneurs create opportunities based on the new technologies, the number of jobs will rebound. That, at least, has always been the pattern. The question, then, is whether today's computing technologies will be different, creating long-term involuntary unemployment.

At least since the Industrial Revolution began in the 1700s, improvements in technology have changed the nature of work and destroyed some types of jobs in the process. In 1900, 41 percent of Americans worked in agriculture; by 2000, it was only 2 percent. Likewise, the proportion of Americans employed in manufacturing has dropped from 30 percent in the post-World War II years to around 10 percent today—partly because of increasing automation, especially during the 1980s.

While such changes can be painful for workers whose skills no longer match the needs of employers, Lawrence Katz, a Harvard economist, says that no historical pattern shows these shifts leading to a net decrease in jobs over an extended period. Katz has done extensive research on how technological advances have affected jobs over the last few centuries—describing, for example, how highly skilled artisans in the mid-19th century were displaced by lower-skilled workers in factories. While it can take decades for workers to acquire the expertise needed for new types of employment, he says, "we never have run out of jobs. There is no long-term trend of eliminating work for people. Over the long term, employment rates are fairly stable. People have always been able to create new jobs. People come up with new things to do."

Still, Katz doesn't dismiss the notion that there is something different about today's digital technologies—something that could affect an even broader range of work. The question, he says, is whether economic history will serve as a useful guide. Will the job disruptions caused by technology be temporary as the workforce adapts, or will we see a science-fiction scenario in which automated processes and robots with superhuman skills take over a broad swath of human tasks? Though Katz expects the historical pattern to hold, it is "genuinely a question," he says. "If technology disrupts enough, who knows what will happen?"

Dr. Watson

To get some insight into Katz's question, it is worth looking at how today's most advanced technologies are being deployed in industry. Though these technologies have undoubtedly taken over some human jobs, finding evidence of workers being displaced by machines on a large scale is not all that easy. One reason it is difficult to pinpoint the net impact on jobs is that automation is often used to make human workers more efficient, not necessarily to replace them. Rising productivity means businesses can do the same work with fewer employees, but it can also enable the businesses to expand production with their existing workers, and even to enter new markets.

Take the bright-orange Kiva robot, a boon to fledgling e-commerce companies. Created and sold by Kiva Systems, a startup that was founded in 2002 and bought by Amazon for $775 million in 2012, the robots are designed to scurry across large warehouses, fetching racks of ordered goods and delivering the products to humans who package the orders. In Kiva's large demonstration warehouse and assembly facility at its headquarters outside Boston, fleets of robots move about with seemingly endless energy: some newly assembled machines perform tests to prove they're ready to be shipped to customers around the world, while others wait to demonstrate to a visitor how they can almost instantly respond to an electronic order and bring the desired product to a worker's station.

A warehouse equipped with Kiva robots can handle up to four times as many orders as a similar unautomated warehouse, where workers might spend as much as 70 percent of their time walking about to retrieve goods. (Coincidentally or not, Amazon bought Kiva soon after a press report revealed that workers at one of the retailer's giant warehouses often walked more than 10 miles a day.)

Despite the labor-saving potential of the robots, Mick Mountz, Kiva's founder and CEO, says he doubts the machines have put many people out of work or will do so in the future. For one thing, he says, most of Kiva's customers are e-commerce retailers, some of them growing so rapidly they can't hire people fast enough. By making distribution operations cheaper and more efficient, the robotic technology has helped many of these retailers survive and even expand. Before founding Kiva, Mountz worked at Webvan, an online grocery delivery company that was one of the 1990s dot-com era's most infamous flameouts. He likes to show the numbers demonstrating that Webvan was doomed from the start; a $100 order cost the company $120 to ship. Mountz's point is clear: something as mundane as the cost of materials handling can consign a new business to an early death. Automation can solve that problem.

Meanwhile, Kiva itself is hiring. Orange balloons—the same color as the robots—hover over multiple cubicles in its sprawling office, signaling that the occupants arrived within the last month. Most of these new employees are software engineers: while the robots are the company's poster boys, its lesser-known innovations lie in the complex algorithms that guide the robots' movements and determine where in the warehouse products are stored. These algorithms help make the system adaptable. It can learn, for example, that a certain product is seldom ordered, so it should be stored in a remote area.

Though advances like these suggest how some aspects of work could be subject to automation, they also illustrate that humans still excel at certain tasks—for example, packaging various items together. Many of the traditional problems in robotics—such as how to teach a machine to recognize an object as, say, a chair—remain largely intractable and are especially difficult to solve when the robots are free to move about a relatively unstructured environment like a factory or office.

Techniques using vast amounts of computational power have gone a long way toward helping robots understand their surroundings, but John Leonard, a professor of engineering at MIT and a member of its Computer Science and Artificial Intelligence Laboratory (CSAIL), says many familiar difficulties remain. "Part of me sees accelerating progress; the other part of me sees the same old problems," he says. "I see how hard it is to do anything with robots. The big challenge is uncertainty." In other words, people are still far better at dealing with changes in their environment and reacting to unexpected events.

For that reason, Leonard says, it is easier to see how robots could work *with* humans than on their own in many applications. "People and robots working together can happen much more quickly than robots simply replacing humans," he says. "That's not going to happen in my lifetime at a massive scale. The semiautonomous taxi will still have a driver."

One of the friendlier, more flexible robots meant to work with humans is Rethinks Baxter. The creation of Rodney Brooks, the company's founder, Baxter needs minimal training to perform simple tasks like picking up objects and moving them to a box. It's meant for use in relatively small manufacturing facilities where conventional industrial robots would cost too much and pose too much danger to workers. The idea, says Brooks, is to have the robots take care of dull, repetitive jobs that no one wants to do.

It's hard not to instantly like Baxter, in part because it seems so eager to please. The "eyebrows" on its display rise quizzically when it's puzzled; its arms submissively and gently retreat when bumped. Asked about the claim that such advanced industrial robots could eliminate jobs, Brooks answers simply that he doesn't see it that way. Robots, he says, can be to factory workers as electric drills are to construction workers: "It makes them more productive and efficient, but it doesn't take jobs."

The machines created at Kiva and Rethink have been cleverly designed and built to work with people, taking over the tasks that the humans often don't want to do or aren't especially good at. They are specifically designed to enhance these workers' productivity. And it's hard to see how even these increasingly sophisticated robots will replace humans in most manufacturing and industrial jobs anytime soon. But clerical and some professional jobs could be more vulnerable. That's because the marriage of artificial intelligence and big data is beginning to give machines a more humanlike ability to reason and to solve many new types of problems.

Even if the economy is only going through a transition, it is an extremely painful one for many.

In the tony northern suburbs of New York City, IBM Research is pushing super-smart computing into the realms of such professions as medicine, finance, and customer service. IBM's efforts have resulted in Watson, a computer system best known for beating human champions on the game show *Jeopardy!* in 2011. That version of Watson now sits in a corner of a large data center at the research facility in Yorktown Heights, marked with a glowing plaque commemorating its glory days. Meanwhile, researchers there are already testing new generations of Watson in medicine, where the technology could help physicians diagnose diseases like cancer, evaluate patients, and prescribe treatments.

IBM likes to call it cognitive computing. Essentially, Watson uses artificial-intelligence techniques, advanced natural-language processing and analytics, and massive amounts of data drawn from sources specific to a given application (in the case of health care, that means medical journals, textbooks, and information collected from the physicians or hospitals using the system). Thanks to these innovative techniques and huge amounts of computing power, it can quickly come up with "advice"—for example, the most recent and relevant information to guide a doctor's diagnosis and treatment decisions.

Despite the system's remarkable ability to make sense of all that data, it's still early days for Dr. Watson. While it has rudimentary abilities to "learn" from specific patterns and evaluate different possibilities, it is far from having the type of judgment and intuition a physician often needs. But IBM has also announced it will begin selling Watson's services to customer-support call centers, which rarely require human judgment that's quite so sophisticated. IBM says companies will rent an updated version of Watson for use as a "customer service agent" that responds to questions from consumers; it has already signed on several banks. Automation is nothing new in call centers, of course, but Watson's improved capacity for natural-language processing and its ability to tap into a large amount of data suggest that this system could speak plainly with callers, offering them specific advice on even technical and complex questions. It's easy to see it replacing many human holdouts in its new field.

Digital Losers

The contention that automation and digital technologies are partly responsible for today's lack of jobs has obviously touched a raw nerve for many worried about their own employment. But this is only one consequence of what Brynjolfsson and McAfee see as a broader trend. The rapid acceleration of technological progress, they say, has greatly widened the gap between economic winners and losers—the income inequalities that many economists have worried about for decades. Digital technologies tend to favor "superstars," they point out. For example, someone who creates a computer program to automate tax preparation might earn millions or billions of dollars while eliminating the need for countless accountants.

New technologies are "encroaching into human skills in a way that is completely unprecedented," McAfee says, and many middle-class jobs are right in the bull's-eye; even relatively high-skill work in education, medicine, and law is affected. "The middle seems to be going away," he adds. "The top and bottom are clearly getting farther apart." While technology might be only one factor, says McAfee, it has been an "underappreciated" one, and it is likely to become increasingly significant.

Not everyone agrees with Brynjolfsson and McAfee's conclusions—particularly the contention that the impact of recent technological change could be different from anything seen before. But it's hard to ignore their warning that technology is widening the income gap between the tech-savvy and everyone else. And even if the economy is only going through a transition similar to those it's endured before, it is an extremely painful one for many workers, and that will have to be addressed somehow. Harvard's Katz has shown that the United States prospered in the early 1900s in part because secondary education became accessible to many people at a time when employment in agriculture was drying up. The result, at least through the 1980s, was an increase in educated workers who found jobs in the industrial sectors, boosting incomes and reducing inequality. Katz's lesson: painful long-term consequences for the labor force do not follow inevitably from technological changes.

Brynjolfsson himself says he's not ready to conclude that economic progress and employment have diverged for good. "I don't know whether we can recover, but I hope we can," he says. But that, he suggests, will depend on recognizing the problem and taking steps such as investing more in the training and education of workers.

"We were lucky and steadily rising productivity raised all boats for much of the 20th century," he says. "Many people, especially economists, jumped to the conclusion that was just the way the world worked. I used to say that if we took care of productivity, everything else would take care of itself; it was the single most important economic statistic. But that's no longer true." He adds, "It's one of the dirty secrets of economics: technology progress does grow the economy and create wealth, but there is no economic law that says everyone will benefit." In other words, in the race against the machine, some are likely to win while many others lose.

Critical Thinking

1. Define productivity and explain why when technology innovation makes one employee more productive it does not automatically cost other employees their jobs.
2. Brynjolfsson demonstrates that something new happened around 2001 so that increased productivity no longer led to a growth in the number of jobs. Generate at least three independent hypotheses as to why there appeared a sudden change in this relationship at that point in time.

Internet References

Andrew McAfee: Are Droids Taking Our Jobs?
www.ted.com/talks/andrew_mcafee_are_droids_taking_our_jobs.html

Robots at Work: Toward a Smarter Factory
www.wfs.org/futurist/2013-issues-futurist/may-june-2013-vol-47-no-3/robots-work-toward-smarter-factory

Should We Fear "The End of Work"?
www.pbs.org/newshour/businessdesk/2013/07/should-we-fear-the-end-of-work.html

Unit 7

UNIT

Prepared by: Liz Friedman, *DePaul University* and
Daniel Mittleman, *DePaul University*

National Security

Prior to 2013, American cyberwar and cyber espionage capabilities were touted as important cogs within our military's arsenal. Stuxnet, for example, leaked into the news in 2010 as a mysterious, very focused attack upon the Iranian nuclear program that must have come from the Americans or Israelis, though neither government owned up to sponsoring it. Stuxnet, while fascinating, has become old news. Much more interesting was Flame, an even-more sinister follow-up attack upon the Iranian nuclear program, so named by the Russian computer security firm that uncovered and publicized its existence. Flame leads one to wonder: Is this what the future of warfare is going to be like?

Things changed in 2013, the year national security and personal privacy found themselves in direct conflict in the United States. The news was dominated by Edward Snowden's exposure of National Security Agency (NSA) information that documents how the U.S. government has been systematically collecting data on Americans for over two generations—even before the existence of the Internet, and has increased and automated that surveillance since September 2001. Some Americans view Snowden as a national hero: a whistleblower who uncovered long-standing unconstitutional activities. Others, including the government national security and homeland security communities, view Snowden as a traitor and seditionist. However, one views the propriety of Snowden's whistleblowing, it is enlightening to read about the processes the U.S. government has used to infiltrate our telecommunications and computing systems to capture and store vast quantities of data. Since 2013—and perhaps due to the Snowden revelations—renewal of security legislation that supports unhindered government access to personal data has been readily challenged and slowed. But, as of this writing, public policy has yet to be fully spelled out.

On other fronts, the emergence of both military and commercial drones is changing the airspace, both at home and in the field of battle. We wrote in this space a few years back that over 500 drone flights had taken place over U.S. airspace between 2010 and 2012. Today, we report that over 300,000 drone aircraft are registered with the FAA (as of early 2016). Drones are being used by consumers for aerial photography, surveillance, and sport. Several businesses are exploring the feasibility of product delivery be drone. And speculation exists that firms such as Apple and Google may be developing drones capable of carrying a human enabling a Uber-like industry of personal human flying transport in the very near future.

Law enforcement agencies are purchasing and deploying drones for surveillance and related activities. But so have criminals. Mexican cartels have been found using drones to smuggle drugs across the border. And the cartels have begun to jam the GPS signals of U.S. Customs and Border Patrol drones as well.[1]

Current statistics capturing military use of drones are a bit harder to come by. The U.S. military reports they undertook 473 drone strikes between 2009 and June 2016, killing approximately 2,400 enemy combatants as well as between 64 and 116 non-combatants.[2] Outside observes suggest the U.S. government significantly understates non-combatants killed. Use of drones goes both ways; ISIS has begun to deploy drones as well, both for reconnaissance and battlefield intelligence as well as offensive strikes.[3]

Other issues emerging this year include the growing domestic use of drone aircraft by Customs and Border Protection and other federal and local agencies. It appears over 500 domestic drone flights have taken place between 2010 and 2012.[3] There exists little or no policy regulating the use of domestic drones nor addressing constitutional issues that might arise from their use. As drone use by multiple law enforcement agencies grows, courts and Congress will no doubt take a stand on their legality.

Omnipresent surveillance of U.S. public space has produced benefits. The 2013 Boston Marathon bombers, for example, were quickly identified by crowdsourcing surveillance video that captured them at the race. A New York City terrorist bomber was similarly identified in 2016. The presence of recording equipment must be presumed today be friend and foe alike, likely modifying behaviors in the public arena.

[1]See: http://www.defenseone.com/technology/2015/12/DHS-Drug-Traffickers-Spoofing-Border-Drones/124613/
[2]See: http://www.nytimes.com/2016/07/04/world/middleeast/drone-strike-statistics-answer-few-questions-and-raise-many.html
[3]See: https://tsasblog.wordpress.com/2016/09/14/drones-simply-a-toy-or-significant-risk-to-national-security/

Prepared by: Liz Friedman, *DePaul University* and
Daniel Mittleman, *DePaul University*

Article

How Technology is Transforming the Future of National Security

PATRICK TUCKER

Learning Outcomes

After reading this article, you will be able to:

- Discuss America's dwindling commitment to developing armed drone technology.

- Describe the Pentagon's interest in climate change.

- Identify the differences between quantum cryptography and pulse position modulation.

Transformative Technology and the Future of National Security

Maintaining technological superiority is a constant challenge for the military, one that U.S. Navy Rear Admiral Mathew Klunder, head of the Office of Naval Research, thinks about in personal terms. "I never want to see U.S. sailors or Marines in a fair fight." Keeping the fight unfair is more complicated than it has ever been. Despite some $63.5 billion of research and development funding allocated to the Defense Department in fiscal year 2015, the proliferation of cheap computers, cheap Internet and cheap drones is changing geopolitical realities faster than Washington can keep up.

This e-book on emerging technologies and their influence on national security seeks to provide a snapshot of the challenges and opportunities of the next several decades. We'll explore the military's ongoing efforts to use big data strategically in an environment where the NSA's data collection activities have provoked backlash from all corners. We'll examine the proliferation of unmanned aerial vehicles and its implications for the future of war and peace. We'll also look at the military's efforts to harness breakthrough technologies from atomic GPS to

synthetic fuel and more. These articles are presented as conversation starters. The discussion of the technologies of tomorrow will be fast-moving in the months ahead, much like the pace of technological advancement itself. Whether or not the fight is fair, it's about to get a lot more interesting.

Every Nation Will Have Armed Drones by 2024

The proliferation of weaponized drone technology is inevitable, and there's nothing the U.S. can do to stop it.

Virtually every country on Earth will be able to build or acquire drones capable of firing missiles within the next 10 years. Armed aerial drones will be used for targeted killings, terrorism and the government suppression of civil unrest. What's worse, say experts, it's too late for the United States to do anything about it.

After the past decade's explosive growth, it may seem that the U.S. is the only country with missile-carrying drones. In fact, the U.S. is losing interest in further developing armed drone technology. The military plans to spend $2.4 billion on unmanned aerial vehicles, or UAVs, in 2015. That's down considerably from the $5.7 billion that the military requested in the 2013 budget. Other countries, conversely, have shown growing interest in making unmanned robot technology as deadly as possible. Only a handful of countries have armed flying drones today, including the U.S., United Kingdom, Israel, China and (possibly) Iran, Pakistan and Russia. Other countries want them, including South Africa and India. So far, 23 countries have developed or are developing armed drones, according to a recent report from the RAND organization. It's only a matter of time before the lethal technology spreads, several experts say.

"Once countries like China start exporting these, they're going to be everywhere really quickly. Within the next 10 years, every country will have these," Noel Sharkey, a robotics and artificial intelligence professor from the University of Sheffield, told *Defense One*. "There's nothing illegal about these unless you use them to attack other countries. Anything you can [legally] do with a fighter jet, you can do with a drone."

Sam Brannen, who analyzes drones as a senior fellow at the Center for Strategic and International Studies' International Security Program, agreed with the timeline with some caveats. Within five years, he said, every country could have access to the equivalent of an armed UAV, like General Atomics' Predator, which fires Hellfire missiles. He suggested five to 10 years as a more appropriate date for the global spread of heavier, long-range "hunter-killer" aircraft, like the MQ-9 Reaper. "It's fair to say that the U.S. is leading now in the state of the art on the high end [UAVs]" such as the RQ-170.

"Any country that has weaponized any aircraft will be able to weaponize a UAV," said Mary Cummings, Duke University professor and former Navy fighter pilot, in a note of cautious agreement. "While I agree that within 10 years weaponized drones could be part of the inventory of most countries, I think it is premature to say that they will. . . . Such endeavors are expensive [and] require larger UAVs with the payload and range capable of carrying the additional weight, which means they require substantial sophistication in terms of the ground control station."

Not every country needs to develop an armed UAV program to acquire weaponized drones within a decade. China recently announced that it would be exporting to Saudi Arabia its Wing Loong, a Predator knock-off, a development that heralds the further roboticization of conflict in the Middle East, according to Peter Singer, Brookings fellow and author of *Wired For War: The Robotics Revolution and Conflict in the 21st Century*. "You could soon have U.S. and Chinese made drones striking in the same region," he noted.

Singer cautions that while the U.S. may be trying to wean itself off of armed UAV technology, many more countries are quickly becoming hooked. "What was once viewed as science fiction, and abnormal, is now normal . . . Nations in NATO that said they would never buy drones, and then said they would never use armed drones, are now saying, 'Actually, we're going to buy them.' We've seen the U.K., France, and Italy go down that pathway. The other NATO states are right behind," Singer told *Defense One*.

Experts suggest its time the U.S. embrace the inevitable and put weaponized drone technology into the hands of additional allies

---

Virtually any country, organization, or individual could employ low-tech tactics to "weaponize" drones right now. "Not everything is going to be Predator class," said Singer. "You've got a fuzzy line between cruise missiles and drones moving forward. There will be high-end expensive ones and low-end cheaper ones." The recent use of drone surveillance and even the reported deployment of booby-trapped drones by Hezbollah, Singer said, are examples of do-it-yourself killer UAVs that will permeate the skies in the decade ahead—though more likely in the skies local to their host nation and not over American cities. "Not every nation is going to be able to carry out global strikes," he said.

Weaponized Drones Are Inevitable: Embrace It

So, what option does that leave U.S. policy makers wanting to govern the spread of this technology? Virtually none, say experts. "You're too late," said Sharkey, matter-of-factly.

Other experts suggest that its time the U.S. embrace the inevitable and put weaponized drone technology into the hands of additional allies. The U.S. has been relatively constrained in its willingness to sell armed drones, exporting weaponized UAV technology only to the United Kingdom, according to a recent white paper, by Brannen for CSIS. In July 2013, Congress approved the sale of up to 16 MQ-9 Reaper UAVs to France, but these would be unarmed.

"If France had possessed and used armed UAVs . . . when it intervened in Mali to fight the jihadist insurgency Ansar Dine—or if the United States had operated them in support or otherwise passed on its capabilities—France would have been helped considerably. Ansar Dine has no air defenses to counter such a UAV threat," note the authors of the RAND report.

In his paper, Brennan makes the same point more forcefully. "In the midst of this growing global interest, the United States has chosen to indefinitely put on hold sales of its most capable [unmanned aerial system] to many of its allies and partners, which has led these countries to seek other suppliers or to begin efforts to indigenously produce the systems," he writes. "Continued indecision by the United States regarding export of this technology will not prevent the spread of these systems."

The Missile Technology Control Regime, or MTCR, is probably the most important piece of international policy that limits the exchange of drones and is a big reason why more countries don't have weaponized drone technology. But China never signed onto it. The best way to insure that U.S. armed drones and those of our allies can operate together is to reconsider the way MTCR should apply to drones, Brannen writes.

"U.S. export is unlikely to undermine the MTCR, which faces a larger set of challenges in preventing the proliferation of ballistic and cruise missiles, as well as addressing more problematic [unmanned]-cruise missile hybrids such as so-called loitering munitions (e.g., the Israeli-made Harop)," he writes.

Weaponized, Yes. Weaponized and autonomous? Maybe.

The biggest technology challenge in drone development also promises the biggest reward in terms of cost savings and functionality: full autonomy. The military is interested in drones that can do more taking off, landing and shooting on their own. UAVs have limited ability to guide themselves and the development of fully autonomous drones is years away. But some recent breakthroughs are beginning to bear fruit. The experimental X-47B, a sizable drone that can fly off of aircraft carriers, "demonstrated that some discrete tasks that are considered extremely difficult when performed by humans can be mastered by machines with relative ease," Brannen notes.

Less impressed, Sharkey said the U.S. still has time to rethink its drone future. "Don't go to the next step. Don't make them fully autonomous. That will proliferate just as quickly and then you are really going to be sunk."

Others, including Singer, disagreed. "As you talk about this moving forward, the drones that are sold and used are remotely piloted to be more and more autonomous. As the technology becomes more advanced it becomes easier for people to use. To fly a Predator, you used to need to be a pilot," he said.

"The field of autonomy is going to continue to advance regardless of what happens in the military side."

4 DARPA Projects That Could Change the World

DARPA director Arati Prabhakar gives a preview of four of the military's mad science projects that could change the way we live.

Forty years ago, a group of researchers with military money set out to test the wacky idea of making computers talk to one another in a new way, using digital information packets that could be traded among multiple machines rather than telephonic, point-to-point circuit relays. The project, called ARPANET, went on to fundamentally change life on Earth under its more common name, the Internet.

Today, the agency that bankrolled the Internet is called the Defense Advanced Research Projects Agency, or DARPA, which boasts a rising budget of nearly $3 billion split across 250 programs. They all have national security implications but, like the Internet, much of what DARPA funds can be commercialized, spread and potentially change civilian life in big ways that its originators didn't conceive.

What's DARPA working on lately that could be Internet big? Last week at the Atlantic Council, DARPA director Arati

Prabhakar declined to name names. Like a good mutual fund manager, she said that her job was to "manage risk through diversity" in her portfolio. But the technologies that she highlighted in her recent testimony (PDF) to the Senate Appropriations Committee look like a list of insider favorites. Many have received much less public attention than DARPA's flashier robot initiatives.

Here are four of DARPA's potential next big things:

1. Atomic GPS

The Global Positioning System, or GPS, which DARPA had an important but limited role in developing, is a great tool but maintaining it as a satellite system is increasingly costly. A modern GPS satellite can run into the range of $223 million, which is one reason why the Air Force recently scaled back its procurement.

DARPA doesn't have an explicit program to replace GPS, but the DARPA-funded chip-scale combinatorial atomic navigation, or C-SCAN, and Quantum Assisted Sensing, or QuASAR, initiatives explore a field of research with big relevance here: the use of atomic physics for much better sensing. If you can measure or understand how the Earth's magnetic field acceleration and position is Effecting individual atoms (reduced in temperature), you can navigate without a satellite. In fact, you can achieve geo-location awareness that could be 1,000 times more accurate than any system currently in existence, say researchers.

The British military is investing millions of pounds in a similar technology. Researchers associated with the project forecast that they will have a prototype ready within five years.

The upshot for quantum navigation for any military is obvious. It arms them with better and more reliable situational awareness for soldiers and equipment and better flying for missiles. Perhaps, more importantly, a drone with a quantum compass wouldn't require satellite navigation, which would make it much easier to fly and less hackable.

The big benefit for everybody else? Future devices that understand where they are in relation to one another and their physical world won't need to rely on an expensive satellite infrastructure to work. That means having more capable and cheaper devices with geo-location capability, with the potential to improve everything from real-time, location-based searches to self-driving cars and those anticipated pizza delivery drones.

The most important civilian use for quantum GPS could be privacy. Your phone won't have to get signals from space anymore to tell you where you are. It would know with atomic certainty. That could make your phone less hackable and, perhaps, allow you to keep more information out of the hands of your carrier and the NSA.

2. Terehertz Frequency Electronics and Meta-Materials

The area of the electromagnetic spectrum between microwave, which we use for cell phones, and infrared, is the Terehertz range. Today, it's a ghost town, but if scientists can figure out how to harness it, we could open up a vast frontier of devices that don't compete against others for spectrum access. That would be a strategic advantage in a time when more military devices use the same electromagnetic spectrum space.

Research into THz electronics has applications in the construction of so-called metamaterials, which would lend themselves to use in cloaking for jets and equipment and even, perhaps, invisibility.

On the civilian side, because THz radiation, unlike X-ray radiation, is non-invasive, metamaterial smart clothes made with small THz sensors would allow for far faster and more precise detection of chemical changes in the body, which could indicate changes in health states. There's the future doctor in your pocket.

3. A Virus Shield for the Internet of Things

CISCO systems has forecast 50 billion interconnected devices will inhabit the world by the year 2020, or everything from appliances to streets, pipes and utilities through supervisory command and control systems. All of that physical and digital interconnection is now known as the Internet of Things.

The High Assurance Cyber Military Systems program, or HACMS, which DARPA announced in 2012, is trying to patch the security vulnerabilities that could pervade the Internet of Things. The agency wants to make sure that military vehicles, medical equipment and, yes, even drones can't be hacked into from the outside. In the future, some of the software tools that emerge from the HACMS program could be what keeps the civilian Internet of Things operating safely. This breakthrough won't be as conspicuous as the Internet itself. But you will know its influence by what does not happen because of it—namely, a deadly industrial accident resulting from a catastrophic cyber-security breach. (See: Stuxnet.)

This breakthrough won't be as conspicuous as the internet itself. But you will know its influence by what does not happen because of it.

Without better security, many experts believe the Internet of things will never reach its full potential. In a recent survey by the Pew Internet and American Life Project about the future of physical and digital interconnection, Internet pioneer Vint Cerf, who was instrumental in the success of ARPANET, said that in order for the Internet of things to really revolutionize the way we live it must be secure.

"Barriers to the Internet of Things include failure to achieve sufficient standardization and security," he said. HACMS could provide the seeds for future security protocols, allowing the Internet of things to get off the ground.

4. Rapid Threat Assessment

The Rapid Threat Assessment, or RTA, program wants to speed up by orders of magnitude how quickly researchers can figure out how diseases or agents work to kill humans. Instead of months or years, DARPA wants to enable researchers to "within 30 days of exposure to a human cell, map the complete molecular mechanism through which a threat agent alters cellular processes," Prabhakar said in her testimony. "This would give researchers the framework with which to develop medical countermeasures and mitigate threats."

How is that useful right now? In the short term, this is another research area notable primarily for what doesn't happen after it hits, namely pandemics. It took years and a lot of money to figure out that H5N1 bird flu became much more contagious with the presence of an amino acid in a specific position. That's what enabled it to live in mammalian lungs and, thus, potentially be spread by humans via coughing and sneezing. Knowing this secret earlier would have prevented a great deal of death.

In the decades ahead, the biggest contribution of the program may be fundamental changes in future drug discovery. "If successful, RTA could shift the cost-benefit trade space of using chemical or biological weapons against U.S. forces and could also apply to drug development to combat emerging diseases," Prabhakar said.

Before any of these four reach Internet-level success, DARPA faces a big challenge despite its continued popularity, in that they remain a government agency at a time when change moves faster than the U.S. government understands.

"We move at a pace measured in decades in an environment that changes every year," Prabhaka said, at the Atlantic Council. In terms of the emerging technology she's most concerned about, it's the unknown unknowns, the U.S. military's "ability to handle this vast changing landscape."

The agency that helped to bring about the Internet, Siri, and GPS will always enjoy a certain cachet, warranted or not. But the world moves faster than even DARPA can keep up. Perhaps the most important thing that DARPA can create in the years ahead is manageable expectations.

How Big Data Could Track the Next Snowden

The U.S. wants intelligence workers put into a big data cloud they can monitor, and it just might work.

National Intelligence Director James Clapper, at a February 11 Senate Armed Services Committee hearing, asserted (again) that malevolent insiders with access to top secret material, like Edward Snowden, constituted a top threat to our nation's national security. The lawmakers agreed and pressed Clapper to explain how he was changing the practices within his office and across the intelligence community to prevent another Snowden-scale data breach. One key step that Clapper outlined: our nation's top intelligence folks will become subject to much more surveillance in the future.

Clapper said he wanted to put more intelligence community communication into a single, massive (enterprise-sized) cloud environment in order to, as he described it, "take advantage of cloud computing and the necessary security enhancements" therein. There are plenty of good reasons for any department head to want that, but chief among them for Clapper is that moving to the cloud will allow monitors to better "tag the data, [and] tag the people, so that you can monitor where the data is and who has access to it on a real-time basis."

Anticipating insider threat behavior is a problem that governments have been wrestling with since the first act of state treason. But the current round of research within the United States goes back before Snowden to Army Pfc. Bradley (now Chelsea) Manning's 2010 arrest for passing top-secret files to Wikileaks. Manning's disclosure prompted President Obama to issue Executive Order 13587, mandating the creation of an insider threat task force.

Mark Nehmer, associate deputy director of cybersecurity and counterintelligence for the Defense Department, said that a possible insider threat signal could include anything from a change in marital status to a trip abroad to unusual online activity. One or two of these signals in isolation don't serve effectively as a red flag, but observed in the context of one another, patterns can emerge.

"Think of statistics and human behavior and think about correlating past and future behavior, that's the future of insider threat, I believe," he said, at Nextgov's Cybersecurity Series in Washington on Tuesday.

Nehmer and several colleagues have offered DOD various recommendations for curing the threat of an insider attack. These include ensuring that more people with top secret clearance have at least one person sign off on work assignments involving sensitive information; stricter punishments for minor infractions involving data loss, glitches, and "spillage"; mandating that all software fixes comply with a single new standard; and the creation of a joint information environment (JIE) allowing all of the services to share information in one secure cloud setting and far more effective monitoring of employee communication and activity.

"We have all these titanium silos of excellence and we replicate all these services and people. That's not getting us very far," Nehmer said, regarding the importance of the JIE. "We need to build an architecture so that a whole department can use enterprise services." The Pentagon already has a JIE in place for e-mail said Nehmer. This will be extended across other military branches soon.

The question becomes, what are the Snowden-like signals to watch for in this new, more transparent environment?

Few people involved in insider threat programs in Washington are eager to talk about what makes a potential traitor conspicuous, but several interesting findings have been published out of Palo Alto, California.

Oliver Brdiczka, a researcher at PARC, and several of his colleagues have set up a number of experiments to observe potential insider threat behavior in closed online environments. In the first of these [PDF], Brdiczka looked at the massively multiplayer online game *World of Warcraft*. The game, which allows users to build characters, join large organizations called guilds, and go on missions and assignments, has been in the news a bit recently after the Snowden leaks revealed that the NSA had been listening in on chat room conversations between *World of Warcraft* players in the hopes of catching potential terrorists.

Brdiczka and his colleagues were after a more ambitious prize—a scientific understanding of how insider threats actually develop in realtime. Players hunting dragons and orcs wind up collaborating with team mates, applying for positions and earning rewards in somewhat the same way that work teams go about attacking big projects. The game thus served as a suitable proxy for a real world work environment. A player who quits her guild has the potential to damage it, perhaps even absconding with goods in much the same way that Edward Snowden defected with flashdrives of classified information. In Brdiczka's experiment, quitting served as a useful stand in for insider-threat behavior.

The researchers found volunteers, looked at each subject's social network presence, and made each fill out a personality survey. They then carefully observed how the players approached the game play, how they acquired items, fought monsters, interacted with one another and performed dozens of other tasks. Result: The researchers found that they could predict who was going to quit in six months with an accuracy rate of 89 percent.

Shortly after the test, Brdiczka and his colleagues expanded the research [PDF] to the real world. They looked to determine if e-mail patterns could predict quitting (attrition) and began by examining two data sets, a small company of 43 employees and a large company of 3,600, for a period of about 20 weeks.

They measured everything from the frequency of e-mail to the time of day it was sent, to whether the e-mail had attachments or came as a forward. They even taught a computer program to categorize the tone in the messages as being positive or negative. In the end, the results of the experiment were a bit less conclusive than the *World of Warcraft* study. They were able to predict quitting with about 60 percent accuracy.

But they did find some important clues that can predict potential insider threat behavior, and they were counterintuitive. The team had expected that the strongest signal of a quitting event would be e-mails with a highly negative tone, full of spit and spite. In fact, the best attrition symptom was fewer e-mails fewer messages after hours, fewer attachments, fewer words all together.

The Snowden in your office is the guy going dark.

Brdiczka's work is currently being funded by a grant from the Defense Advanced Research Projects Agency, or DARPA. The goal of the Anomaly Detection at Multiple Scales, or ADAMS, program is to "create, adapt, and apply technology to the problem of anomaly characterization and detection in massive data sets. . . . The focus is on malevolent insiders that started out as 'good guys.' The specific goal of ADAMS is to detect anomalous behaviors before or shortly after they turn."

Of course, polls indicate public ambivalence as to whether Edward Snowden is a malevolent insider, a "good guy," or something else entirely. Also, varying bodies have differing definitions of what constitutes an insider in a military context. From a purely technological perspective, these aren't critical points to the functioning of an insider threat computer model. Brdiczka told me that, with some small modification to account for different feature sets, the model could scale up to apply to virtually any domain where online social interaction can be observed and measured. That includes the JIE that the Pentagon wants to build across all service branches, or, for that matter, all of Facebook.

Congratulations. You're an insider now.

The Military is Planning for Climate Change

While the rest of the world continues to debate climate change, the Pentagon has long been preparing for a more unstable environment.

The White House released its National Climate Assessment this May, a 1,100 page document by more than 300 experts examining the effects of man-made climate change on various aspects of American life. While 97 percent of climate scientists agree that climate change is occurring and that human factors are largely the cause, public debate persists around climate change, humanity's role in it, and whether or not its effects will be as severe as the Obama administration and the scientific community are projecting.

But there's little debate over climate change at the Pentagon, where the realities of temperature increases are now a part of everyday planning.

"We have to be concerned about all of the global impacts [of climate change], including here at home, where the Defense Department does have a mission in supporting civil authorities in the event of natural disasters. We have to be concerned about all of it," Sharon Burke, Assistant Secretary of Defense for Operational Energy Plans and Programs told *Defense One*.

"We have to be pragmatic about it," Burke said. "The question is, how is this changing facts on the ground? If we're seeing salt water intrusion at an aquifer at a base in North Carolina, we have to deal with it."

The report's broadest points mirror those of the 2013 Intergovernmental Panel on Climate Change: There will be a rise in global temperature that varies significantly depending on how much more CO_2 is released into the atmosphere in the coming decades. Projections vary from a few degrees' rise to more than 10 degrees by the year 2100. The hottest days of the year would be as much as 15 degrees hotter on average. Sea levels could rise by as much as four feet.

Not everyone agrees with the dire assessment. Paul Knappenberger and Patrick Michael of the CATO Institute were quick to dismiss the report as "biased toward pessimism." "The report overly focuses on the supposed negative impacts from climate change while largely dismissing or ignoring the positives from climate change," they said.

"I'm not seeing intransigence [on the issue] in the Pentagon," retired Army Brig. Gen. John Adams told *Defense One*. Adams is an advisor to the Center for Climate Security, which looks at the intersection of climate change and national security. 'The Pentagon is seeing this as a problem. Instability is accelerating. Climate change is an accelerator of instability. The Pentagon understands that. They're looking at what sorts of force structures and equipment they're going to need to have available to deal with increasing instability that will be most effected by climate change."

Adams, who lives in Pensacola, Fl., spoke specifically about how climate change is influencing military decision-making near him. "We have major installations in this area. We predict the sea level will rise here. That means that Navy ship berths will have to change, because they're not floating docks, they're built into the land. And when the sea level rises above the point where it's safe to berth a Navy ship, then you have to change the berthing structure . . . so climate change will have an effect on our basing structures."

Climate change will also alter the way the military acquires equipment, Adams said. "If we're going to find ourselves operating in littoral areas that are affected by climate change, where the instability will be most accelerated by climate change, we have to have the force structure to be able to operate."

The White House report makes note of the changing arctic as a future destination for increased U.S. naval activity. "With sea ice receding in the Arctic as a result of rising temperatures, global shipping patterns are already changing and will continue to considerably in the decades to come."

It's also a concern that Defense Secretary Chuck Hagel reiterated in a major speech in Chicago in May. "The melting of gigantic ice caps presents possibilities for the opening of new sea lanes and the exploration for natural resources, energy, and commerce. The Defense Department is bolstering its engagement in the Arctic and looking at what capabilities we need to operate there in the future," he said at the Chicago Council on Global Affairs.

Adams says "there will be new competitors for that route. The United States has a big role to play in any of the sea lanes."

Climate change is already influencing the military mission, Burke said, as the U.S. builds up its military-to-military relationships around the world. "We had 14,000 people who deployed to support [relief] efforts for Hurricane Sandy. We also had a lot of people who deployed to support relief efforts for the typhoon in the Philippines. We're already seeing increased demands on our time," she said.

While the military faces the effects of climate change head on, it also contributes to the problem. In 2013, the Defense Department burned more than 12 million gallons of oil a day. But the department has also offered some potential solutions to military dependence on fossil fuels. The Office of Naval Research recently announced the successful creation of a synthetic fuel from seawater. But much of the innovation taking place to green the military is far more subtle. DOD plans to invest $1.7 billion in fiscal year 2015 on initiatives to improve energy efficiency and energy performance, Burke said.

Climate and weather has been part of the military conversation since the dawn of armies, but the current conversation between the Obama administration and the military is rooted in the 2010 Quadrennial Defense Review, which observed: "DOD will need to adjust to the impacts of climate change on our facilities and military capabilities. . . . While climate change alone does not cause conflict, it may act as an accelerant of instability or conflict, placing a burden to respond on civilian institutions and militaries around the world. In addition, extreme weather events may lead to increased demands for defense support to civil authorities for humanitarian assistance or disaster response both within the United States and overseas."

The next National Climate Assessment is due within four years and will look squarely at the national security implications of climate change. "Right now everyone is looking at health, environment, and economy and how those things fit together and those are really important. But we also feel it's a good time to look specifically at security," Burke said. "I do think there's a dialogue between the scientists, engineers, and policymakers to have actionable information. That's a conversation that needs to deepen."

The Most Secure E-mail in the Universe

Here's how you will one day be able to send invisible messages on your future quantum cell phone.

Say you wanted to send an e-mail more secure than any message that had ever been transmitted in human history, a message with *absolutely* no chance of being intercepted. How would you do it?

You may have encrypted your message according to the highest standards, but encryption doesn't guarantee secrecy. The fact that you sent it is still detectable. An intercepting party in possession of just a few clues such as your identity, the receiver's identify, the time of the message, surrounding incidents and the like can infer a great deal about the content of the message in the same way that the NSA can use your metadata to make inferences about your personality. You need to conceal not just what's in the message but its very existence.

The answer? Make your message literally impossible to detect. A team of researchers from the University of Massachusetts at Amherst and Raytheon BBN Technologies led by Boulat A. Bash have created a method for doing just that, cloaking electronic communications so that the communication can't be seen. They explain it in a paper titled Covert Optical Communication.

The question of exactly how secure any communication can be is of no small relevance either to national security watchers worried about losing secrets or to a public increasingly concerned about governmental invasion of digital privacy. The breakthrough shows that it is possible to send a message that can't be intercepted, no matter how determined the National Security Agency is to intercept it.

The practice of embedding secret messages in computer files is called digital steganography. Steganography has been around since the days of ancient Greece. The term simply refers to the deliberate hiding of a message within a message. Dissidents in Laos, the United Arab Emirates, Saudi Arabia, and especially China use *digital* steganography to send secret messages. But these methods are far from fully secure.

Today, we send a lot of messages over fiber-optic cable, essentially using light as a communications medium. It's instant and cheap but someone monitoring the photons passing through those cables can detect when one party is sending a message to another (it is just *light*, after all.) Photon detectors are extremely accurate, able to detect single photons passing between two points, but they aren't perfect and sometimes they read false positives. Bash's technique makes use of that flaw using pulse position modulation—and it's not much more complicated than Morse code.

Take a unit of time, like a second, and chop it up into smaller parts that vary in size, one-fourth, one-eighth, and so on. Then assign each band a corresponding symbol. There's your code. You can transfer a photon-based message over a fiber-optic cable that corresponds to the code and—so long as the message sender and the receiver of the message both have the key to the code—then each can read the message.

Pulse position modulation is not new. The formula that Bash and his colleagues created takes this process to the next step rendering it far more useful. It solves for how many bits of message a sender can pack into a certain interval of time in order for the message to always appear like background noise to any detector currently in existence.

In addition to light-based communication, the formula would render undetectable cell phone-based text messages. Cell phones use microwaves to send and receive data, which is a very noisy area of the electromagnetic spectrum. More noise is good in Bash's communication-concealing scheme in the same way that it's easier to hide in dense jungle foliage than it is in open desert.

Unfortunately, you and the person you are sharing the message with must agree in advance on the code and exchange it, which presents something of an obstacle.

While there is no way to share a secret code in an invisible e-mail there is a way to share it in an encrypted e-mail that would destroy itself if viewed by an outsider. Using quantum encryption, you could send a message between two parties containing the deciphering key and that message, while detectable, would also be unhackable.

University of Oxford quantum physicist Artur Ekert calls quantum encryption the ultimate physical limits of privacy. Other key distribution schemes such as the Diffie Hellman scheme, rely on the difficulty of mathematical problems to work, whereas quantum encryption does not. According to Heisenberg's uncertainty principle, objects viewed on the atomically small quantum scale change their behavior when viewed. Quantum encryption offers the possibility of a message so secure that any attempt to read it without authorization will destroy it, not because of some programmer's whim but because of the way subatomic particles operate.

"For quantum cryptography we need 'only' to transit quantum particles over a certain distance, and this is relatively easy. Quantum cryptography has been demonstrated in practice and there are even companies that can sell it to you," Ekert told *Defense One*.

Quantum cryptography and Bash's pulse position modulation technique are two very different animals. Cryptography makes messages difficult to decipher and pulse position modulation cloaks them so that they can't be detected. But Bash's method could go hand-in-hand with something like quantum key distribution, which a message sender would use in advance to share the key code. That, in turn, would be used in the future for covert communication.

Here's what the most secure electronic message exchange in the history of humanity would look like: You would first exchange the code key in a quantum encrypted message, and then, when the receiver and the sender both had the code, they could exchange an invisible—thus perfectly secure—message. A third party might be able to detect that two parties had exchanged a single message that had been quantum encrypted, containing the key code, but that third party wouldn't be able to see any of the exchanges that passed after that or open the key code message.

The breakthrough shows that it is possible to send a message that can't be intercepted, no matter how determined the national security agency is to intercept it.

Right now, quantum encryption is not the sort of service you can use on your iPhone or some common device. It requires dedicated devices and a connection between two points. But that will change, according to Ekert. "We will probably demonstrate device independent quantum crypto soon in the labs, but it will take some time before we turn them into a commercial proposition," he said.

How soon? Perhaps sooner than many think. Back in August, members of a team from the University of Bristol published a paper outlining ideas for how to do it.

Secure? Yes. Practical for all communication? No. Bash's method is not one you would use for everything. The laws of physics that make photon cloaking possible impose a stingy limit on the size of the message that is transferable over that medium, limited to tens to hundreds of bits of per second according their paper. That's enough space to send yes or no signals or small values, but sending an entire Word document at that rate would take a very long time.

The NSA is spending nearly $80 million on a program called Penetrating Hard Targets to build a quantum computer to de-encrypt the most expertly encoded communications, according to *The Washington Post*. The government has been funding quantum computer research for more than a decade to develop techniques for super hacking. So far, the record suggests that they have little to show for their efforts.

"Purely on numbers, the agency would appear to be lagging behind major labs such as the Institute for Experimental Physics at the University of Innsbruck in Austria," noted Jon Cartwright in a recent piece for *Physics World*.

Despite the agency's reputation for digital omnipresence, their real capabilities are far from godlike.

"The recent Snowden revelations confirm something we've long suspected: NSA does not really have a supercomputer that can break all of our standard cryptography. What they've resorted to is colluding with equipment manufacturers to include 'back doors' in encryption products and software," Johns Hopkins University cryptology expert Matthew Green told *Defense One,* referring to the recent revelations that the NSA had given security industry provider RSA multiple encryption tools. "All of this discussion about quantum crypto is moot if someone puts a back door into the hardware responsible for performing the encryption."

For the majority of the public, the best way to secure your personal e-mail is to use some commonly available tools, Green said.

"Our current practical encryption schemes are all extremely secure, and there's no reason to believe that your communications aren't confidential—provided you're using encryption and it's properly implemented," he said. "In theory, these schemes can be broken, but the computational effort to do it is far beyond what humans will ever muster."

Critical Thinking

1. Use an example to illustrate why the "upshot for quantum navigation for any military is obvious."
2. Is it a practical suggestion that "more people with top secret clearance" have at least one person sign off on work assignments involving sensitive information? Why or why not?
3. Which of the public's ambivalent assessments of Edward Snowden is most appropriate: he is a malevolent insider, a "good guy," or something else entirely? Explain.

Internet References

engadget: "Google tests the performance limits of D-Wave's quantum computers"

    www.engadget.com/2014/01/20/google-tests-the-performace-limits-of-d-wave-quantum-computers

International Committee of the Red Cross: "The use of armed drones must comply with laws"

    www.icrc.org/eng/resources/documents/interview/2013/05-10-drone-weapons-ihl.htm

New York Times: "Pentagon Signals Security Risks of Climate Change"

    www.nytimes.com/2014/10/14/us/pentagon-says-global-warming-presents-immediate-security-threat.html?_r=0

Popular Science: "DARPA To Scientists: Find A Better Way To Study Chemical Weapons"

    www.popsci.com/technology/article/2013-05/darpa-scientists-find-better-way-to-study-chemical-weapons

RT: "Pentagon increasing surveillance to prevent another Snowden-style leak"

    http://rt.com/usa/188824-pentagon-intelligence-monitoring-leak

PATRICK TUCKER is technology editor for *Defense One.* He's also the author of *The Naked Future: What Happens in a World That Anticipates Your Every Move?* (Current, 2014). Previously, Tucker was deputy editor for *The Futurist,* where he served for nine years. Tucker's writing on emerging technology also has appeared in *Slate, The Sun, MIT Technology Review, Wilson Quarterly, The American Legion Magazine, BBC News Magazine* and *Utne Reader* among other publications.

Prepared by: Liz Friedman, *DePaul University* and
Daniel Mittleman, *DePaul University*

Article

The Snowden Effect: Privacy Is Good for Business

Laura Hautala

Learning Outcomes

After reading this article, you will be able to:

- Understand the inherent conflicts between free speech and government policing of online speech to protect its citizens.

- Be able to articulate what Edward Snowden did and offer an informed opinion as to whether he was right in doing it.

- Be able to discuss the free speech implications of government monitoring of online political speech. Be able to offer an informed opinion as to whether the benefits of government monitoring of this speech outweigh the costs.

O n June 6, 2013, Edward Snowden—holed up in a Hong Kong hotel room with two Guardian reporters and a filmmaker—told the world about a secret surveillance program that let the US National Security Agency grab people's emails, video chats, photos, and documents through some of the world's biggest tech companies.

That program was called Prism, and the journalists revealed the extent of its reach just one day after reporting that the NSA was collecting phone records in bulk from Verizon. Top-secret slides intended for NSA senior analysts—and leaked by Snowden—listed Apple, Google, Microsoft, Yahoo, AOL, Facebook and a video chat company called PalTalk as willing partners in the surveillance program. The public uproar was immediate, even as all of the companies denied giving the NSA unfettered access to such data.

All of the companies, except Microsoft and PalTalk, declined to discuss this story on the record.

Prism was just one of Snowden's many revelations, but its disclosure kicked off a crisis of confidence and conscience throughout the technology industry. In the three years since Snowden's initial leak, Apple, Google, Microsoft, Facebook, and Yahoo have become some of the biggest advocates of consumer privacy. They've beefed up encryption and other safeguards in their products and services. A few have challenged the US government in courts—and in the court of public opinion—in the debate over national security and personal privacy.

"These companies are now engaged in a genuine commitment to demonstrate that they're willing to protect privacy even against the US government," says Glenn Greenwald, who broke the Snowden story while a reporter for the Guardian. "That has really altered the relationship between the US government and these tech companies, and made it much, much harder to spy."

That debate reached a crescendo early this year when Apple resisted a court order forcing it to write software that would have circumvented encryption built into an iPhone 5C used by a terrorist in San Bernardino, California. Such software "would be the equivalent of a master key, capable of opening hundreds of millions of locks—from restaurants and banks to stores and homes," CEO Tim Cook wrote in an open letter in February to customers. "No reasonable person would find that acceptable."

Good for business

Since 2013, Snowden has been called everything from a whistleblower and patriot to a criminal and traitor.

That characterization seems to be fluid. Take former US Attorney General Eric Holder. He oversaw the Department of Justice when it unsealed charges against Snowden on two counts of violating the Espionage Act of 1917 and theft of government property.

But earlier this week, Holder told political commentator David Axelrod he thought Snowden had performed a "public service by raising the debate that we engaged in and by the changes that we made." That said, Holder also believes that Snowden should return from his self-imposed exile in Russia to stand trial for his actions.

"I think there has to be a consequence for what he has done," Holder says. "But I think in deciding what an appropriate sentence should be, I think a judge could take into account the usefulness of having had that national debate."

Holder's softening perspective shows just how much the debate colors our worldview.

Consider the tech giants' public stance on privacy, which coincidentally (or not) happens to be good for business, says Greenwald. He believes they're "petrified" of being seen as NSA collaborators and of losing customers to rivals based outside the US.

Yahoo provided the first glimpse of pushback against surveillance demands. As the public uproar began in 2013, company higher-ups immediately saw the value of telling the public another story: Yahoo had its customers' backs. They even had proof: The company had already fought and lost a constitutional challenge to the law that authorizes Prism's collection of user data.

In 2007, the online media portal and email service fought a court order under Section 702 of the Foreign Intelligence Surveillance Act Amendments Act that compelled it to disclose the content of email and other communications so long as 51 percent of the people targeted were foreign.

A week after Snowden spilled the beans on Prism, Yahoo filed a request to unseal documents from that challenge. Why the rush to go public? To make sure Yahoo's 225 million monthly email users didn't lose their trust in the company, says Chris Madsen, Yahoo's assistant general counsel.

Or put another way, to protect business. All of the other companies named as Prism participants faced the same issue.

"A failure to do that in this particular industry means a significant loss in market share," Madsen says candidly.

Battle lines

But losing customers wasn't these companies' only concern. The tech industry sincerely wants to push back, says Snowden's attorney, Ben Wizner of the American Civil Liberties Union. That's because Snowden disclosed the frightening power of the NSA's other technology efforts. These include the Muscular program, which exploited weak points in Yahoo's and Google's data centers to scoop up unencrypted data, and Bullrun, which used superfast computers to decipher encrypted emails and documents.

"There was material in the Snowden disclosures that was genuinely shocking," Wizner says. "That radicalized a lot of people in the technology community."

Encryption became the tech industry's best defense in its advocacy for consumer privacy.

Apple put itself at the vanguard of that battle, upgrading its Mac OS and iOS mobile software with stronger encryption. It also showed a very public willingness to defy the FBI and courts that demanded Apple create backdoors into its most important product.

"When the FBI has requested data that's in our possession, we have provided it," Cook wrote in an open letter to customers on February 16. "Apple complies with valid subpoenas and search warrants. . . . We have also made Apple engineers available to advise the FBI, and we've offered our best ideas on a number of investigative options at their disposal."

But the company won't bend on encryption, according to Cook, signaling his willingness to challenge the FBI in front of a federal judge. In March, more than 40 top tech companies signed amicus briefs supporting Apple as it prepared to face the government in a court case that, ultimately, never took place. Then last month, Apple rehired crypto expert Jon Callas, who co-founded PGP (Pretty Good Privacy), Silent Circle and Blackphone. Callas had worked for Apple in the 1990s and again between 2009 and 2011.

Google is fighting its own encryption battle in several undecided court cases related to phones running its Android mobile software.

That means we can expect governments to escalate their efforts to get around encryption, says Greenwald. "It's going to be like an arms race," he says. As governments develop new tools for spying, "private companies and privacy activists [will try] to use math to build a wall of numbers, essentially, around people's communication."

That's how it should be, says Denelle Dixon-Thayer, chief legal and business officer at Mozilla, which coordinates the development of the Firefox open-source web browser.

Governments spy, she says. "It's not our job to make that easy for them."

The great debate

Snowden's revelations did more than pit the tech industry against government and law enforcement, and spotlight the warring demands of personal privacy and national security.

Ironically, even unexpectedly, it also made the US government more transparent about its efforts. Less than two months after those first disclosures in 2013, the office of the Director of National Intelligence declassified documents explaining the government's bulk collection of US phone records.

In March 2014, President Barack Obama said that the government should stop acquiring phone data in bulk from the phone companies. That June, the Director of National Intelligence released its first annual transparency report, revealing more than 1,760 court orders to collect personal data.

In November 2015, five public advocates, all private attorneys with expertise in privacy law, began advising the courts on ways to minimize the impact of foreign surveillance on people in the US.

And last month, Reuters reported Congress no longer supported draft legislation that would have let judges force tech companies to help law enforcement crack encrypted data.

None of this means the US and other governments will end their widespread surveillance. It does, however, signal a degree of openness in telling the public how often the US goes after that data.

"Government officials have been more willing to engage in a conversation," says Margaret Nagle, Yahoo's head of US government affairs. "That has made it increasingly important that providers engage in that conversation as well."

It's a beginning.

Snowden says his goal wasn't to personally end surveillance. It was to alert people that surveillance was actually happening.

"The public needs to decide whether these programs and policies are right or wrong," Snowden says in a video published by the Guardian in June 2013. "This is the truth. This is what's happening. You should decide whether we should be doing this."

For now, the tech industry has become our proxy in that debate.

Critical Thinking

1. To what extent should the government monitor free speech activities on the Internet? When, if ever, should the government attempt to identify anonymous participants engaging in political speech?

2. Were Edward Snowden actions in publicizing classified materials showing the US Government was spying on Americans and allied nations a service or disservice? Should he be awarded or condemned for his actions?

3. Under what circumstances, and with what protections for individuals, should the US government be able to use cyber tools to spy on American citizens?

Internet References

Edward Snowden on Cyber Warfare [Video]
    https://goo.gl/JhvaAU
The Most Wanted Man in the World
    https://goo.gl/ogWdpl
The Snowden Effect: 8 Things That Happened Only Because Of The NSA Leaks
    https://goo.gl/2WL0EU

LAURA writes about cybersecurity and privacy.

Article

Prepared by: Liz Friedman, *DePaul University* and
Daniel Mittleman, *DePaul University*

New Study: Snowden's Disclosures about NSA Spying Had a Scary Effect on Free Speech

JEFF GUO

Learning Outcomes

After reading this article, you will be able to:

- Understand the inherent conflicts between free speech and government policing of online speech to protect its citizens.

- Articulate what Edward Snowden did and offer an informed opinion as to whether he was right in doing it.

- Discuss the free speech implications of government monitoring of online political speech. Be able to offer an informed opinion as to whether the benefits of government monitoring of this speech outweigh the costs.

I n June 2013, reporters at The Washington Post and the Guardian ran a series of stories about the U.S. government's surveillance programs. According to documents leaked by Edward Snowden, the National Security Agency was harvesting huge swaths of online traffic—far beyond what had been disclosed—and was working directly with top Internet companies to spy on certain people.

Glenn Greenwald, one of the Guardian journalists who reported the disclosures and a surveillance skeptic, argued in a 2014 TED talk that privacy is a critical feature of open society. People act differently when they know they're being watched. "Essential to what it means to be a free and fulfilled human being is to have a place that we can go and be free of the judgmental eyes of other people," he said.

Privacy advocates have argued that widespread government surveillance has had a "chilling effect"—it encourages meekness and conformity. If we think that authorities are watching our online actions, we might stop visiting certain websites or not say certain things just to avoid seeming suspicious.

The problem, though, is that it's difficult to judge the effect of government-spying programs. How do you collect all the utterances that people stopped themselves from saying? How do you count all the conversations that weren't had?

A new study provides some insight into the repercussions of the Snowden revelations, arguing that they happened so swiftly and were so high-profile that they triggered a measurable shift in the way people used the Internet.

Jonathon Penney, a PhD candidate at Oxford, analyzed Wikipedia traffic in the months before and after the NSA's spying became big news in 2013. Penney found a 20 percent decline in page views on Wikipedia articles related to terrorism, including those that mentioned "al-Qaeda," "car bomb," or "Taliban."

"You want to have informed citizens," Penney said. "If people are spooked or deterred from learning about important policy matters like terrorism and national security, this is a real threat to proper democratic debate."

Even though the NSA was supposed to target only foreigners, the immense scale of its operations caused many to worry that innocent Americans were getting caught in the dragnet. A Pew survey in 2015 showed that about 40 percent of Americans were "very" or "somewhat" concerned that the government was spying on their online activities.

The same survey showed that about 87 percent of American adults were aware of the Snowden news stories. Of those people, about a third said they had changed their Internet or phone habits as a result. For instance, 13 percent said they "avoided using certain terms" online; and 14 percent said they were having more conversations face to face instead of over the phone. The sudden, new knowledge about the surveillance programs had increased their concerns about their privacy.

Penney's research, which is forthcoming in the Berkeley Technology Law Journal, echoes the results of a similar study conducted last year on Google Search data. Alex Marthews, a privacy activist, and Catherine Tucker, a professor at MIT's business school, found that Google activity for certain keywords fell after the Snowden stories were splashed on every front page. Both in the United States and in other countries, people became reluctant to search for terrorism-related words such as "dirty bomb" or "pandemic."

Penney focused on Wikipedia pages related to sensitive topics specifically flagged by the Department of Homeland Security. In a document provided to its analysts in 2011, the DHS listed 48 terrorism terms that they should use when "monitoring social media sites." Penney collected traffic data on the English Wikipedia pages most closely related to those terms.

This chart from the paper shows how the number of views dropped after the June 2013 news articles. The amount of traffic immediately dropped and stayed low for the subsequent 14 months.

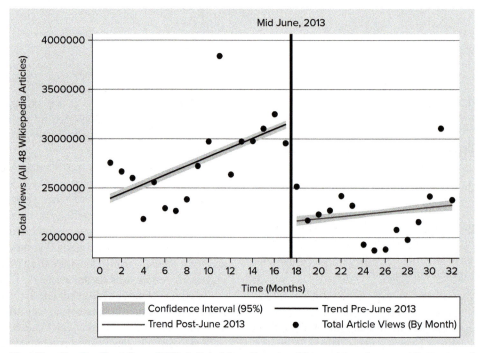

First Results: Pre/Post June 2013 Article View Trends   The sudden drop, and flatter trend or slope in the data, after June 2013 surveillance revelations consistent with a chilling effect

To be clear, this traffic drop could have come from anywhere—Penney did not track the country of origin—but the United States accounts for 43 percent of English Wikipedia traffic, more than any other country.

Penney narrowed the list to the most suspicious-sounding articles, as judged by an online survey he administered. The results became even more dramatic.

Here, in black, are the combined monthly traffic totals for the Wikipedia pages related to the 31 top words on the DHS list. In the year and a half before the Snowden revelations, traffic to these pages was rising. After June 2013, traffic not only fell immediately but continued to decline over the next dozen months.

Terrorism Articles vs. Control Group   The sudden drop and trend reversal for the terrorism-related articles is consistent with chilling effects. The security-related articles control group shows little impact.

For comparison, the chart also shows the combined page views for 25 Wikipedia pages that are security-related but not terrorism-related. These are less provocative articles containing the words "Border patrol" or "Central Intelligence Agency." There was a slight but statistically insignificant dip in traffic for these pages, which makes sense because people may not be as worried about visiting these kinds of pages.

The Wikipedia data suggest that the Snowden revelations had a noticeable impact on people's Wikipedia behaviors, says Penney. "I expected to find an immediate drop-off in June, and then people would slowly realize that nobody is going to jail for viewing Wikipedia articles, and the traffic would go back up," he said. "I was surprised to see what looks to be a longer-term impact from the revelations."

Penney has provided evidence that spying programs, once the public knows about them, cause collateral damage. It's unlikely, of course, that the patterns here were caused by actual terrorists changing their Internet habits.

Instead, the study suggests that the shift in Wikipedia traffic was the result of people who stifled their curious impulses because they didn't want to seem like they were doing anything wrong. "This is measuring regular people who are being spooked by the idea of government surveillance online," Penney said.

That's one plausible conclusion we could draw from the data. There is, however, an alternative explanation for these results.

The Snowden revelations ignited a huge debate about the NSA. Stories about government surveillance dominated the news cycle for months. Perhaps people stopped looking at terrorism-related Wikipedia articles not because the Snowden leaks made them paranoid, but because the news distracted them from their previous curiosity about terrorism.

In other words, maybe it wasn't a "chilling effect" that caused the dip in terrorism-related Wikipedia traffic—but rather the short attention spans of online audiences.

It will require more research to fully understand what happened. But even if the evidence is still being examined, chilling effects continue to occupy a prominent position in privacy debates.

In March 2015, the American Civil Liberties United filed a lawsuit in federal district court challenging the NSA's surveillance practices, with Wikipedia's parent organization as one of the eight plaintiffs. Writing with his colleague Lila Tretikov in the New York Times, Wikipedia founder Jimmy Wales accused the NSA of tracking Wikipedia users:

So imagine, now, a Wikipedia user in Egypt who wants to edit a page about government opposition or discuss it with fellow editors. If that user knows the N.S.A. is routinely combing through her contributions to Wikipedia, and possibly sharing information with her government, she will surely be less likely to add her knowledge or have that conversation, for fear of reprisal.

The result, argued Wales and Tretikov, "represents a loss for everyone who uses Wikipedia and the Internet—not just fellow editors, but hundreds of millions of readers in the United States and around the world."

In October, a judge threw out the case, declaring that the plaintiffs "have not alleged facts that plausibly establish an injury attributable to the NSA's Upstream surveillance." In other words, there wasn't enough evidence that anyone was harmed. The decision has been appealed.

Critical Thinking

1. To what extent should the government monitor free speech activities on the Internet? When, if ever, should the government attempt to identify anonymous participants engaging in political speech?

2. Were Edward Snowden actions in publicizing classified materials showing the US Government was spying on Americans and allied nations a service or disservice? Should he be awarded or condemned for his actions?

3. Under what circumstances, and with what protections for individuals, should the US government be able to use cyber tools to spy on American citizens?

Internet References

Edward Snowden on Cyber Warfare [Video]
https://goo.gl/JhvaAU

The Most Wanted Man in the World
https://goo.gl/ogWdpl

The Snowden Effect: 8 Things That Happened Only Because Of The NSA Leaks
https://goo.gl/2WL0EU

JEFF GUO is a reporter covering economics, domestic policy, and everything empirical. He's from Maryland, but outside the Beltway.

Article

Prepared by: Liz Friedman, *DePaul University* and
Daniel Mittleman, *DePaul University*

America Is 'Dropping Cyberbombs'— but How Do They Work?

Richard Forno, and Anupam Joshi

Learning Outcomes

After reading this article, you will be able to:

- Undertand the basic weapons and attacks available in a cyberwar.

- Discuss implications of war moving from a physical battlefield to a cyber battlefield (or a combination of the two).

- Discuss ethical similarities and difference of cyberwar versus physical military war.

Recently, United States Deputy Defense Secretary Robert Work publicly confirmed that the Pentagon's Cyber Command was "dropping cyberbombs," taking its ongoing battle against the Islamic State group into the online world. Other American officials, including President Barack Obama, have discussed offensive cyber activities, too.

The American public has only glimpsed the country's alleged cyberattack abilities. In 2012 The New York Times revealed the first digital weapon, the Stuxnet attack against Iran's nuclear program. In 2013, former NSA contractor Edward Snowden released a classified presidential directive outlining America's approach to conducting Internet-based warfare.

The terms "cyberbomb" and "cyberweapon" create a simplistic, if not also sensational, frame of reference for the public. Real military or intelligence cyber activities are less exaggerated but much more complex. The most basic types are off-the-shelf commercial products used by companies and security consultants to test system and network security. The most advanced are specialized proprietary systems made for exclusive—and often classified—use by the defense, intelligence, and law enforcement communities.

So what exactly are these "cyberbombs" America is "dropping" in the Middle East? The country's actual cyber capabilities are classified; we, as researchers, are limited by what has been made public. Monitoring books, reports, news events, and congressional testimony is not enough to separate fact from fiction. However, we can analyze the underlying technologies and look at the global strategic considerations of those seeking to wage cyber warfare. That work allows us to offer ideas about cyber weapons and how they might be used.

A collection of capabilities

A "cyberbomb" is not a single weapon. Rather, cyberweapons are collections of computer hardware and software, with the knowledge of their potential uses against online threats. Although frequently used against Internet targets such as websites and forums, these tools can have real-world effects, too. Cyberattacks have disrupted cellphone networks and tricked computers controlling nuclear centrifuges into functioning differently from how they report their status to human operators. A simulated attack has shown how an enemy can remotely disrupt electric power generators.

The process of identifying potential targets, selecting them and planning "cyberbomb" attacks includes not only technological experts but military strategists, researchers, policy analysts, lawyers, and others across the military-industrial complex. These groups constantly analyze technology to develop the latest cyber weapons and tactics. They also must ensure the use of a given "cyberbomb" aligns with national interests, and follows national and international laws and treaties.

For example, as part of their counterterrorism efforts, electronic intelligence services (such as the American NSA and British GCHQ) routinely collect items like real names, user IDs, network addresses, Internet server names, online discussion histories and text messages from across the Internet. Gathering and analyzing these data could use both classified and unclassified methods. The agencies could also conduct advanced Google searches or mine The Internet Archive's Wayback Machine. This information can be linked with other data to help identify physical locations of target computers or people. Analysts can also observe interconnections between people and infer the types and strengths of those relationships.

This information can clue intelligence analysts in to the existence of previously undiscovered potential Internet targets. These can include virtual meeting places, methods of secure communications, types of phones or computers favored by the enemy, preferred network providers or vulnerabilities in their IT infrastructures. In some cases, cyberattacks need to be coordinated with spies or covert agents who must carry out physical aspects of the plan, especially when the electronic target of a "cyberbomb" is hard to reach—such as the computers inside the Iranian nuclear facility targeted by the Stuxnet worm.

Cyberattack purposes can vary widely. Sometimes, a government entity wants to simply monitor activity on a specific computer system in hopes of gaining additional intelligence. Other times, the goal is to place a hidden "backdoor" allowing the agency to secretly take control of a system. In some cases, a target computer will be attacked with the intent of disabling it or preventing future use by adversaries. When considering that kind of activity, planners must decide whether it's better to leave a site functional so future intelligence can be collected over the long term or to shut it down and prevent an adversary from using it in the near term.

Although not strictly a "cyber" attack, "cyberbombing" also might entail the use of decades-old electronic warfare techniques that broadcast electromagnetic energy to (among other things) disrupt an adversary's wireless communications capabilities or computer controls. Other "cyberbombing" techniques include modifying or creating false images on an enemy's radar screens ahead of an air attack, such as how Israel compromised Syria's air defense systems in 2007. These may be done on their own or to support more traditional military operations.

Finally, using an electromagnetic pulse (EMP) weapon to disrupt and/or disable all electronic circuits over a wide area—such as a city—could be considered the "Mother of All Cyber Bombs." As such, its effect would be felt both by enemy forces and local (likely) noncombatant citizens, all of whom suddenly would be unable to obtain fresh water and electricity, and find their local hospitals, banks and electronic items ranging from cars to coffee pots unable to function. Depending on the heat and blast from the bomb's detonation, some people might not notice—though those dependent on electronic medical devices like pacemakers probably would feel effects immediately. EMP is commonly associated with nuclear weapons, but even using nonnuclear EMP devices in a populated area would presumably cause enough "collateral damage" that it would violate international laws.

Fighting against nongovernment groups

In addition to the above techniques, and particularly when fighting opponents that are not foreign governments—such as ISIS—a unique type of "cyberbombing" seeks to target the online personas of terror group leaders. In this type of attack, one goal may be to tarnish their online reputations, such as publishing manipulated images that would embarrass them. Or, cyber weaponry may be used to gain access to systems that could be used to issue conflicting statements or incorrect orders to the enemy.

These types of "cyberbombs" can create psychological damage and distress in terrorist networks and help disrupt them over time. The United Kingdom's JTRIG (Joint Threat Research Intelligence Group) within GCHQ specializes in these tactics. Presumably similar capabilities exist in other countries.

Until recently, few nations publicly admitted planning or even thinking about waging offensive warfare on the Internet. For those that do, the exact process of planning a digital warfare campaign remains a highly guarded military and diplomatic secret.

The only people announcing their cyberattacks were assorted hacktivist groups such as Anonymous and the self-proclaimed "Cyber-Caliphate" supporting ISIS. By contrast, the most prominent cyber attack waged by a nation-state (2011s Stuxnet)—allegedly attributed to the United States and Israel—was never officially acknowledged by those governments.

Cyber weapons and the policies governing their use likely will remain shrouded in secrecy. However, the recent public mentions of cyber warfare by national leaders suggest that these capabilities are, and will remain, prominent and evolving ways to support intelligence and military operations when needed.

Critical Thinking

1. Should your country be investing in offensive cyberbombing technologies? Should your country be investing in technologies to defend against cyberbombing?

2. Do you think innocent civilians are more or less likely to be impacted by a cyberbomb versus a physical bomb? Why? Would you be more worried to know an enemy has the capability of launching a physical bombing attack or a cyberbomb attack against your location?

3. How do the ethics of cyberwar compare to the ethics of physical war?

Internet References

Cyberwarfare Greater Threat to US Than Terrorism, Say Security Experts
https://goo.gl/0UPz7Z

Stop Saying We're Dropping 'Cyber Bombs' On ISIS
https://goo.gl/fvdP9u

These 5 Facts Explain the Threat of Cyber Warfare
https://goo.gl/EMksOo

Prepared by: Liz Friedman, *DePaul University* and
Daniel Mittleman, *DePaul University*

Article

The Internet of Things We Don't Own?

Who will control the 'ordinary pursuits of life' in the digital economy?

JASON SCHULTZ

Learning Outcomes

After reading this article, you will be able to:

- Understand the traditional role of the First Sale Doctrine in establishing and protecting the rights of consumers, and changes to this doctrine now occuring with the advent of digital products and digital components within traditional physical products.

- Articulate pros and cons of the changes to the First Sale Doctrine from both the seller's and buyer's points of view.

- Articulate direct and indirect systemic implications, including unintended implications due to a shift in consumer ownership rights in the digital age.

Cars, refrigerators, televisions, wristwatches. When we buy these everyday objects, we rarely give much thought to whether or not we own them. We pay for them, we possess them, we wear them or put them in our garages or on our shelves, so we have very little reason to question their legal status or their loyalties. Yet in the last decade or so, we have witnessed a subtle and effective shift to cede control over our purchases, especially when they contain software.

It began with digital content. Movies started telling us where and when they could be played. Soon our music informed us how many devices it would live on. Then our library books began to automatically re-encrypt themselves on the date they became overdue. Now our phones will not allow us to delete certain apps; our televisions listen for when we take a bathroom break, and mattresses can keep tabs on where we slept last night.

The integration of such smart product features with ubiquitous network connectivity, microscopic sensors, large-scale analytics, social information sharing platforms, and cloud storage has created a new generation of embedded systems, the Internet of Things (IoT). It is not like the Internet we once knew, and it is not a particularly new idea: embedded computing systems have been around for decades. But the speed of adoption and the diverse capacities of these devices are unprecedented.

The era of IoT has brought more than technological and social shifts. It has also created unusual legal uncertainties. Historically, purchasing consumer goods, even electronic ones, was largely governed by two areas of law: property and contract. The good was a piece of property. The purchase agreement was a contract. Apart from the occasional equipment rental or lease, if money changed hands, the good went home with its new owner. Quid pro quo.

Even goods subject to other laws, such a copyright or patent, generally fell within this framework. As patent or copyright owners sold off individual books, movies, or machines, the law would "exhaust" any remaining intellectual property rights in that particular copy, prohibiting the IP owner, in the words of the U.S. Supreme Court, from interfering with the rights of purchasers to use it "in the ordinary pursuits of life." That meant the purchaser could use the item as she saw fit and then dispose of it, including reselling it, under whatever conditions she chose. These exhaustion rules originated from the long-standing common law regime of personal property, which generally forbids subjecting objects to ongoing restrictions, especially restrictions on resale.

But that approach is under threat. Digital goods have pushed us away from traditional legal models, and, drawing from the world of software, now come with ubiquitous "Terms of Service" that few if any of us read. Within the dense legalistic language of these documents, IoT manufacturers and distributors are quietly attempting to shift the rules of ownership. For example, many now claim we do not own our phones, our cars, or even our televisions: we are merely "licensing" them. Others assert that when our devices break, it is illegal for anyone other than the manufacturer to diagnose the problem, let alone fix it. And others go even further, claiming any data captured by the device belongs to them and not the users who bought the device and created that data. And while users and consumer advocates have generally pushed back on these assertions, device manufacturers continue to push this view of the world upon us.

The exact origin of this shift is difficult to pinpoint, but one significant moment in its early history was the introduction of the iPhone on January 9, 2007. Steve Jobs told the assembled crowd, "Today, Apple is going to reinvent the phone." Like nearly every Apple product, the iPhone user experience was carefully choreographed and tightly controlled. What Jobs did not tell the crowd was that Apple's legal strategy to maintain ownership and control of the devices in our pockets and purses was equally choreographed and controlled.

Eleven days after the iPhone debuted, a group of skillful Apple enthusiasts decided to test its technological and legal limits by "jailbreaking" the phone. This led to a cycle where Apple would upgrade its systems to break the jailbreak and the jail breakers would upgrade their breaks to free their phones from the upgrade. This battle over who "owns" the device continues to this day, with Apple insisting that "iPhone users are licensees, not owners, of the copies of iPhone operating software."

As contested ownership over smartphones has become more of a mainstream debate, the battle over IoT ownership has moved into more traditional pursuits of ordinary life.

For example, just last year, farmers found out that many of them may no longer own the equipment they purchased, including even vehicles such as tractors and combine harvesters. Even the iconic John Deere tractor now contains no less than eight control units—hardware and software components that regulate various functions, ranging from running the engine to adjusting the armrest to operating the hitch. When tractors were purely mechanical, farmers could easily maintain, repair, and modify their own equipment as needed. But now, software stands in their way. Tired of losing revenue to industrious farmers who repaired their own tractors or bargain hunters who took their equipment to an independent repair shop, John Deere decided to interpose a software layer between farmers and their tractors, claiming it retained ownership and that farmers merely had "an implied license for the life of the vehicle to operate the vehicle."

John Deere is not alone. Other vehicle manufacturers including Ferrari, Ford, General Motors, and Mercedes-Benz are finding new ways to use technology and law to weaken the property interests of drivers. These efforts take a number of forms—DRM that prevents repair and customization, software that monitors and controls your driving, even restrictions on vehicle resale. The car, once a symbol of freedom and independence, is increasingly a tool for control. Modern cars, much like John Deere's tractors, rely on dozens of electronic control units. Access to the software code on those control units is necessary for many common repairs. The code is also crucial if a driver wants to change the default tuning of her vehicle to get more horsepower or better fuel efficiency from the engine, the ambition of a growing group of car purchasers concerned about the environment calling themselves "eco-modders" and "hyper-milers." Yet under the ownership rules of the auto manufacturers, these hobbyists run the risk of becoming copyright infringers.

Such shifts in the battle over IoT ownership are also reaching into the security and safety research communities. As our vehicles incorporate greater computational systems with increased complexity, independent testing of their safety and security will increasingly require access to the copyrighted code inside them. Under the traditional law of personal property ownership, all researchers had to do was purchase a vehicle and then test it; manufacturers had no power to object other than to void the warranty. Despite Ford recalling half a million vehicles due to software glitches, Chrysler recalling 1.4 million vehicles because their infotainment systems were vulnerable to hackers, and notorious scandals such as the Volkswagen's "Defeat Device" that allowed it to cheat on emissions tests for diesel vehicles, we see more and more automakers claiming the code inside our cars is proprietary and access to it without their authorization is illegal. Consumer advocates have pushed back against these efforts, passing a Right to Repair law in Massachusetts and pressuring manufacturers to negotiate a Memorandum of Understanding with aftermarket repair shops and part suppliers that allows those businesses access to diagnostic information for repair and replacement purposes. But this does not cover automobile owners.

Nor are our children immune from this shift. Most children have imaginary friends and/or play with dolls. And while we are often surprised at the intensity of these relationships, we have historically understood they were private and ephemeral. Not anymore. Mattel's new WiFi-enabled Hello Barbie doll comes fully equipped with a built-in microphone and a cloud-based machine learning system to "personalize" your child's experience. However, what Barbie won't tell you or your child is that every single word or sound made in her presence will be recorded and transmitted back to Barbie's ML master archive for research purposes. In order to discover that, you would have to read her online Privacy Policy and Terms of Use. With the introduction of this capacity in our children's toys and other home devices such as the Nest thermostat and the Samsung "listening" Smart-TV, the sense of privacy and autonomy we used to enjoy in our homes and with the objects we owned has become yet another contested space in the IoT era.

So what does the law have to say about the question of IoT ownership? To date, neither the courts nor Congress have resolved the question. In general, the courts are split on the exact rules for who "owns" embedded copyrighted media, including software. Some have taken a somewhat technocratic approach, simply deferring to whatever words the maker puts in her license or TOS, regardless of whether or not those words accurately reflect the realities of the transaction. Other judges, however, have been more cautious, recognizing that consumer expectations play an important role in transactions, especially those involving physical objects. The Supreme Court has come close to weighing in on the issue in some of its recent patent and copyright cases, but has not given us a definitive rule.

Even the Copyright Office has avoided opining, for example, choosing to grant smartphone jail breakers an exemption from anti-circumvention liability under copyright law's fair use doctrine instead of declaring them owners with the right to modify embedded software. Recently, Congress has taken more action with Rep. Blake Farenthold introducing the You Own Devices Act (YODA), both houses beginning to examine the possibility of updating the copyright exhaustion rules for the digital age, and Senators Grassley and Leahy specifically asking the Copyright Office to analyze "how copyright shapes our interactions with software in things we own." The Commerce Department also recently issued a White Paper expressing concerns for consumers and the market if IoT manufacturers begin placing restrictions on the freedom to resell devices. But while many of these voices are asking good questions, none have provided the answers we need.

To find the answers, we will need to have a more open and honest conversation about ownership—in the courts, in Congress, and in the technical communities that are designing the IoT ecosystem. Hiding these conflicts and questions in shadowy TOS and embedded firmware code will only further confuse consumers and courts and ultimately complicate instead of clarify the rules we want when it comes to our ability to enjoy the ordinary use of these objects, including our ability to use them privately, to customize them to our needs, and even to part with them as we please.

Critical Thinking

1. How are the rules of ownership shifting due to the fact digital information is included in traditional products from books, to music, to smartphones, to cars and televisions? How does this rules of ownership shift impact our ability to modify, repair, and resell products we purchase?

2. What are the pros and cons of the changes to the First Sale Doctrine from both the seller's and buyer's points of view?

3. What, if any, are the unintended consequences of the changes to the First Sale Doctrine that is now occuring? Who are the winners and losers of these consequences?

Internet References

John Deere Clarifies: It's Trying to Abuse Copyright Law to Stop You from Owning Your Own Tractor . . . Because It Cares About You
https://goo.gl/LSfTx9

LG Will Take the 'Smart' Out of Your Smart TV If You Don't Agree to Share Your Viewing and Search Data with Third Parties
https://goo.gl/k4gBp3

Supreme Court Justices Worry About 'Parade of Horribles' If They Agree You Don't Own What You Bought
https://goo.gl/Oi4rmt

Jason Schultz (SchultzJ@exchange.law.nyu.edu) is Professor of Clinical Law at New York University's School of Law.

Prepared by: Liz Friedman, *DePaul University* and
Daniel Mittleman, *DePaul University*

Article

Know Your Rights!

Hanni Fakhoury and Nadia Kayyali

Learning Outcomes

After reading this article, you will be able to:

- Articulate the basic principles of the U.S. Constitution Fourth Amendment, and the implications for those principles with the advent of digital communication and storage technologies.

- Understand both the rights and the limitations on search and seizure protections you have under the U.S. Constitution.

- Understand appropriately both legal and behaviors to exhibit if law enforcement requests to search or seize your property in the United States.

Your computer, phone, and other digital devices hold vast amounts of personal information about you and your family. This sensitive data is worth protecting from prying eyes, including those of the government.

The Fourth Amendment to the U.S. Constitution protects you from unreasonable government searches and seizures, and this protection extends to your computer and portable devices. But how does this work in the real world? What should you do if the police or other law enforcement officers show up at your door and want to search your computer?

EFF has designed this guide to help you understand your rights if officers try to search the data stored on your computer or portable electronic device, or seize it for further examination somewhere else. Keep in mind that the Fourth Amendment is the minimum standard, and your specific state may have stronger protections.

Because anything you say can be used against you in a criminal or civil case, before speaking to any law enforcement official, you should consult with an attorney. Remember, generally the fact that you assert your rights cannot legally be used against you in court. You can always state: "I do not want to talk to you or answer any questions without my attorney present."

If they continue to ask you questions after that point, you can say: "Please don't ask me any further questions until my attorney is present." And if the police violate your rights and conduct an illegal search, often the evidence they obtain as a result of that search can't be used against you.

We've organized this guide into three sections:

- Overview: When can the police search my devices?
- The police have a warrant. Now what?
- The police can't get into my computer. Now what?

Overview: When can the police search my devices?

- If you consent to a search, the police don't need a warrant.
- Law enforcement may show up at your door. Apart from a few exceptions, police need a warrant to enter your home.
- Be aware that the police can ask your roommate/guest/spouse/partner for access to your computer if they don't have a warrant.
- Even if you're arrested, police can only search your phone under limited circumstances.
- Police can search your computer or portable devices at the border without a warrant.

If you consent to a search, the police don't need a warrant.

The most frequent way police are able to search is by asking you for permission. If you say "yes" and consent to the search, then police don't need a warrant. You can limit the scope of that consent and even revoke or take it back after the officers begin searching, but by then it may be too late.[1] That's why it's better not consent to a search—police may drop the matter. If not, then they will generally need to get a search warrant to search.

Law enforcement may show up at your door. Apart from a few exceptions, police need a warrant to enter your home.

The police can't simply enter your home to search it or any electronic device inside, like a laptop or cell phone, without a warrant.

When the police knock on your door, you do not have to let them in unless they have in their possession and show you a valid search warrant. The safest thing to do is step outside and shut the door behind you. They may or may not indicate right away why they are there. If they have a warrant, ask to see it. If they offer to simply "interview" you, it is better to decline to speak until your attorney can be present. You can do this by telling the officer: "I do not want to talk to you. I do not consent to a search. I want to speak to my attorney."

There are two major *exceptions* to the warrant requirement. First, if you consent to a search, then the police can search within the scope of your consent.[2] That's why it is usually better to not consent to a search.

Second, if police have probable cause to believe there is incriminating evidence in the house or on an electronic device that is under immediate threat of destruction, they can immediately search it without a warrant.[3]

Be aware that the police can ask your roommate/guest/spouse/partner for access to your computer if they don't have a warrant.

The rules around who can consent to a search are fuzzy. The key is who has control over an item. Anyone can consent to a search as long as the officers reasonably believe the third person has control over the thing to be searched.[4] However, the police cannot search if one person with control (for example a spouse) consents, but another individual (the other spouse) with control explicitly refuses.[5] It's unclear, however, whether this rule applies to items like a hard drive placed into someone else's computer.[6] And even where two people have control over an item or place, police can remove the non-consenting person and return to get the other's consent to search.[7]

You may want to share this know your rights guide with everyone in your home and ask them not to consent to a search by law enforcement.

Even if you're arrested, police can only search your phone under limited circumstances.

After a person has been arrested, the police generally may search the items on her person and in her pockets, as well as anything within her immediate control, automatically and without a warrant. But the Supreme Court has ruled that police cannot search the data on a cell phone under this warrant exception.[8] Police can, however, search the physical aspects of the phone (like removing the phone from its case or removing the battery) and in situations where they actually believe evidence on the phone is likely to be immediately destroyed, police can search the cell phone without a warrant.

Police can search your computer or portable devices at the border without a warrant.

Fourth Amendment protection is not as strong at the border as it is in your home or office.[9] This means that law enforcement can inspect your computer or electronic equipment, even if they have no reason to suspect there is anything illegal on it.[10] An international airport, even if many miles from the actual border, is considered the functional equivalent of a border.[11] However, border officials in Alaska, Arizona, California, Guam, Hawaii, Idaho, Montana, Northern Mariana Islands, Oregon and Washington can only confiscate an electronic device and conduct a more thorough "forensic" examination of it if they have reasonable suspicion you've engaged in criminal behavior.[12]

The police have a warrant. Now what?

- Ask to see the warrant.
- The warrant limits what the police can do.
- Although the warrant limits what the police can look for, if they see something illegal while executing a warrant they can take it.
- If the police want to search your computer, it doesn't matter whether you're the subject of their investigation.
- You do not have to assist law enforcement when they are conducting their search.
- You do not have to answer questions while law enforcement is searching.

Ask to see the warrant.

A warrant is a document signed by a judge giving the police permission to either arrest you or search your property and take certain items from that property. You have the right to see the warrant and should check to make sure it is valid.

A warrant should contain:

- The correct name of the person arrested or the correct address of the specific place to be searched;
- A list of the items that can be seized or taken by the police;
- The judge's signature;
- A deadline for when the arrest or search must take place

The police must take the warrant with them when executing it and give you a copy of it.[13] They must also knock and announce their entry before they try to forcefully enter your home,[14] and must serve the warrant during the day in most circumstances.[15]

The warrant limits what the police can do.

The purpose of the warrant is to give the judge, not the police, the discretion to decide what places can be searched and which items can be taken.[16] That's why a warrant is supposed to state exactly what the police can search and seize.[17] However, if the warrant authorizes the police to search for evidence of a particular crime, and such evidence is likely to be found on your computer, some courts have allowed the police to search the computer without a warrant.[18]

And remember, if you consent to a search, it doesn't matter if the police have a warrant; any search is permissible as long as the search is consistent with the scope of your consent.

Although the warrant limits what the police can look for, if they see something illegal while executing a warrant they can take it.

While the police are searching your home, if they observe something in "plain view" that is suspicious or incriminating, they may take it for further examination and can rely on their observation to later get a search warrant.[19] For example, if police see an open laptop with something obviously illegal on the screen, they could seize that laptop.

If the police want to search your computer, it doesn't matter whether you're the subject of their investigation.

It typically doesn't matter whether the police are investigating you, or think there is evidence they want to use against someone else located on your computer. If they have a warrant, if you consent to the search, or they think there is something incriminating on your computer that may be immediately destroyed, the police can search it. But remember, regardless of whether you're the subject of an investigation, you can always seek the assistance of the lawyer.

You do not have to assist law enforcement when they are conducting their search.

You do not have to help the police conduct the search. But you should not physically interfere with them, obstruct the search or try to destroy evidence, since that can lead to your arrest. This is true even if the police don't have a warrant and you do not consent to the search, but the police insist on searching anyway. In that instance, do not interfere but write down the names and badge numbers of the officers and immediately call a lawyer.

You do not have to answer questions while law enforcement is searching.

You do not have to answer any questions. In fact, because anything you say can be used against you and other individuals, it is best to say nothing at all other than "I do not want to talk to you. I do not consent to a search. I want to speak to my attorney." However, if you do decide to answer questions, be sure to tell the truth. In many contexts, it is a crime to lie to a police officer and you may find yourself in more trouble for lying to law enforcement than for whatever it was on your computer they wanted.[20]

The police can't get into my computer. Now what?

- The police can take your computer with them and search it somewhere else.
- You do not have to hand over your encryption keys or passwords to law enforcement.
- You may be able to get your computer back if it is taken and searched.
- There is less protection against a search at a place of employment.

The police can take your computer with them and search it somewhere else.

As long as the police have a warrant, they can seize the computer and take it somewhere else to search it more thoroughly. As part of that inspection, the police may make a copy of media or other files stored on your computer.[21]

You do not have to hand over your encryption keys or passwords to law enforcement.

The Fifth Amendment protects you from being forced to give the government self-incriminating testimony. Courts have generally accepted that telling the government a password or encryption key is "testimony." A police officer cannot force or threaten you into giving up your password or unlocking your electronic devices. However, a judge or a grand jury may be able to force you to decrypt your devices in some circumstances. Because this is a legally complicated issue, if you find yourself in a situation where the police, a judge or grand jury are demanding you turn over encryption keys or passwords, you should let EFF know right away and seek legal help.

You may be able to get your computer back if it is taken and searched.

If your computer was illegally taken, then you can file a motion with the court to have it returned.[22] If the police believe that evidence of a crime has been found on your computer (such as possessing "digital contraband" like pirated music and movies, or digital images of child pornography), the police can keep the computer as evidence. They may also attempt to keep the computer permanently, a legal process known as forfeiture, but you can challenge forfeiture in court.[23]

There is less protection against a search at a place of employment.

Generally, you have some Fourth Amendment protection in your office or workspace.[24] This means the police need a warrant to search your office and work computer unless one of the exceptions described above apply. But the extent of Fourth Amendment protection depends on the physical details of your work environment, as well as any employer policies. For example, the police will have difficulty justifying a warrantless search of a private office with doors and a lock and a private computer that you have exclusive access to. On the other hand, if you share a computer with other co-workers, you will have a weaker expectation of privacy in that computer, and thus less Fourth Amendment protection.[25] However, be aware that your employer can consent to a police request to search an office or workspace in your absence.[26] Plus, if you work for a public entity or government agency, no warrant is required to search your computer or office as long as the search is for a non-investigative, work-related matter.[27]

Want to learn more about how to protect yourself from unreasonable government searches and surveillance on your computer or portable electronic devices?

- EFF's newly relaunched Surveillance Self-Defense (SSD) is a guide to defending yourself and your friends from digital surveillance by using encryption tools and developing appropriate privacy and security practices.
- EFF's recently updated Cell Phone Guide for U.S. Protestors explains your rights, and how best to protect the data on your phone, at protests.

Notes

1. *Florida v. Jimeno*, 500 U.S. 248, 252 (1991).
2. *Schneckloth v. Bustamonte*, 412 U.S. 218, 219 (1973); *United States v. Lopez-Cruz*, 730 F.3d 803, 809 (9th Cir. 2013); *United States v. Vanvliet*, 542 F.3d 259, 264 (1st Cir. 2008).
3. *Ker v. California*, 374 U.S. 23, 39 (1963).
4. *Illinois v. Rodriguez*, 497 U.S. 177, 181 (1990); *United States v. Stabile*, 633 F.3d 219, 230–31 (3d Cir. 2011); *United States v. Andrus*, 483 F.3d 711, 716 (10th Cir. 2007).
5. *Georgia v. Randolph*, 547 U.S. 103, 106 (2006).
6. *United States v. King*, 604 F.3d 125, 137 (3d Cir. 2010).
7. *Fernandez v. California*, 134 S.Ct. 1126, 1134 (2014).
8. *Riley v. California*, 134 S.Ct. 2473, 2493 (2014).
9. *United States v. Flores-Montano*, 541 U.S. 149, 152–53 (2004).
10. *United States v. Arnold*, 533 F.3d 1003, 1009 (9th Cir. 2008); *United States v. Ickes*, 393 F.3d 501, 507 (4th Cir. 2005).
11. *Almeida-Sanchez v. United States*, 413 U.S. 266, 273 (1973); *Arnold*, 533 F.3d at 1006 (9th Cir. 2008); *United States v. Romm*, 455 F.3d 990, 996 (9th Cir. 2006); *United States v. Roberts*, 274 F.3d 1007, 1011 (5th Cir. 2001).
12. *United States v. Cotterman*, 709 F.3d 952, 957 (9th Cir. 2013) (en banc).
13. Federal Rule of Criminal Procedure 41(f)(1)(C).
14. *Wilson v. Arkansas*, 514 U.S. 927, 929 (1995).
15. Federal Rule of Criminal Procedure 41(e)(2)(A)(ii).
16. *Marron v. United States*, 275 U.S. 192, 196 (1927).
17. *Andresen v. Maryland*, 427 U.S. 463, 480 (1976).
18. *United States v. Mann*, 592 F.3d 779, 786 (7th Cir. 2010); *Brown v. City of Fort Wayne*, 752 F.Supp.2d 925, 939 (N.D. Ind. 2010).
19. *Horton v. California*, 496 U.S. 128, 133 (1990); *United States v. Walser*, 275 F.3d 981, 986 (10th Cir. 2001); *United States v. Carey*, 172 F.3d 1268, 1272 (10th Cir. 1999).
20. *Compare* 18 U.S.C. § 1001(a) (maximum punishment for first offense of lying to federal officer is 5 or 8 years) *with* 18 U.S.C. §§ 1030(a)(2) and (c)(2)(A) (maximum punishment for first offense of exceeding authorized computer access is 1 year).
21. *United States v. Hill*, 459 F.3d 966, 974 (9th Cir. 2006); *In re Search of 3817 W. West End, First Floor Chicago, Illinois 60621*, 321 F.Supp.2d 953, 958 (N.D. Ill. 2004); *see also* Federal Rule of Criminal Procedure 41(e)(2)(B).
22. Federal Rule of Criminal Procedure 41(g).

23. *See* 18 U.S.C. §§ 982, 983; Federal Rule of Criminal Procedure 32.2.

24. *Mancusi v. DeForte*, 392 U.S. 364, 369 (1968); *United States v. Ziegler,* 474 F.3d 1184, 1189 (9th Cir. 2007).

25. *Schowengerdt v. United States*, 944 F.2d 483, 488-89 (9th Cir. 1991).

26. *Ziegler*, 474 F.3d at 1191.

27. *City of Ontario v. Quon*, 560 U.S. 746, 748 (2010); *O'Connor v. Ortega*, 480 U.S. 709, 722 (1987).

Critical Thinking

1. Of the questions answered at the site, which answer surprised you the most? Of the questions answered at the site, did you disagree with any of the rights currently in force? If so, which ones and why?

2. Research online the historical motivation for creating the Fourth Amendment to the U.S. Constitution. As the framers of the Constitution were naïve to electronic technologies, what rules do you think they would have found appropriate for protecting against unreasonable search and seizure of digital information?

3. Since this article was published in 2011, we have learned the NSA has been collecting vast amounts of electronic information on Americans under provisions of the Patriot Act that render national security considerations sufficient to collect such information. How do you think national security considerations should be balanced against Fourth Amendment protections against unreasonable search and seizure?

Internet References

Bruce Schneier: The Security Mirage [TED Talk]
www.ted.com/talks/bruce_schneier.html

Era of Online Sharing Offers Benefits of 'Big Data,' Privacy Trade-Offs
www.pbs.org/newshour/bb/science/jan-june13/nsa2_06-12.html

4 Things You Should Know about Metadata, Hackers And Privacy That Edward Snowden Would Never Tell You
www.forbes.com/sites/gregsatell/2013/08/03/4-things-you-should-know-about-metadata-hackers-and-privacy-that-edward-snowden-would-never-tell-you

Hasan Elahi: FBI, Here I Am! [TED Talk]
www.ted.com/talks/hasan_elahi.html

Mikko Hypponen: Three Types of Online Attack [TED Talk]
www.ted.com/talks/mikko_hypponen_three_types_of_online_attack.html

Fakhoury, Hanni and Kayyali, Nadia. "Know Your Rights!" *Electronic Frontier Foundation*, October 21, 2014. Copyright © 2014 by Electronic Frontier Foundation. Creative Commons Attribution License. Used with permission.

Unit 8

UNIT

Prepared by: Liz Friedman, *DePaul University* and
Daniel Mittleman, *DePaul University*

Projecting the Future

As Yogi Berra once famously said, "It's tough to make predictions, especially about the future." And indeed it is. For example, Thomas Watson Jr., then the Chairman of IBM, predicted in 1953 that IBM would be able to market "maybe five computers."[1] (That is not a typo; although to his credit, at the time each 701 computer was the size of a backyard shed, required more air conditioning than a commercial freezer, and rented for $12,000 to $20,000 a month.) Twenty-four years later, Ken Olson, President of Digital Equipment Corporation (DEC) then one of the largest computer companies in the world, looked at the newly released Apple II computer by an unknown start-up in California and surmised, "There is no reason anyone would want a computer in their home." IBM, in 1981, released the IBM PC that lead to a mass adoption of personal computers with at least one, today, in almost every home. Apple, in turn, has led the push to put a computer in almost everyone's pocket, and in doing so has become the most valuable company in the world. And Apple's iPhone 7 is, by measure of instructions per second, about 1 million times faster than the first IBM PC.

Clearly, predicting the future is risky business. We tend to view the future through the lens of the present day, thinking the future will simply be an improved variation of what is now. In the short term, this sometimes works, but the history of technology shows that every so often a new technology completely reshapes not only that technological domain, but economic, social, and political structures impacted by it. This certainly was true with Gutenberg's printing press, which in the mid-15th century changed not only the field of printing, but became a catalyst for the Protestant movement against the Church, increased levels of literacy, and, therefore, the end of the middle ages. Watt's steam engine, in 1781, led to revolutions in transportation (both railroad and shipping) as well as factory work, making it a principal catalyst of the Industrial Revolution. Not to mention the sweeping effects of the commercialization of the automobile at the beginning of the 20th century.

Since the commercialization of the computer in the 1950s, we have experienced a punctuated leap in technological capability roughly once a decade. Computers in the first decade of commercialization were large, expensive, and difficult to program. Only the largest, most data-intensive organizations considered acquiring them. Each computer was handcrafted, sometimes modified for individual customers.

The integrated circuit was invented in 1958 and found its way into mass-produced computers by the mid-1960s. This reduced the size and price of computers, making them affordable for many more businesses—and large organizations often bought several. This generation of computers led to computerization of government records, computerized billing by utility companies and department stores, and—because information now had to fit into limited fields of data records—standardization among almost everything business and government did.[2] At about the same time, the U.S. Department of Defense commissioned the development of a self-healing network technology with no central hub that would be impossible for the enemy to defeat with a single well-placed strike. This network was named ARPANET and is the precursor to today's Internet.[3] ARPANET, which went live in 1969, enabled e-mail, electronic file transfers, remote computer login, and discussion boards. Though access to these networking features was largely limited to government workers and academics, within those communities, they were widely used by the late 1970s.

The microprocessor was invented in 1971 and it led to later inventions at both ends of the spectrum. At the high end, Cray Computers shipped the world's first supercomputer in 1976 enabling sophisticated computational intensive simulation and modeling applications. And the low end, the microprocessor enabled personal computers beginning with the Altair 8800 in 1975. Other computers quickly followed, including the original Apple II in 1977. IBM released its PC in 1981 and brought this form factor into the mainstream. PC-sized computing, along with parallel developments in Ethernet networking technology enabled computing on almost every office desktop, shared file space within a company, and e-mail. It also enabled people to have computers in their homes.

---

[1] This quote is often attributed to his father, Thomas Watson Sr., as saying he predicted a world market of maybe five computers. But there is no evidence Watson Sr. ever said such a thing. Watson Jr. did say something to this effect as IBM began marketing their first commercial computer, the 701, in 1953. While he predicted they would sell five of them, they actually sold 18 during their first sales pitch.

[2] For those of you interested in the societal impact of this standardization, read Les Earnest, Can Computers Cope with Human Races, *Communications of the ACM*, February 1989, v32, n2, 174–182.

[3] The Internet is simply the interconnection of many networks that run on TCP/IP, a descendent of the ARPANET protocol.

In 1993, Marc Andreessen built Mosaic, the first graphical browser, and ushered in the era of the World Wide Web (WWW), which is primarily a file sharing application that runs on top of the basic Internet protocols. And in 1995, the WWW went commercial with the founding of Yahoo, eBay, and Amazon, initiating the era of e-commerce. By the middle of the following decade, an amalgam of technical developments improved synchronous interactivity on the web. These developments enabled social media and social networking, what we now call Web2.0.

At about the same time, improvements in wireless connectivity (both WiFi and cellular) made rich mobile computing possible. The introduction of the iPhone in 2007 solidified the user interface and led to mass adoption.

Every one of the computing epochs recounted above contributed to significant shifts in economic, social, and political institutions and behaviors. There is no reason to believe this timeline has run its course. And that is why we are interested in predictions. Were the future easy to predict, we all would have bought IBM stock in 1952, Microsoft stock in 1986, and Apple in 1997 (when Steve Jobs returned). But the future is so hard to predict that CEOs of major computer companies got it wrong in embarrassing ways.

Today we are on the cusp of Web 3.0. The mobile marketplace is saturated with smartphones so much so that more computing takes place today by phone and tablet than by desktop and laptop computers. Users enter peta bytes of data onto the Internet, much of retained for analysis in huge repositories owned by Google, Facebook, Amazon, and the like. We interact with the Internet not only through keyboard and mouse, but by voice talking with smart agents like Siri, Alexa, and Cortana. And they, in turn, can talk to our home appliances and soon, perhaps, our cars.

Article

Prepared by: Liz Friedman, *DePaul University* and
Daniel Mittleman, *DePaul University*

What the Future of Home Automation Can Learn from Back to the Future

Learning Outcomes

After reading this article, you will be able to:

- Understand the traditional role of the First Sale Doctrine in establishing and protecting the rights of consumers, and changes to this doctrine now occuring with the advent of digital products and digital components within traditional physical products.

- Articulate pros and cons of the changes to the First Sale Doctrine from both the seller's and buyer's points of view.

- Articulate direct and indirect systemic implications, including unintended implications due to a shift in consumer ownership rights in the digital age.

Recently, I was channel surfing for something good on TV when I came upon "Back to the Future II." It had been a while since I've watched it, so I was pretty entertained by 1989s campy idea of what 2015 might look like. Flying cars, hover skateboards, and a "1980's themed nostalgia restaurant" highlight some of the predictions that were made about how the future will look. While some of it was hilariously wrong in so many ways, some things weren't completely off target. For example, the scene where Marty Jr. talks to the television asking for multiple channels is something that is not far off. A setup like that is something that we here at Josh.ai think is a perfect solution for voice that will make life easier, and we are working to make that a reality.

It all got me thinking, though, about how the path for future smart homes and smart home technology will twist and turn. It's pretty easy to simply jump 25 years into the future and hypothesize wildly about some fantastical ideas that may or may not come to pass, like they did in *"Back to the Future."* Instead, I'm going to try and evolve my ideas gradually starting with the problems we face now and slowly solving them toward a (*hopefully*) more realistic future.

The Present

For more than 10 years, people have been able to purchase home installations from companies like Crestron or Savant. These companies make it possible to achieve almost full control from a single control panel. However, these installations can be difficult to use and are often incredibly expensive. This is to say nothing of the devices themselves, which are often fairly pricey. These points naturally combine to limit the reach of the smart home. How are people able to immerse themselves in the idea of a fully automated home when many of them can only afford a fraction of the necessary hardware?

Contrast that with the DIY market of products. This includes lights from Hue, thermostats from Nest, and speakers from Sonos. Each product has its own app. So now you have an app for some of your lights, maybe another app for others, an app for your thermostats, and an app for music. It quickly gets out of hand and becomes an incredibly annoying experience switching from one app to another. More-so, maybe users have a hard enough time learning how one app works, let alone a dozen.

Performing anything aside from a simple task takes a number of taps and swipes, and even simple tasks can be taxing when they are hidden behind layers and layers of UI and submenus. Right now, even the best case scenario has work to do before it can be mass consumed.

Near Future (3 Years from Now)

So where do we go from here? There are a number of startups being created and partnerships being formed to help try and solve the app bloat issue. It's not a feasible long-term solution to expect users to open separate apps to perform different actions. The goal of these startups and partnerships are good but often fail to recognize the bigger problem: a well-designed clean user interface. No matter how many ways you combine all the devices into one app, if the UI for that app is non-intuitive, then there isn't much in the way of progress.

Josh.ai, a home automation client, is an attempt to solve both problems. Not only will it be able to interact with multiple devices and services used throughout the home, it will also make interacting with those devices and services easier to use through flexible voice control and a learning intelligence that grows as you use it.

By reducing complex tasks like "wake me up at 6:30 and play my theme song and brew some coffee" to a single voice command instead of a minimum of 6 button presses, we've removed the annoyance and difficulty of talking to your home. Suddenly, there's not a bloat of apps you use to talk to your devices. There's a brain in your home that understands natural language and controls your devices for you.

Sounds awesome, but it's certainly far from perfect. There are always more devices to control, and while voice recognition has gotten good over the past few years, it's nowhere near the comprehension of a human. Proper artificial intelligence is also considerably further behind than what a human brain can do, not to mention other functionality that opens up now that there is a brain in the home.

10 Years from Now

You wake up in 2025 to the shades being pulled open electronically next to you, letting the sun fill the room. Josh greets you good morning and informs you that your coffee is ready. As you grab your cup of coffee, Josh starts reading you today's news, cultivated from a few of your favorite websites and any topics that he knows you tend to find interesting. You're not really in the best of moods so you tell him to shut up. You hear the shower start to turn on, since you always shower in the morning after your coffee. Afterward, you get dressed (by yourself, Josh can't do that for you) and open the door to the garage where your car engine revs up and the door starts to open upon your entry. You get in and your car drives you to work. The garage door closes and everything in your home that is no longer needed turns off.

Above, I paint a fairly idealized description of what your future smart home can do. And there's good reason to believe that it's overly optimistic. But at the same time, the technology to do almost everything above exists today—we just haven't yet put the substantial work required to make it as seamless as described. The beauty of it isn't that everyone would have to live in the house that I just described, it's that you could live in the house that you want to describe. Don't want to have a conversation with a robot in the morning? No problem. Do you

want some level of control over everything you do instead of something doing it for you? Go for it! The idea isn't to force everyone into my idea of a smart home, it's to build out a system that lives alongside *you* and caters to *you*. This isn't some robot that says here is the functions I will provide, it's a system that can learn your patterns and understand exactly what functionality you want to have provided for you.

So what problems do we face now? It seems like that whole "smart home" thing is pretty well accomplished for the most part. Aside from the perpetually unsolved problems surrounding speech recognition and artificial intelligence, what else is there to do?

25 Years from Now

Projecting further into the future is a much more difficult task. It's hard to make it seem familiar, yet more advanced. If someone from 1990 were to be transported to today, although there would be an obvious shock at the sort of technology we take for granted, not much of it would be terribly unrecognizable or unfamiliar. Everything would be novel and exciting, but at the same time neighborhoods would look largely the same, streets and cities would operate largely the same, and people would still be largely the same. For as much as there is that changes, so much of what our 1990's traveler recognizes about humanity and day-to-day life would be familiar, and they could relatively easily assimilate to our modern way of life.

Odds are that the same will be true 25 years from now. I feel that our homes will operate largely the same way that they do today and in the above example 10 years into the future. Although, with the increasing amount of energy consumption, I would guess that the biggest difference would be that homes have now effectively become batteries. Energy is less of a worry since homes produce much of their own power through wind, solar or other renewable energy sources (while still probably connected to the grid for supplemental energy). Phones and other devices within the home draw from that power wirelessly such that you don't really need to worry about plugging your phone in for a charge. In fact, homes are smart enough to share power with one another, or neighborhoods are all treated as a large power source. Maybe even an entire city. The technology described in the "10 Years From Now" section will be more ubiquitous, and since most homes have a brain, communication amongst the homes can happen more freely (if you so choose, you can always opt out of such connectivity).

Maybe this makes it easier to meet people and connect with them in a more personal way than the current Facebook and other internet models. Maybe some of these changes means our day to day lives are easier, freeing us up to discover new things that I don't have the creativity to imagine. Maybe I'm just being optimistic. But this whole exercise has really only helped to reinvigorate my passion for building this potential future, and I know that everyone else helping to make Josh a reality feels a similar optimism for what we're building and the future we're helping create. Regardless of whether Marty had it right with hoverboards and kitchens that cook for you, one thing is for certain, the future of home automation is exciting to think about!

Critical Thinking

1. How are the rules of ownership shifting due to the fact digital information is included in traditional products from books, to music, to smartphones, to cars and televisions? How does this rule of ownership shift impact our ability to modify, repair, and resell products we purchase?

2. What are the pros and cons of the changes to the First Sale Doctrine from both the seller's and buyer's points of view?

3. What, if any, are the unintended consequences of the changes to the First Sale Doctrine that is now occuring? Who are the winners and losers of these consequences?

Internet References

John Deere Clarifies: It's Trying To Abuse Copyright Law To Stop You From Owning Your Own Tractor . . . Because It Cares About You
https://goo.gl/LSfTx9

LG Will Take The 'Smart' Out Of Your Smart TV If You Don't Agree To Share Your Viewing And Search Data With Third Parties
https://goo.gl/k4gBp3

Supreme Court Justices Worry About 'Parade Of Horribles' If They Agree You Don't Own What You Bought
https://goo.gl/Oi4rmt

Article

Prepared by: Liz Friedman, *DePaul University* and
Daniel Mittleman, *DePaul University*

To Automate Everything, Solve These Three Challenges

ALISON BRUZEK

Learning Outcomes

After reading this article, you will be able to:

- Understand the current barriers and problems that must be solved before automated home technologies are widely used in the vast majority of homes.

- Understand the trade-offs among the convenience, complexity, customization, control, and privacy in the implementation of automated home technologoies.

- Understand the security issues that surface when automated home technologies are placed on the Internet.

"It was a pain," my dad says of the programmable thermostat we had in my childhood home. It was a plastic rectangle the size of a small envelope that jutted out from the wall. He would flip down the protective cover and tap the buttons to make the numbers on the digital display slowly tick up and down.

"I could never remember how to do it. I would have to find the manual and try to read and do it at the same time," he recalls. "When the power went out, we would have to start over." His countless minutes of frustrated button-pushing made sure that the house was cool during muggy summers or toasty when we woke up on cold winter mornings—a common occurrence in Minnesota. Yet, despite his best efforts, there were times when the temperature still wasn't quite right. The air conditioner would keep blowing, for example, when we left the house on weekends. And he'd have to manually override the settings to keep out the chill of a blustery snow day.

It's hard to imagine that same thermostat being cutting edge, but that's exactly what it was more than 20 years ago. It was

programmable, but in no way was it intelligent. The only intelligence it contained was that which the user transferred to it. Today, most people's thermostats aren't much different, but that's starting to change.

Thermostats are relatively banal devices, but as the startup Nest has shown, they are ripe for an overhaul. Nest's thermostats can sense when people are home, monitor weather reports, and respond to commands from a smartphone, adjusting the temperature as needed. "In some ways, it is a first step in the right direction," says Lorna Goulden, a technology consultant, regarding Nest and the incoming tide of smart devices. Indeed, the thermostat is just one of a slew of new devices that blur the boundary between virtual and physical worlds. They promise to make our built environments more intelligent, responsive, and efficient.

Collectively, they are called the internet of things or the internet of everything. The concept was first envisioned back in the late 1990s during the dot-com bubble. Then, people anticipated a near-future where computers and the internet were everywhere. Now, 14 years later, connected devices are just beginning to slip into homes, from smart thermostats to apps that unlock your door without a key. Smart objects are slowly transitioning from pioneering to practical.

Yet just as the internet of things is poised to remake our homes and offices, it's facing perhaps its most critical test: adoption by the average consumer. The intelligent future promised by entrepreneurs won't catch on if those devices can't connect to each other automatically, lack intuitive programmability, or aren't appealing designed. If they fail at any one of these, automating our homes may be more trouble than its worth.

But if engineers and designers can nail each of those requirements, then much like electricity did a century ago, the internet will course through our homes so seamlessly we may pay little attention to it as we go about our daily lives.

Connecting Everything

There's a good chance that you already have an internet-connected device in your home. It may be a DVR or a set of wireless speakers. These are early components of the internet of things, but they're missing something important—the ability to interact with the other objects in your home. "They've got a little bit of a learning curve," says Craig Miller, vice president of worldwide marketing at Sequans Communications, which creates computer chips for smart devices.

The most intelligent smart devices may need not just one connection, but two: one to the internet and another to fellow smart objects. We know how to handle the first one—just add a chip for Wi-Fi or cellular service such as LTE and you're online. Coordinating with other smart objects can pose a problem, though. Currently, device-to-device communication is experiencing some growing pains, much like wireless networking for computers did in the 1990s. It took a few years for competitors to settle on a standard, Wi-Fi, and a few more before it became widely adopted.

"It's not a lack of standards, it's the fire hose of standards that's the problem," says Rob Faludi, an adjunct professor in the Interactive Telecommunications program at New York University and chief innovator at Digi International, a networking company. "But that's always a problem with devices," he adds, referring to the historical differences between computer platforms such as Windows and Mac. In that case, users felt computers were valuable enough to put up with the problem of incompatible devices. Eventually, a consensus developed around key standards, and the market coalesced around them.

For now, the torrent of different networking standards poses a problem for average users, who don't want to—and shouldn't have to—think about how their refrigerator might talk with their dishwasher. Most smart devices currently require users to delve into application programming interfaces, known as APIs, for which you need a good deal of programming knowledge to use properly. Companies such as Microsoft are hoping to simplify the operation of a smart home, building dashboards that allow users to control disparate smart objects from their PCs or an all-controlling smartphone. But even these tools require some effort and knowledge to implement. Simplifying this process won't be easy—the more devices in a network, the harder it is to coordinate.

Engineers have a long road ahead of them, but if they can make communication seamless, there's a lot of potential in that connectivity. Faludi offers the example of a home air conditioner and a security system: Say it's been a hot three days and the air conditioner hasn't turned on. There's a good chance the occupant isn't home, and, if the front door is unlocked, it might be time to close that deadbolt.

Programming It All

Connecting devices is only part of the challenge. To really unlock the power of the internet of things, smart devices' functions must be accessible to average users without making them cede too much power. If people don't feel in control, they'll be hesitant to adopt the technology. "It can be very discomforting to come into a house and all [these] things start happening," explains Jason Johnson, co-founder of the Internet of Things Consortium. In reality, intelligent homes will be only partly automated, giving users final say over what happens, just like our current relationship with computers.

Even one of the closest examples of full automation today, Alex Hawkinson's SmartThings, prompts users for guidance at the outset and later allows its decisions to be overridden through a smartphone app. For example, objects connected to the bathroom fan and the shower faucet may prompt the user whether they want the vent to turn on or the heater to fire up. Another may connect to the blinds and default to raise in the morning and lower in the evening, but will still allow people to raise and lower them manually. That way, there aren't any surprises.

As more smart devices are added to a home, the number of possibilities—but also the complexity—could grow exponentially. Finding the balance will be tricky. "If the usability is lacking at any step of the way, and frequent updates present more frustration than excitement and delight," explains Goulden, the consultant, "then interest will quickly fade." What people really want, Goulden says, is "the Apple experience"—pull it out of the box and it's ready to start using.

Designing for Everyone

There's one final, and often overlooked, challenge—design. It's easy to see how bad design can frustrate a user—take the baffling array of buttons on the thermostat at my parents' home. The buttons' position, hidden behind a panel, made the whole package nicer to look at but not any easier to use.

Contrast that with Nest, which has no buttons. Rather, its physical interface consists of one rotary dial. Not only does it pay homage to old thermostats—making the device seem less threatening—it's also intuitive: turn right to raise the temperature, left to lower it. "It was born out of frustration, which I think many people can relate to when they've tried to program their programmable thermostat," says Kate Brinks, director of communications for Nest.

The best, easiest-to-use smart objects will likely look no different than devices we use today, Faludi points out. "A big chunk of this will just be baked into things that we buy," he says. "You won't buy an 'internet of things.'"

There will be entirely new products, but that shouldn't unte-ther design from reality, Johnson says. "Technology products shouldn't look like technology products." Developers should shoot for "something that either spouse could bring home and put on the kitchen counter," he says. "And it gets past that 'Ew, what is that thing.'"

And rather than just being "smart" for technology's sake, the devices should also address people's actual needs, he says. "We need to develop products that are very practical, that are solving very real problems," he says. "Not just, 'Gee whiz, wouldn't it be cool if I could turn on the lights from my phone?'"

Goulden adds that, in her consulting, she advises clients that smart objects should act as an extension of the user. "How do you take an individual's identity and how do you relate that to the objects that are around them?" The more relatable the object, the simpler it is to understand.

Too Smart a Future?

As the internet of things becomes a larger—and less visible—part of our lives, it could change the entire meaning of privacy. The media went wild in July when two security researchers turned a Jeep Cherokee into a child's toy, controlling it remotely through the car's digital diagnostic port. But future security hacks need not be so flashy to be concerning. The internet of things has the potential make not just individuals but also hospitals, governments, and cities vulnerable. If everything—from medical devices such as pacemakers or pill dispensers to infrastructure such as bridges and railroads—is on the network, then the consequences can be deadly.

The number of vulnerable points—the "surface area" for attacks—with a connected device is often greater than people realize, says Chris Poulin, a research strategist with IBM Security. For example, if you have a Nest, it's not just that someone could get into the physical blob on your wall. There's also, "the mobile app, which connects to Nest's [data servers], and then to the Nest in the house, which connects to the WiFi, which again connects to Nest's data servers...the surface is just really broad."

That's part of what the Federal Trade Commission worried about in their report last January. People need to consider not just unauthorized access to their smart fridge or connected garage door, they stated. Consumers should also be aware that their personal information being collected from their smart objects could potentially be accessed by future banks, employers, or insurers who might make decisions based on that information.

In September, the FBI released a cyber crime public service announcement (http://www.ic3.gov/media/2015/150910.aspx), explaining how the internet of things can be exploited.

Among their recommendations for how to defend against those exploits is a simple suggestion: "Consider whether IoT devices are ideal for their intended purpose." In other words, the first step for a consumer should be, is that smart fridge really necessary? Lee Tien, a specialist in privacy and civil liberties at the Electronic Frontier Foundation, says consumers must watch out for themselves because the companies aren't always able to. Especially when devices are made by small startups, he says, and "not in the first tier of expertise of security." Bruce Schneier, a computer security and privacy expert, says after devices are shipped, companies have no incentive to update old software or computer chips to ensure future loopholes are fixed—they're too busy working on their next thing. He says until the makers of devices go open-source and allow outside engineers to help find and fix security problems, this will always be the case. However, the new problems are slowly growing interesting solutions. Companies such as Honeywell that once were known for protecting your home now protect industrial plants working in oil, gas, chemicals, or minerals and use the internet of things. For consumers, Schneier says large companies that control your entire ecosystem of technology, whether it be Google or anyone else, will be how people keep their hardware and software up-to-date. "Apple does security for all iOS users. This is the future." Yet there is a contingent that doesn't see privacy concerns holding up adoption. Faludi argues that people are "always going to have concerns about security and privacy," adding that, "they're problems for developers to solve, but they're not really any kind of barrier." Researchers such as Faludi are wary that a lack of confidence in the future could stop adoption.

On the Cusp

Despite the hurdles, the potential for the internet of things is enormous. Not only could it simplify many aspects of our daily lives, it could also make our homes more energy efficient, saving us money and reducing our environmental footprint. And few stand to benefit more than people with disabilities. For some, even simple tasks take an inordinate amount of time and effort. Automating those would allow them to direct their energy toward more important things in their lives.

It may take some time for that to happen, though. Smart objects are starting to trickle into the marketplace, but widespread use of the internet of things is still 5 to 10 years off, according to industry analysts at Gartner, a market research firm. That's good news for the engineers, developers, and designers who are trying to work out the many kinks that remain.

Should they succeed in making smart objects intuitive, transparent, and minimally invasive, though it's likely that people like my parents, who are sick of tapping buttons to program everyday life, will adopt them. There are signs they're getting closer; my dad called the other day, clearly smiling through the phone. "Your mom and I are thinking about getting a Nest."

Critical Thinking

1. The article quotes Lorna Goulden saying "In some way, [Nest] is a first step in the right direction." If so, what steps do you foresee following in the near future? What are some problems you would like automated home technology to solve for you?

2. What unforseen big new idea (see Postman model in Unit 1 Introduction) might be enabled by automated home technologies?

3. Would you trust living in an automated home? If no or you aren't sure, what safety, privacy, or security concerns do you have? What would it take for a home technology to gain your trust?

Internet References

Amazon Wants Alexa to Take Control of Your Smart Home
https://goo.gl/VqjpJ2
Welcome To Privacy Hell, Also Known As The Internet Of Things
https://goo.gl/UjhQMH
We Can't Let Our Toasters Become Smarter Than We Are
https://goo.gl/Fzvcn6

ALISON BRUZEK is a science writer based in Cambridge, Mass.

Article

Prepared by: Liz Friedman, *DePaul University* and
Daniel Mittleman, *DePaul University*

The Murky Ethics of Driverless Cars

A new study explores a moral dilemma facing the creators of self-driving vehicles: In an accident, whose lives should they prioritize?

TOM JACOBS

Learning Outcomes

After reading this article, you will be able to:

- Recognize that there are ethical trade-offs we make doing routine activities in our everyday lives, such as driving.

- Recognize that the ethical choices we think we might make in abstract situations may or may not differ from what we would do if actually faced with the choice.

- Articulate the dilemma encountered if one is asked to make a decision that trades off one set of lives for another set of lives.

So you're driving down a dark road late at night when suddenly a child comes darting out onto the pavement. Instinctively, you swerve, putting your own safety in jeopardy to spare her life.

Very noble of you. But would you want your driverless vehicle to do the same?

That question, which can be found idling at the intersection of technology and ethics, is posed in the latest issue of *Science*. A variation on the famous trolley dilemma, it won't be theoretical for long: Self-driving vehicles are coming soon, and they will need to be programmed how to respond to emergencies.

A research team led by Iyad Rahwan of the Massachusetts Institute of Technology argues that this poses a huge challenge to their creators. In a series of studies, it finds people generally agree with the "utilitarian" argument—the notion that cars should be programmed to spare as many lives as possible.

However, when asked what they would personally purchase, they tended to prefer a vehicle that prioritized the safety of its riders. And a theoretical government regulation that would mandate a spare-the-greatest-number approach significantly dampens their enthusiasm for buying a driverless car.

"Figuring out how to build ethical autonomous machines is one of the thorniest challenges in artificial intelligence today," the researchers write. "For the time being, there appears to be no way to design algorithms that would reconcile moral values and personal self-interest."

Rahwan and colleagues Jean-Francois Bonnefon and Azim Shariff describe six studies, all conducted online via Amazon's Mechanical Turk. In the first, the 182 participants "strongly agreed that it would be more moral for autonomous vehicles to sacrifice their own passengers when this sacrifice would save a greater number of lives overall."

Another study found this still held true even when the passengers were described as "you and a family member," as long as it meant saving the lives of multiple pedestrians. The 451 participants, however, "indicated a significantly lower likelihood of buying the autonomous vehicle when they imagined the situation in which they and their family member would be sacrificed for the greater good.

In still another study, the 393 participants "were reluctant to accept government regulation" that would mandate programming the cars to ensure the fewest lives were lost. "Participants were much less likely to consider purchasing an autonomous vehicle with such regulation than without."

That suggests such regulations "could substantially delay the adoption" of driverless cars, the researchers write. That would be unfortunate, they note, since these cars are much safer than those driven by humans, and more lives will be saved as more of them are on the road.

Altogether, the results suggest people approve of self-driving cars "that sacrifice their passengers for the greater good, and would like others to buy them—but they would themselves prefer to ride in autonomous vehicles that protect their passengers at all costs."

A dilemma indeed. If you'd like to explore the specific ethical questions in more detail—which may or may not clarify your thinking—you may do so at http://moralmachine.mit/edu.

Or you can just give it some serious thought while you sit in traffic.

Critical Thinking

1. Should we be able to program ethical decision-making parameters into automated technologies? Why or why not?

2. Articulate how comfortable you are in permitting an automated technology to make a life or death ethical decision for you. Would you be more comfortable if you were able to give it instructional parameters ahead of time? If you are not comfortable, what is it about the situation that makes you uncomfortable?

3. Is there a way to avoid encountering the ethical dilemmas articulated in this article? [The third Internet Resource may assist you in answering this question.]

Internet References

Engineers Say If Automated Cars Experience 'The Trolley Problem,' They've Already Screwed Up
https://goo.gl/R13m5P

The Ethics of Autonomous Cars
https://goo.gl/YJuZxJ

When Should Your Driverless Car From Google Be Allowed To Kill You?
https://goo.gl/8bO3MA

TOM JACOBS is a staff writer with Pacific Standard magazine.